Breaking the Exclusion Cycle

4—
Jun

Breaking the Exclusion Cycle

*How to Promote Cooperation between
Majority and Minority Ethnic Groups*

ANA BRACIC

OXFORD
UNIVERSITY PRESS

OXFORD
UNIVERSITY PRESS

Oxford University Press is a department of the University of Oxford.
It furthers the University's objective of excellence in research, scholarship,
and education by publishing worldwide. Oxford is a registered trade mark of
Oxford University Press in the UK and certain other countries.

Published in the United States of America by Oxford University Press
198 Madison Avenue, New York, NY 10016, United States of America.

Library of Congress Control Number: 2019955807

ISBN 978-0-19-005067-2

1 3 5 7 9 8 6 4 2

Printed by Marquis, Canada

Contents

Preface

For Roma, the easiest document to obtain, by far, is the death certificate.
Anonymous, Prague 2010

I heard this statement on my first trip to the field in 2010, and have since heard similar versions of it repeated in Hungary, Slovakia, Czech Republic, and Croatia. I did not set out in 2010 with the intent of writing a book, but if I were to trace this book back to its beginning, it would start there. This statement, wryly passed around as a joke within circles of government experts, NGO workers, and activists, speaks clearly to the depth of discrimination Roma encounter in Central and Eastern Europe today. It refers to administrative barriers that Roma face when trying to obtain personal documents. Often, these barriers are not a matter of bureaucracy. Intolerant administrative officials may hinder the process of their own accord, by withholding information or aid, by repeatedly sending those who seek documents to the wrong place, and, in extreme cases, by stating that obtaining documents is simply not possible. Tellingly, no such barriers exist when a death certificate is needed.

Individual behavior matters for exclusion. Social exclusion endures because of multiple intersecting exclusionary forces, including structural inequalities—but individual behaviors, like those of the intolerant bureaucrats, play a critical role in helping exclusion persist. Even if all structural barriers to equality were eliminated, our conversation went in 2010, mere individuals could keep exclusion going. This is why I focus on them here.

My choice to examine Roma and non-Roma predates the conversation about death certificates and individual behaviors, and stems entirely from the fact that Roma and non-Roma can be found in many places, and have fraught relationships in most of them. Roma are the largest ethnic minority in Europe. They make up millions (somewhere between 10 and 12) and are tremendously diverse and complex. Yet, while there isn't a state in Europe without a Roma population, Roma/non-Roma relations are relatively understudied, especially in political science. Given their numbers and the extent to which some Roma are excluded, this lack of attention is conspicuous. The oversight merits correction not only because Roma communities are numerous, but also because their dispersal and diversity may offer sources of variation that scholars often seek to leverage when looking for analytical clarity. While I initially decided to focus on Roma and non-Roma because of the possibility to study the two across different states, I ultimately chose a narrower focus. Still, this book contributes to the correction of the oversight.

A word on positionality. The main feature of this book is the exclusion cycle, a dynamic that consists of Roma and non-Roma attitudes, behaviors, and interpretations. The cycle is sustained by members of both groups, but non-Roma play a much larger role. As a result, the empirical portion of this book allots more pages to non-Roma. As I am a Slovene non-Roma myself, those pages came faster. Grappling with the Roma portion of the exclusion cycle was more demanding and took longer. This makes sense; trying to see the world through someone else's eyes is never easy and the challenge grows substantially when our life experiences are fundamentally different. I anticipated this challenge and I tried to contend with it to the best of my ability. I tried to remain aware of my position both while in the field and while writing. I discovered (some) blind spots and corrected them. I am certain others remain. I consulted both Roma and non-Roma when designing the research protocols and their delivery; where appropriate, I consulted Roma and non-Roma from the localities where I fielded the studies, and where not, I sought help from Roma and non-Roma from other localities. I discussed my conclusions with members of both communities. Nevertheless, readers should remain mindful of my positionality as they continue reading. Knowing where I stood when I made my observations, collected my data, and wrote my conclusions—even as I interrogated that place—matters for understanding and critically evaluating my work.

This book combines several methods—semi-structured interviews with experts and regular citizens, field observations, surveys, and experiments—to ask how individual behaviors by both Roma and non-Roma help social exclusion persist. I do not try to explain the persistence of all exclusion everywhere; this study is focused in place and time, and any generalizations require a volume of caveats and a heap of salt. But I do aim to provide one explanation of how individual behaviors can contribute to a self-sustaining cycle of exclusion, and an exploration of how we might think about breaking that cycle.

Acknowledgments

I would first like to thank 670 anonymous participants, Roma and non-Roma, for giving me their time, their attention, and their patience. Without them, there would be no experiments, no games, and no book. I owe a debt of gratitude to all who spoke with me regarding Roma exclusion over the past 8 years, formally or informally. I am especially grateful to Dušica Balažek, Stane Baluh, Stanko Daniel, Marek Hojsik, Jožek Horvat Muc, Vera Klopčič, Djordje Jovanović, Marian Mandache, Martin Martinek, Margareta Matache, Vera Messing, Bogdan Miklič, Delia Nita, Laco Oravec, Stepan Ripka, Janja Rošer, Eva Salnerova, Monika Sandreli, Filip Škiljan, Anton Štihec, Haris Tahirović, Brano Tichy, Milena Tudija, Galbea Vasile, anonymous government employees, anonymous European Commission employees, and others who wish to remain unnamed.

Fielding the two experimental studies in Slovenia and conducting interviews in Slovenia, Croatia, Hungary, Czech Republic, Slovakia, and Romania would have been impossible without the financial support I received from New York University (Departmental Travel Grant, Departmental Summer Field Research Grant, George Downs's research funds), the American Political Science Association (Rita Mae Kelly Endowment Fellowship Grant), the University of Oklahoma (Junior Faculty Summer Fellowship, Faculty Investment Program), and the International Studies Association (Deborah Gerner Grant for Professional Development Award). The Ed Cline Faculty Development Award from the University of Oklahoma (OU) helped fund my book conference, which I held at OU in August 2017.

I began exploring Roma/non-Roma relations as a graduate student at New York University (NYU); I fielded the first study, a part of which I present in this book, to produce my third dissertation paper. At NYU, I am especially grateful to Becky Morton for advice on experimental research design; to Kanchan Chandra for introducing me to ethnic politics and for pushing me to think more deeply and more carefully; to Neal Beck for his generous advice on scholarship and life; and to Diana Barnes for helping with fieldwork-related administrative challenges. I would like to thank Anjali Thomas Bohlken, Yael Zeira, Anna Getmansky, and Manuela Travaglianti for countless conversations, many regarding research. I am grateful to my committee members—to

David Stasavage for his immediate, ready support and quick feedback; to Mike Gilligan for telling me to "just *go* to the field;" and to Josh Tucker for telling me to "go home and just think for a month" when I returned from the field the first time, unsure of what to make of the first set of findings. Bringing up these moments may seem trivial, but it isn't; each marks a crucial turning point on my journey towards writing this book and becoming a better scholar. No one, however, prepared me better for this book than George. George Downs taught me how to think. When I met with him during my first year of graduate school I kept a notebook in which I wrote down everything he said; he was making so many connections at the same time I was afraid that I would miss them if I didn't write them down immediately. He once asked me to stop, laughing, and I flatly refused. Eventually, though, I wrote less and less. This book differs substantially from his work, but he was the first to see it taking shape and put me on a path towards it. It is an honor to have been his student.

During my time as a postdoctoral fellow at the Center on Democracy, Development, and the Rule of Law at Stanford University, I began to develop the second study, which makes up the bulk of this book. For feedback, I owe gratitude to Steve Stedman, Anna West, and members of the 2014 spring Flavor Lab—Darin Christensen, Nick Eubank, Francisco Garfias, Grant Gordon, Eric Kramon, Dorothy Kronick, Avital Livny, Ramya Parthasarathy, Melina Platas, Bilal Siddiqi, Manuela Travaglianti, and Kelly Zhang.

I fully developed, fielded, and wrote up the second study while working as an Assistant Professor at the University of Oklahoma. I am grateful to Paul Goode for his mentorship; to Keith Gaddie and Scott Robinson for their support as chairs; to Marilyn Korhonen for helping me construct a viable research plan; to Keith Gaddie and Alisa Fryar for their help in putting on a book conference; and to Cathy Brister and Jamie Vaughn for working a minor miracle to get me to the field on time, with funding. For feedback on portions of the book, I would like to thank Collin Barry, Mike Crespin, Christian Davenport, Siduri Haslerig, Allen Hertzke, Hank Jenkins-Smith, Charlie Kenney, Katy Schumaker, and Carol Silva. For advice regarding publishing, I am grateful to Michele Eodice and Justin Wert. While at OU, I found a new mentor in Will Moore, who was incredibly generous with his time and advice. I will pay it forward.

Claire Adida, Alisa Fryar, Don Green, David Laitin, Isabela Mares, and Scott Robinson attended my book conference and engaged with my work deeply and thoughtfully, for hours. This conference was the single most extraordinary academic experience I have ever had and I am grateful to these scholars beyond measure. The book you have before you bears their mark.

I would like to thank Angela Chnapko, Alexcee Bechthold, Lucy Hyde, Rajeswari Sathiyamoorthy, Balasubramanian Shanmugasundaram, and the editorial team at Oxford University Press for guiding me through the publication process. I am grateful to two anonymous reviewers for their comments and suggestions, which have made the book stronger.

I would like to thank Amy Liu and the participants of the Multiculturalism in Europe Workshop in the Center for European Studies at the University of Texas at Austin; Jim Curry and the participants of the Political Research Colloquium in the Department of Political Science at the University of Utah; Zoltan Barany and the participants of the Comparative Speaker Series in the Department of Government at the University of Texas at Austin; Isabela Mares, Dan Corstange, and the participants of the Comparative Politics Seminar in the Department of Political Science at Columbia University; and Lisa Baldez, Kyle Dropp, and the participants of the Department Speaker Series in the Department of Government at Dartmouth. I have also received great feedback during talks at Michigan State University, Florida State University, The Ohio State University, and the University of California, Santa Barbara; I thank all the participants for their insight.

I am grateful to Milena Tudija, Štefan Bajič, Monika Sandreli, Jožek Horvat Muc, Vera Klopčič, and Julija Sardelić for making fieldwork possible. I thank Chris Eades, Tanner Davis, and Eva Trapečar for putting the tower game into Unity, for recording and cutting vocals in a language they didn't speak (except Eva), and for patiently adjusting the game during the pilot phase. I owe a debt of gratitude to my enumerators, who braved 95 degree heat and conscientiously followed the protocols: Mojca Bečaj, Lorena Bogataj, Bernarda Bračič, Živa Kleindienst, Tija Kuhar, Jaka Kukavica, Manja Munda, Maša Rozman, Tjaša Stopar, Natalija Trunkelj, Eva Trapečar, Lucija Vihar and Evgen Šmit Žagar.

I would like to thank my first undergraduate reader, Soraya Sadik Peron, for reading the book for clarity and accessibility. Turning the wheel back to my own undergraduate years, I would like to thank Pat Kain and Will Evans, who taught me expository writing. Will once told me to "listen to sentences" as if they were music. I try my best to listen. I thank my second undergraduate reader, Thomas Larkin, for his precise and thorough edits. He listens to sentences too. I would like to thank the members of our political science "writing club" at OU. Mackenzie Israel-Trummel, Allyson Shortle, Kathleen Tipler, and Solongo Wandan have, between them, read all the chapters, several of them more than once. I am grateful for their attention to detail; for their suggestions regarding the literature, the theory, and the empirics; and for their unending support and patience while I worked on this book. I also cherish their friendship. Being a young assistant professor has its ups and downs. Along with Siduri Haslerig, these four women have been there for everything.

Different members of my family have had a hand in almost every part of this project. I thank my dad, Slavko, for folding and helping deliver several hundred envelopes to the mailboxes of potential participants. I thank my sister, Eva, for being a punctilious enumerator, enforcing the research protocols as strictly as I would have, were I not on another enumerator team (and for the envelopes). Eva also designed the cover of this book, which I adore, and recorded the vocal instructions and commentary for the tower-building videogame. I would like to thank my mom, Bernarda, who walked the entire field with me. She, too, was a punctilious enumerator, in all locations, in both studies, every time. She observed all the pilots and did not hold back when telling me what went wrong when or who didn't understand me and why. She, too, folded and delivered envelopes. And she helped me enter data late at night, only to wake up in the morning and go to the field again. Finally, I would like to thank my husband, Nicholson. While he missed the fieldwork, he was there for the rest. Many of the leaps I needed to make, whether in design or theory or writing, I made while talking with him (or, sometimes, at him). He sat with me through grant applications, puzzled with me through unexpected findings (and celebrated the good ones), and argued with me about the finer points of various claims and assumptions I'd made. Nicholson talked me down when I was stressed and had confidence in me when I lacked it. He read and edited this book twice. I will be forever grateful for his love, his perseverance, and his faith.

1

Introduction

On the evening of 18 December 2011, a breaking and entering took place in Boston. Police officer Luis Anjos patrolled the blocks surrounding the crime scene for suspects: three Black men, one wearing a red hoodie and two in dark clothing. He found none. On his way back to the police station, away from where the suspects had allegedly gone, he saw two Black men walking near a park. Anjos rolled down his window and yelled for them to stop. Jimmy Warren and his companion made eye contact with the officer, and ran.[1]

To many, this story might seem simple. "The two men shouldn't have run," they might think. "If they had nothing to hide, they wouldn't have run," they might reason. "Since they did run, they must be guilty of something," they might conclude.

But reality is not so simple. Our societies systematically view and treat some people as less trustworthy, less capable, less intelligent, and less deserving than others. Jimmy Warren is such a person. He belongs to a group stereotyped as criminal. Following a crime, a police officer may be quick to consider every member of this minority in the vicinity a potential suspect; after all, his fellow officers have arrested a fair number of such men in the past. Having seen men who look like him arbitrarily arrested and mistreated while in custody, Warren, who was innocent, may have chosen to run rather than risk humiliation and possible abuse by the police. Blind to Warren's reasoning and armed with a powerful stereotype, the police officer likely interpreted running as guilt, confirming his bias. When someone steals again, the police might once more look for a suspect who resembles Warren, and the individual approached might, once more, run.

This book is about situations like this one; seemingly small, but central to the persistence of social exclusion. The brief interaction between Warren and the police captures a dynamic through which members of the majority and the minority contribute to this exclusion. It starts with anti-minority culture. In the case of Warren, this culture includes the widespread belief that people like him are criminals. Anti-minority culture then gives rise to discrimination.

[1] For details, see Commonwealth v. Jimmy Warren (2016), p.337.

Breaking the Exclusion Cycle: How to Promote Cooperation between Majority and Minority Ethnic Groups.
Ana Bracic, Oxford University Press (2020). © Oxford University Press. DOI: 10.1093/oso/9780190050672.001.0001

Chances are the police officer felt little compunction in pursuing Warren and his companion, even as they were not in the vicinity of the crime and did not fit the description of suspects provided by the injured party. Members of the stereotyped minority must know how to live in a world where anti-minority culture is inescapable. They must anticipate discrimination, must cope with it, and must strive to improve their lives in spite of it. Perhaps this is why Jimmy Warren ran. When he did, the police officer made a mistake. He interpreted Warren's running as an admission of guilt, and not as an act of self-preservation to which Warren had to resort because of racial profiling. The officer's mistaken interpretation further reinforces the stereotype that led him to suspect Warren in the first place. This fuels the anti-minority culture that's already in place, ensuring that the dynamic repeats.[2]

I call this dynamic the exclusion cycle. Anti-minority culture comes first. Discrimination follows, as do minority survival strategies. The errors in interpretation—attribution errors—then feed anti-minority culture, and the cycle starts over. In this book, I explore this cycle and propose a way to break it.[3]

The main contribution of my cyclical theory lies in its comprehensive approach. In studying discrimination, we rightly tend to focus on those who discriminate. To fully understand intractable cases of exclusion, however, a more expansive approach is needed. We must not only look at those who discriminate but also at their targets. I theorize that behaviors of both interact and feed into one another, resulting in a state that at best preserves the rift between the two communities and, at worst, widens it beyond mending. Exclusion is so intractable for precisely this reason. I then empirically examine the behaviors and attitudes of both—the majority that discriminates and the marginalized minority they target—and demonstrate that both groups

[2] The Supreme Judicial Court recognized the nature of this dynamic, stating the following (Commonwealth v. Jimmy Warren (2016), p.337). As the police officer had very few details describing the suspects—only that there were three, that one wore a red hoodie and the others dark clothing, and that they were Black—he had no ability to reasonably target the defendant or any other Black male as a suspect in the crime; in addition, the two Black men did not actually fit the description. The opinion further states that in light of a recent police report stating that Black men in Boston were disproportionately more likely to be targeted in police-civilian encounters, flight of a Black suspect is "not necessarily probative of a suspect's state of mind or consciousness of guilt" (Commonwealth v. Jimmy Warren, SJC 11956, 342 (2016)). Instead, disproportionate targeting of Black men suggests that "[s]uch an individual, when approached by the police, might just as easily be motivated by the desire to avoid the recurring indignity of being racially profiled as by desire to hide criminal activity" (Commonwealth v. Jimmy Warren (2016), p.342). The Supreme Judicial Court found that the police lacked reasonable suspicion for the investigatory stop of the defendant and vacated the judgment of conviction.

[3] Elsewhere, this dynamic has been discussed by Adida et al. (2010, 2016), Loury (2002) (economics) and Rusche and Brewster (2008) (sociology).

play a part in perpetuating exclusion, but that the responsibility lies with the majority.

The exclusion cycle is about the behaviors and the beliefs of individuals. As this book is confined to the personal, individual sphere, it cannot tell the full story. What individuals think and do is the smallest building block of a much larger system. Some have called it systemic racism (Feagin 2000; Ture and Hamilton 1967), some social exclusion (Madanipour et al. 1998),[4] others über discrimination (Reskin 2012). This system is comprised of institutionalized disparities, "codified in our institutions of custom, practice, and law" (Phyllis Jones 2000), which interact with and reinforce one another, resulting in entrenched inequality that is passed on from one generation to the next. Sometimes, these systems are recognized and challenged by state actors and private citizens, but they are intractable and change slowly. Other times they are not challenged at all, but instead fortified and exploited by those in power. What happens at the higher levels of the system matters for how individuals behave. I do not explore that here, however, and so I implore the reader to bear in mind that the exclusion cycle does not exist in a vacuum.

To study the exclusion cycle, I capture interactions between Roma and non-Roma in a Slovene town that is typical of other towns in Central and Eastern Europe where Roma and non-Roma live.[5] Roma, a diverse ethnic minority, are often derogatively called "Gypsies". While widely used by non-Roma across the globe, and sometimes without knowledge that it is derogatory, this word is, to many Roma, a hurtful racial slur (Oprea 2012). As the communities whose members participated in my studies prefer to use the word Roma (Miklič 2013), I consistently use this word here, unless directly quoting a participant.

Roma are widely stereotyped as cheaters, thieves, and takers by non-Roma. I leverage this stereotype in my field experiments that use games played with modest amounts of money, and demonstrate the following. First, anti-Roma culture has a strong presence in this town. Second, non-Roma discriminate against the Roma, particularly so if they are prejudiced against

---

[4] I chose the language of exclusion for this book because this is the term commonly used when talking about marginalized Roma in Europe. Policy makers at the EU and state levels refer to social exclusion, as do Roma NGOs and Roma and non-Roma in general.

[5] By speaking broadly about Roma and non-Roma, this work runs the risk of reifying the Roma/non-Roma divide. What it means to be Roma and non-Roma of course changes and evolves over time and across experiences. Using a two-word dichotomy as a basis for comparison is therefore reductive, but it reflects a difficult reality. Whatever the categories of Roma and non-Roma mean at a particular moment in time, to particular people, the divide is salient, especially as it is reinforced by the experience of past discrimination (Wimmer 2013). Examining behaviors along this divide is thus useful, even if limited.

them. Third, Roma use survival strategies, but not uniformly: Roma who have personally experienced discrimination are more likely to resort to them. Finally, non-Roma are inclined to interpret Roma uses of survival strategies as quintessentially Roma, instead of attributing them to discrimination. Roma/non-Roma relations in this town thus appear to follow the logic of the cycle.

I examine one intervention that might break this cycle: NGO-based promotion of intergroup contact. I compare Roma/non-Roma interactions in the typical town to those in a different Slovene town which matches the first on all relevant factors, but which has a Roma-led NGO that promotes intergroup contact and dialogue (the first town has a Roma-led NGO that focuses on service provision). My findings suggest that intergroup contact can help break the exclusion cycle. I find that while anti-Roma sentiment is present in the town with the contact-promoting NGO, there is less of it and, more importantly, non-Roma there do not appear to act on it. Non-Roma in this town do not discriminate against the Roma. Roma still use survival strategies, but to a lesser extent. Since the use of survival strategies is tied to personal experience of discrimination, and since there is less discrimination in this town, fewer Roma resort to these strategies. Likewise, non-Roma in this town still commit the error of attributing Roma uses of survival strategies to the Roma as such and not the discrimination, but they do that far less often than non-Roma from the first town. NGO promotion of intergroup contact thus appears to be effective in breaking the cycle—primarily through curtailing discriminatory behaviors by the majority.

Two additional, and important, findings emerge from this study. First, Roma do not uniformly behave as stereotyped. Some do, as do some non-Roma, but many do not. I find the need to explicitly state this obvious fact distasteful. However, we far too often make remarks that treat the stereotype of Roma as cheaters and thieves as given. Around the world, people say "I was gypped!" when they mean to say that they felt cheated, and many tourists have been warned about Roma pickpockets in particular on the streets of Paris, Rome, or Prague. Stereotyping the Roma is rote. It is therefore important, sadly, to empirically demonstrate that it is wrong. Second, Roma do not discriminate against non-Roma. Despite generations of mistreatment and exclusion, and despite discrimination they experience today, Roma treat non-Roma no differently than they treat their own. This is remarkable.

I collected the data I draw on in this book between the summers of 2010 and 2018. I use a number of empirical approaches. The centerpiece are two lab-in-field experiments that capture discriminatory behavior by non-Roma and survival strategies by Roma. One of these experiments uses a tower-building videogame, which I created to visualize the public goods game (Marwell and Ames 1979). The videogame is a significant departure from the way this game is typically delivered and offers more precision in inference because I am able to capture how different people react to the exact same play scenario, as well as how the same person reacts to different play scenarios. The videogame also enables the most vulnerable among the Roma to participate. The multi-round public goods game requires repeated interactions and is typically played in a group, face-to-face. Asking Roma and non-Roma participants to play the game in a group was untenable as such interactions can be fraught and contentious. Typical alternatives are fielded online and tend to involve a computer interface, which requires participants to read. A substantial proportion of older Roma participants, especially women, cannot read and would automatically be excluded from participating in any such study. The videogame resolves this problem. I use original survey data, field observations, and semi-structured interviews to fill in the gaps and to provide context for participant behaviors that I capture through the experiments.

Although I use the case of Roma and non-Roma to explore the exclusion cycle, the insights apply more broadly. The example of Jimmy Warren illustrates how an exclusion cycle can take root in Boston. Similarly, we might find such cycles among Haitians and non-Haitians in the Dominican Republic, Batwa and non-Batwa in Uganda, Blacks and non-Blacks in Rio de Janeiro, and Muslim immigrants and the "rooted French" in France (those French citizens with four grandparents born within the French hexagon; see Adida et al. (2010)).

Importantly, the dynamic I describe with the exclusion cycle is not the only one that perpetuates exclusion at the individual level, nor is it the only possible manifestation of a cycle of exclusion. It is, perhaps, the simplest form of such a cycle, to be complicated and built upon in the future. It is also not an absolute and all-encompassing explanation of exclusion; instead, it is only a small piece of a much larger and complex whole. What this book offers is an illustration of *one* way in which exclusion can be cemented at the level of the individual. Variations of and deviations from the cycle provide numerous fruitful and necessary avenues for future research.

In what follows, I first briefly discuss social exclusion and then explain why I focus on individual behavior. The section after that describes the exclusion cycle and discusses why the promotion of intergroup contact and dialogue could help in breaking it. Next, I discuss the scope of the argument. The conclusion offers brief descriptions of the remaining chapters.

Social exclusion

The concept of social exclusion is contested and constantly evolving.[6] Madanipour et al. (1998) write:

> Social exclusion is defined as a multi-dimensional process, in which various forms of exclusion are combined: participation in decision making and political processes, access to employment and material resources, and integration into common cultural processes. When combined, they create acute forms of exclusion that find a spatial manifestation in particular neighbourhoods.
>
> (Madanipour et al. 1998, 22)

The basic components of exclusion or, rather, their relative importance, vary based on the environment. In the UK, for example, poverty is perhaps the most crucial building block of exclusion (Burchardt et al. 2002). In stronger welfare states where social benefits ensure basic subsistence, political, social, or cultural exclusion may take precedence (Newman and Massengill 2006). In the US, scholars tend not to talk about exclusion at all, and refer instead to "'ghettoization,' 'marginalization,' and the 'underclass'" (Burchardt et al. 2002). These concepts and their permutations, however, are roughly speaking about the same group of people: individuals or groups who cannot participate fully in typical activities of the societies in which they live.

Generally, this tends to happen for reasons beyond their control, though exclusion can also be voluntary as "individuals or members of a group may withdraw from participation in the wider society in response to experience of hostility and discrimination" (Barry 2002, p.14). Likewise, while those who are excluded usually want to participate, the desire to be included is not required; even if a Traveller has no interest in eating in a restaurant with a "polite notice—positively no travellers" (BBC 2008) sign on the door, he is still excluded.

Social exclusion can be wide-ranging. A young Black man in America who is still in high school, for example, faces disproportionately high risks of exclusionary school punishment, such as suspension or expulsion (Fenning and Rose 2007). Overrepresentation of students of color in exclusionary punishment is linked to the same phenomenon in the juvenile justice and prison systems (Wald and Losen 2003). Early on, Black (and Latino) boys are more likely to be labeled as potentially dangerous and systematically pushed

---

[6] See Barry (2002) and Byrne (2005) for in-depth discussions on definitions of social exclusion.

out of school (Casella 2003); later, they are far more likely to end up in prison for offenses that go unpunished when committed by Whites (Alexander 2010), more likely to be systematically excluded from the job market (Pager 2007), and more likely to be kept out of quality housing by way of discrimination in sales, rental, or lending markets (Pager and Shepherd 2008). Convicted felons are further excluded from public benefits that others enjoy, like access to food stamps, public housing, and federal educational assistance, as well as fundamental forms of political participation, like voting and serving on juries (Alexander 2010).

Of course, not all instances of social exclusion are as pervasive. Some individuals are excluded on a single dimension, like young people in numerous European countries today who complete their educations but cannot get hired, contributing to youth unemployment rates as high as 50 percent (Eurostat 2017).[7] As individuals who are excluded on a single dimension are likely to remain insulated from other spheres of exclusion, their experience of social exclusion is fundamentally different from that of people who are excluded intentionally and systematically, based on their racial or ethnic identity, their country of immediate or distant origin, their faith, their sexual orientation, and more. This book is about the latter type of exclusion— intentional, systematic, all-encompassing.

As it exists on multiple dimensions, pervasive social exclusion has multiple immediate causes: an individual might be denied a job opportunity because an intolerant employer refuses to interview minority candidates; a family might be excluded from living in a neighborhood because landlords there tend to quote higher rent prices to people who don't look like them; a local hospital might have an unwritten policy for placing minority patients in some rooms, and majority patients in others (as I find to be the case in one field site); a municipality might skip roads in a minority neighborhood as it works on repaving potholes. Poverty-stricken school districts might be forced to spend fewer funds on more students. A country might refuse to grant driving licenses to a portion of its population.

The power to exclude thus lies in the hands of individuals, businesses, health care and other service providers, municipalities, states, countries, and more. These individual and systemic modes of exclusion then intersect and interact, leading to exclusion that is deeply embedded and intractable. In this book,

---

[7] While high youth unemployment rates are present in almost all European countries, they are particularly high in Greece, Spain, Croatia, and Italy, where they ranged between 40 and 50 percent in 2013 (Eurostat 2017).

I have chosen to examine individuals alone. With this focus, the story that I tell is necessarily limited as the dynamics I study are in real life complicated by the systemic factors I leave out. However, those complications might be better addressed once their component parts are understood. Here, I look at the smallest of those parts.

Why focus on individuals?

Just above, I wrote that young Black men are more likely than young White men to face exclusionary punishment in school. This is not so because of differences in socio-economic status, or higher rates of misbehavior among Black students. Instead, this stems from systematic differences in teacher referrals to the principal's office (Skiba et al. 2002). Teachers are substantially more likely to send Black boys to the principal's office, and often for infractions that are less serious.[8] If being sent to the principal's office does not seem foreboding, recall that rates of suspension in schools closely correspond to rates of juvenile or later incarceration that label people felons for the rest of their lives, thereby ensuring exclusion across several dimensions. A young person could thus be pushed towards intractable exclusion by a single individual who may or may not be aware of her bigotry (Sheets 1996).

The idea that a single individual could so meaningfully contribute to the exclusion of another might appear improbable at first, but in truth individuals make decisions that matter all the time. Social spaces and institutions that support exclusion rest on the attitudes and the behaviors of individuals. Even where laws and policies reflect a commitment to inclusion, inclusion in practice may prove elusive if the citizenry is reluctant to embrace it. For a vivid example, recall the racial harassment of 6 year-old Ruby Bridges, who was the first Black student attending a formerly all-White elementary school in New Orleans, following the Brown v. Board of Education decision. White protesters, mostly women, harassed the girl throughout the year, using not only protest signs but also props like a Black baby doll in a coffin (Junn 2017). Of course, I do not claim that social exclusion would disappear if actions of individuals did not support it; structural exclusion is too deeply embedded in our institutions. Instead, I maintain that social exclusion *cannot* disappear as long as the attitudes and behaviors of individuals fuel it. Addressing individual

---

[8] Skiba et al. (2002) find that Black and Latino boys are sent most often, followed by White boys, Black girls, and White girls.

behaviors is thus necessary, but insufficient, to efforts that aim to eliminate exclusion completely.

Individual behaviors can perhaps cause most harm when the individuals who engage in them are state actors. The degree of harm varies from state to state; today, state actors in the Philippines under President Rodrigo Duterte operate quite differently from those in Austria, but regardless of where they are, state actors are granted a degree of license and protection that ordinary citizens tend not to have, while their actions often carry consequences that cannot be ignored. Police brutality, rampant in Brazil and in recent years receiving more and more attention in the United States, provides an example of individuals perpetuating exclusion while operating as state actors. In the United States, victims of police brutality are disproportionately people of color (Swaine et al. 2015); in Rio de Janeiro, the majority of victims are young Black men (Amnesty International 2016). Research suggests that in the US, excessive attention paid to men of color in stop-and-frisk operations (Gelman et al. 2007) and traffic stops (Horrace and Rohlin 2016) is not due to a higher rate of infractions by men of color. There is no explicit policy that demands racial profiling in police stops. The decision about whom to stop and whether to shoot rests with individuals.

An individual can also contribute to exclusion as a private citizen. For instance, a number of Indian states implement a mid-day meal scheme, which provides children in government schools with a hot lunch every day (Thorat and Lee 2005). Often, dominant caste communities mobilize against the participation of Dalits, members of former "untouchable" castes and groups, in the scheme. Some pressure local administrators to hire dominant caste cooks by forbidding their children to eat food prepared by a Dalit cook or by enrolling their children in a different school, one without a Dalit cook (Thorat and Lee 2005). Others mobilize to exclude Dalit children from the scheme altogether, or, if that fails, to segregate mid-day meals, to serve Dalit children insufficient portions of inferior food, and to serve the meals in dominant caste localities such that Dalit children are forced to walk through tense and threatening areas to receive the meals to which they are entitled (Thorat and Lee 2005). Here, private citizens—parents or prominent members of the dominant caste—are the primary actors behind denying Dalit children their right to food.

Those who exclude are not the only individuals whose behaviors help perpetuate social exclusion. The excluded also contribute. Consider the "new poor," a distinct social group of squatters and slum dwellers in Iran in the middle of the 20th century (Bayat 1997). This social group of disenfranchised people developed in the wake of modernization policies pursued by both Shahs since the 1930s, which resulted in rapid urban growth, urban migration, and marginalization of the urban poor. Many of the "new poor" settled in illegally established sites. As the neighborhoods grew, slum dwellers demanded public goods, like water and electricity. In response to refusals or delays, they acquired the goods themselves. They built roads and clinics, tapped into electricity lines, and built a subsistence economy based on street services and street vending (Bayat 1997). Having secured access to public goods on their own, they sought autonomy from "the state and from modern institutions" (Bayat 1997, 11), which often subject people to surveillance and regulate how they live their daily lives. This autonomy enabled them to thrive on their own, through cooperation, self-regulation, moral economies, and local conflict resolution. But it also solidified their exclusion.

In sum, individuals play a crucial part in perpetuating exclusion. Those who exclude may do it as private citizens or as agents of the state; actions legitimized by the state can be particularly impactful. Those who are excluded may help reinforce exclusion by seeking alternative ways of existence—ways that deepen the rift between communities, but allow the excluded not only to survive but also to improve their lives.

Presenting the case: Roma, non-Roma, Novo mesto, and Murska Sobota

Roma are Europe's largest ethnic minority. Recent estimates suggest that 10 to 12 million Roma live across Europe today (Matache and Mark 2014). They emigrated from India over 900 years ago, and over time followed a number of migration routes to virtually every state in the European space, as well as many beyond (Mendizabal et al. 2012). While popular depictions of Roma tend to focus on their nomadic way of life, not all Roma travelled, and most of those who did are no longer itinerant (Barany 2002). Their language, Romani, which is closely related to early modern languages of central and northern India (Matras 2002), is perhaps their most distinctive cultural feature (although some Roma do not speak it). It has six major dialect branches, each consisting of numerous dialects, as well as a separate group of dialects that are not categorized within any of those major branches (Matras 2002). The Romani language thus perfectly illustrates a fundamental fact about the Roma: they are complex and diverse.

Although a superordinate "umbrella" Romani identity exists and many Roma identify as such in relation to non-Roma and within their own subgroup, their subgroup identity may take precedence in relation to other Roma (Bodnárová 2018). Subgroup names are often based on traditional professions, geographical location, religion, and group lifestyle. Romani subgroups which traditionally engaged in training bears (or are thought to have done so), for example, are called Ajdžides in Turkey, Mečkara in Bulgaria, and Ursari in Romania. The names are based on their respective local non-Roma words for "bear," but despite the shared traditional occupation, the three subgroups are not related (Bodnárová 2018). Among numerous other subgroup names based on traditional professions are Colari (carpet dealers), Kanaloš (spoon makers), Lovari (horse-dealers), Rudari (miners), and Musicians; named instead for geography, Vlaxi Roma historically come from the principality of Wallachia (in Romania), while the Bergitka Roma reside in the Carpathian highlands in Poland (Bodnárová 2018).[9] While the legacies of traditional occupations are quite meaningful, members of most Romani communities today no longer engage in these trades and instead have taken up mainstream professions.

Roma heterogeneity manifests itself in a rich array of cultural practices and traditions. Gábor Roma communities from Transylvania, for example, tend to engage in international trade and gutter construction (Jacobs 2018). Men traditionally wear black hats and mustaches, while women wear long floral pleated skirts (Jacobs 2018). Hungarian Roma, a large heterogeneous group of Roma who live in Hungary and parts of Slovakia, typically don't speak Romani. Many are believed to be descended from musician families, but not all are; those who are musicians are also called Musician Roma (Bodnárová 2018).[10] The highly influential tradition of the Musician Roma has given life to greats like János Bihari who pioneered the *verbunkos* style that later became known as "Magyar-Hungarian national music *par excellence*" (Lajosi 2014, p.643). Many Roma communities across the Balkans are Muslim and often called "Turkish;" many Roma there do indeed speak Turkish, in addition to Romani, and identify as Turks—a testament to the lasting influence of the Ottoman Empire on the region (Marushiakova and Popov 2018). And some Norwegian Romanifolk/Tatere communities, while no longer completely itinerant, still travel from village to village in the summer, either trading goods or selling their

---

[9] Bergitka is based on the German word "Berg," which means mountain.
[10] The term "Musician Roma" is sometimes used to describe non-musicians as well (Bodnárová 2018).

own products (Wiedner 2018). They are particularly well known for elaborate metal works, crafting knives and kitchen tools, and for the production of textiles.

While the histories and experiences of Romani communities vary, many have historically experienced gross mistreatment and discrimination, including slavery in Moldavia and Wallachia (Barany 2002), genocide during World War II (Lewy 2000), and forced assimilation in the second half of the 20th century (Barany 2002). As diverse as the Roma are, they remain commonly reduced to a number of stereotypes and are often seen as tourist-terrorizing pickpockets, as curse-wielding fortune tellers, as bohemian musicians, and as a burden on the social welfare state. Non-Roma discrimination against the Roma coupled with institutional mechanisms that further cement inequality has resulted in the social exclusion of many. This is not to say that all Roma experience social exclusion—many do not—or that those who do experience it in the same way. Indeed, Roma/non-Roma relations are context- and experience-specific such that an account of relations in one place does not necessarily generalize to all relations everywhere. Certainly, however, socially excluded Romani communities can be found in any European country from Ireland to Russia. This includes Slovenia.

Slovenia is a country of about 2 million people located between Italy, Austria, Hungary, and Croatia. If one were to ask a few strangers on the streets of Ljubljana what part of Europe the country belongs to, the answers would likely differ. One might claim Central, pointing to its place in the former Austro-Hungarian Empire; another might say Eastern, as Slovenes are a Slavic people; another still might say neither, pointing South to the Balkans and Slovenia's recent history as a part of Yugoslavia. According to the contemporary division of Slavs, mainly constructed on a linguistic basis, ethnic Slovenes are Southern Slavs, along with Bosnians and Herzegovinians, Bulgarians, Croatians, Macedonians, and Serbs, though they may be more closely related to Slavs from the West, particularly Slovaks and Czechs (Zupan et al. 2013). The first written record of Roma in Slovenia is from 1387 (Štrukelj 1980).

Before Slovenia became a member of the European Union (EU) in 2004, its treatment of the Roma was subject to scrutiny, as is typically the case during EU accession negotiations. The European Commission found that the country had made sufficient progress in this general area since negotiations started in 1998. The reality on the ground casts a shadow over this conclusion. In 1997, for example, non-Roma villagers from Maline set up explosives around the house a Roma family had recently bought and set up an armed patrol to prevent the family from moving in (Erjavec et al. 2000). The villagers succeeded. In

Ambrus, in 2006, several hundred non-Roma armed with clubs, guns, and chainsaws forcibly evicted a Roma family from land they had owned and lived on for decades (Traynor 2006). This family has not yet returned home. Slovenia is no outlier. Such events have happened in a number of other EU member states, particularly those that have joined during the Eastern Expansions in 2004 and 2007 (Matache 2014). In Baia Mare, Romania, for example, local Roma were forcibly re-settled into hazardous laboratory spaces of a decommissioned chemical plant (Lacatus 2012). In Vitkov, Czech Republic, a three year-old Roma girl lost 80 percent of her skin after far-right extremists threw a Molotov cocktail into her family's home (Tkach 2010). And in Gemerská Poloma, Slovakia, a mob of forty to fifty young men repeatedly attacked three Roma families over the Easter weekend, ransacking their homes and beating the adults. The mayor of the town suggested that the families lock their doors (Albert 2011).

When it comes to Roma, Slovenia is relatively understudied. The country was not included in either of the two large surveys of Roma in Europe, both conducted in 2011, of which one covered 11 and the other 12 states (FRA 2014a; Ivanov et al. 2012).[11] We therefore have less systematic information about Slovene Roma than we do about their counterparts in Hungary or Czech Republic. The lack of attention, however, should not lead one to conclude that Roma/non-Roma relations in Slovenia are superior to those in a dozen of countries across Europe, or that the lives of Roma in Slovenia are better by comparison. In fact, based on a range of socioeconomic and quality of life indicators, the lives of Roma in my two field sites, Novo mesto[12] and Murska Sobota, are quite similar to the lives of Roma across 12 European states.[13]

Novo mesto, the first of my field sites, is the regional capital of Dolenjska. The city lies in the south-eastern corner of the country, about 10 miles away from the Slovene-Croat border. Novo mesto has the largest Roma population in the region, and second largest in Slovenia. Official and unofficial population counts differ; the unofficial estimate, based on a source in town, suggests that Roma make up 2.8 percent of the town population. At 1.2 percent, the

---

[11] The first survey is the European Union Agency for Fundamental Rights (FRA) Roma Pilot Survey (FRA 2014a); the second is the UNDP-World Bank-European Commission Regional Roma Survey (Ivanov 2012).

[12] To readers in English, capitalizing "Novo" but not "mesto" might look unusual. The word "mesto" means "city" in Slovene and is therefore not capitalized even when it is a part of a proper name.

[13] These countries are Albania, Bosnia and Herzegovina, Bulgaria, Czech Republic, Hungary, Croatia, Moldova, Montengro, Macedonia, Romania, Serbia, and Slovakia. The data for these countries is from the UNDP-World Bank-European Commission Regional Roma Survey (Ivanov et al. 2012). I collected the data for Novo mesto and Murska Sobota myself. For more information, see Table 7.1 in Chapter 7.

estimate based on the 2002 Census is much lower (SURS 2002). Novo mesto has had a settled Roma population for over 200 years, though some Roma have arrived more recently. Most live in isolated, segregated neighborhoods; the vast majority lives in Brezje-Žabjak, which is separated from the rest of town by a stretch of fields and woods. Roma have had a representative in the local government since 2002 (Dedić 2003b). Each local school employs one Romani assistant who helps Roma students with Slovene, which is their second language (Rajšek 2014). The schools do not teach Romani and their syllabi do not include lessons on Roma history, culture, tradition, or past mistreatment.

My second field site, Murska Sobota, is the regional capital of Prekmurje, in the north-eastern corner of the country. I selected the two sites using nearest neighbor matching (Ho et al. 2007a, 2007b), which ensured that they matched on a number of relevant factors. Like Novo mesto, Murska Sobota is approximately 10 miles from the Slovene-Croat border; it has the largest Roma population in the region, and the largest in the country. Roma make up 2.3 percent of the town population (SURS 2002). Like in Novo mesto, the Roma in Murska Sobota have been settled there for over 200 years, live predominantly in isolated, segregated neighborhoods, and have a representative in the local government (Dedić 2003b). Local schools do employ Romani assistants, but do not teach Romani or put lessons on the Roma on their syllabi (Rajšek 2014). While the two towns are quite similar, they differ in one crucial aspect. Novo mesto has a Roma NGO that provides socio-economic services to the Roma. Non-Roma are typically not involved in its activities. The Roma NGO in Muska Sobota, in contrast, focuses on Roma/non-Roma relations, fostering positive intergroup contact and dialogue.

The first site, Novo mesto, serves as the baseline case which I use to describe how an exclusion cycle can come about in a community where Roma and non-Roma live. Murska Sobota provides an example of a case where intergroup contact strategies can be used to break an exclusion cycle. In the section that follows, I present the Roma exclusion cycle using general examples as well as some findings from Novo mesto. Later in this chapter, I will briefly turn to Murska Sobota and intergroup contact.

The exclusion cycle

As previously mentioned, the exclusion cycle has four parts. Anti-minority culture is first, followed by discriminatory behavior by the majority. Survival strategies used by the minority are next, and the attribution error, committed by the majority, is last. Such errors then feed anti-minority culture and the cycle starts over. The starting point of the cycle is arbitrary. Indeed, for members of groups that have been excluded for generations, seeking to identify the beginning would be futile and likely impossible. The four parts of the cycle also do not necessarily follow a clearly defined progression; instead of strictly playing out between two particular individuals, constant interactions between different people can make up complete or partial cycles, which then interweave to reinforce group divisions.

Anti-minority culture

Humans have a fundamental need to belong. We also have a need to be unique (Allport 1954; Brewer 1991). To balance these countervailing forces, we form ingroups and outgroups (Campbell 1958). As we derive our self-esteem from our ingroups (Tajfel and Turner 1979), we constantly compare them to relevant outgroups. This results in ingroup favoritism as well as, sometimes, outgroup derogation (Gaertner et al. 1999). While we require next to nothing to maintain divisions (Billing and Tajfel 1973; Wright et al. 1997), characteristics that are socially meaningful, like race or gender, make it much easier. Historical inequalities in power, wealth, and opportunity have created frameworks that accommodate privileged groups' need for higher self-esteem. The resulting anti-minority cultures not only provide space for prejudice, but also normalize it.

While anti-minority culture can endure, it is not static. It is continually evolving, being remade with new, updated expressions of prejudice that man-ifest as personal opinions and spread through informal social networks; as stories that popular media choose to report and curate by using particular language; or as depictions in popular culture that create new imagery of old, limited, and damaging tropes. In the case of the Roma, one can simply search one's memory for romanticized, outdated, and stereotypical images of the Roma as transient, bohemian folk of wily ways and unbridled passions. Carmen, of the eponymous opera by Bizet, is one such character. Her aria from the first act, "Habanera," is among the most well known in history. Its message—that love is rebellious and wild, and knows no law—is borne out in full by Carmen herself, and so constantly reinforces the popular per-ception of the Roma as opera houses stage the blockbuster time and time again. The less operatically inclined might have instead run across Esmeralda, the main character in Victor Hugo's *Notre-Dame de Paris* (1833; in English

"The Hunchback of Notre Dame"), either as a character in the original work or in one of numerous adaptations, including the Disney movie in 1996.[14] In both works and some of their adaptations, the romanticized images appear alongside depictions of the Roma as conniving, hyper-sexual, dangerous, and criminal—say, when the beautiful and generous Esmeralda is revealed to have been French all along, and just kidnapped by Roma as a child.

Alongside popular depictions of Roma, anti-Roma culture is rooted in everyday speech. English-speaking societies, for example, commonly use the word "gyp" to express indignation about feeling cheated. This phrase is so banal that many English-speakers who say "I was gypped!" are not aware of its connotations. As such, the phrase perfectly illustrates how deep-seated anti-minority culture can be: by using the phrase, one can contribute to it without ever harboring anti-Roma sentiment. This is, of course, not always the case; often speech is quite explicitly prejudiced. When they want to accuse someone of a great deal of lying, ethnic Slovenes say "he lies like a Gypsy" (SSKJ 2008). When they want to describe someone as dirty or as having darker skin, they say he is "black like a Gypsy" (SSKJ 2008).[15] The authoritative Dictionary of the Standard Slovene Language (or SSKJ) describes neither of these phrases as derogatory.

Non-Roma study participants from Novo mesto, the first of my field sites, thus did not refrain from open prejudice. When asked about the Roma, one said that they "[b]eg from house to house despite social benefits and government child support, that they steal . . . that they don't work, they are not clean." Another warned: "they are cunning; you can't trust everything they say," and another still that "they extort rights and social benefits from the state." Overall, 62 percent of the participants agreed with the damning statement that "the Roma cannot be trusted."[16] Anti-minority culture sustains a social space in which non-Roma are not only able to openly express prejudice, but do so expecting support. This is then embraced by various entities that can profit from promoting open bigotry, ranging from the press (Glücks 2016) to individuals running for and serving in office (Rajšek 2011).

Discrimination

Anti-minority culture creates space for maltreatment. Discrimination is unfair or unequal treatment of an individual based on certain characteristics, like

---

[14] See Oprea (2012) for an exploration of the gendered nature of stereotyping of the Roma.

[15] In Slovene, the two phrases are "laže kot cigan" and "črn kot cigan," respectively.

[16] For details, see Chapter 5.

gender, race, ethnicity, age, sexual orientation, religion, disability, and more. For someone who harbors anti-minority sentiment, the step from an adverse attitude to adverse behavior can be challenging in a social space that condemns discrimination. If anti-minority culture is pervasive, such a step is easier. This appears to be the case across a number of spheres in European countries with Romani populations.

Schools often segregate. Perhaps the most extreme example comes from the Czech Republic,[17] where some school officials routinely place Roma children with no disabilities in schools for mentally disabled children. In Croatia, where Romani students attend regular schools along with non-Roma, they have been placed in separate, Roma-only, classrooms.[18] And, where Roma and non-Roma students do attend classes together, teachers often practice segregation within their own classrooms by placing Roma children in the last row of seats (Matache 2014).

Discrimination continues in the realm of employment. In Bulgaria, the Czech Republic, Hungary, Romania, and Slovakia, employers typically do not take measures to comply with anti-discrimination legislation and often feel little compunction in openly discriminating, going so far as telling candidates that they do not employ Roma (Hyde 2006). Individuals who work at state employment offices contribute to the problem by allowing potential employers to opt out of seeing Roma job candidates, which results in Roma job seekers never finding out about the opportunity at all (Hyde 2006).

Roma further face mistreatment in healthcare. In some hospitals in Slovenia, for example, Roma patients are segregated and placed in Roma-only rooms.[19] As recently as 2001, doctors in Slovakia and the Czech Republic (Stejskalová and Szilvási 2016) sterilized Roma women without their consent or awareness, or with consent extracted under duress, during labor. Finally, law enforcement often alternates between two extremes, targeting Roma under some circumstances, while not providing enough protection in others (recall the hate crimes I briefly mentioned just a few pages ago). A particularly sobering example of police targeting comes from Sweden, where in 2013 the press revealed the existence of a secret illegal registry of resident Roma—including over 1000 entries for children, some of them toddlers—compiled and maintained by police officers in the southern part of the country under the guise of fighting violent crime (Mansel 2013).

[17] D.H. and others v. Czech Republic, 57325/00, 13 November 2007, European Court of Human Rights.

[18] Oršuš and others v. Croatia, 15766/03, 16 March 2010, European Court of Human Rights.

[19] Survey and interview evidence collected as part of this study.

As discrimination against the Roma can be widespread, capturing discriminatory behaviors among non-Roma is challenging. A teacher may discriminate in the classroom, a doctor in the hospital, and a police officer on the street. Documenting these varying behaviors as they occur in real life and all at once is nearly impossible. I therefore turn to games that capture other-regarding behaviors. The games approximate a real-life interaction in a controlled environment, giving participants an opportunity to discriminate (or not to discriminate). Since anyone can play the games, teachers, doctors, and police officers alike may reveal their underlying propensity to discriminate in real life through their game behaviors. Both games I use are games of cooperation, where high levels of cooperation make all players better off, but only if everyone cooperates; if a player defects while others cooperate, the defector is best off. Once other players defect, cooperating is no longer an optimal strategy. The games exploit the stereotype of Roma as cheaters, thieves, and takers such that non-Roma who subscribe to the stereotype— and thus expect that Roma players will not cooperate—might discriminate by cooperating less when playing with Roma. Detailed descriptions of the trust game (Berg et al. 1995) and the public goods (Marwell and Ames 1979) videogame are in Chapter 4.

Fielding these games among randomly sampled non-Roma in Novo mesto, Slovenia, I find the following. First, non-Roma discriminate against the Roma in a single interaction setting, where two players interact once and never again. Second, non-Roma also discriminate against the Roma in a repeated interaction setting, where participants interact with the same players several times over the course of the game. Third, non-Roma who express anti-Roma prejudice discriminate against the Roma, while non-Roma who reject the prejudice do not discriminate. Finally, and most devastatingly, non-Roma not only discriminate against the Roma in anticipation of future Roma behavior but also when evaluating past Roma behaviors. Specifically, reacting to *identical* past Roma and non-Roma game behaviors, non-Roma reward Roma *less* for cooperating and punish them *more* for not cooperating.

My findings from the games, while somewhat abstract, echo Roma reports of discrimination. Eighty-two percent of randomly sampled Roma from Novo mesto reported experiencing at least one type of mistreatment and believed that it happened because they were Roma. Examples include being refused entry into a pub or restaurant, seeing non-Roma passengers blatantly secure their bags upon entering a bus, and having non-Roma switch to a different seat when sitting next to them in the waiting room at the doctor's office.

There are, of course, instances in which the source of discrimination does not lie with individuals, but with institutions. As I focus on individuals in this book, institutional sources are not considered here. It would be careless, however, to forget that in addition to the many examples of individual-based discrimination discussed, there are also others that Roma must contend with on a daily basis.

Survival strategies

Members of marginalized groups are not passive. While they often cannot escape discrimination altogether, they react to it, anticipate it, and devise strategies that let them live and improve their lives. I use the term "survival strategies" to refer to a broad set of behaviors in which individuals engage because discrimination has severely curtailed their options. Survival strategies are defined by their circumstances. Playing the accordion on the street is not a survival strategy if the musician merely wishes to share music with strangers, but it is one if performing on the street allows the musician to make ends meet. While I call them strategies, these behaviors are not necessarily strategic. Some may be automatic, some may be adopted because other group members engage in them, and some may be a matter of tradition, particularly for members of groups that have been excluded for generations. In favor of focusing on strategies of survival, there are a number of other strategies that I neglect here, most notably behaviors that are "surreptitiously offensive" (Bayat 1997, p.6) or aimed at resistance. I focus on survival strategies because the Roma I have interviewed frame the behaviors I discuss as geared towards survival.

Consider the Roma in Novo mesto. Ninety percent of randomly sampled Roma who live there do not have a job; some are retired, but most are unemployed. According to the Republic of Slovenia Statistical Office, the overall unemployment rate in Slovenia that year (2015) was 9 percent. When asked whether they had ever applied for a job with the aid of the Employment Service of Slovenia, as most Slovenes do, 73 percent of Roma said they had; of those, only 10 percent got a job. Over ninety percent live below the poverty line. Facing extraordinary barriers to employment, Roma resort to a number of survival strategies. Many collect and sell scrap metal; some collect it fairly close to home, while others travel all over the country in search of customers. Some Roma do seasonal agricultural work. Others harvest produce that they then sell at the farmers market, particularly mushrooms and blueberries. Some sell various goods door to door. Many rely on social assistance.

Counting on social assistance to make ends meet is a fairly common practice among Slovenes. The government typically spends 1.1 billion euros per year on social transfers; in 2016, social assistance of various forms took up just over 800 million euros. Certainly, there are far more ethnic Slovenes than Roma among those who receive assistance; even if every Roma person in the country were to subsist on social assistance, which is not the case, ethnic Slovenes who do the same would outnumber them by at least an order of magnitude, if not two.[20] And yet, the survival strategy is ethnicized.[21] When they complain that some people receive more from the government than they deserve, Slovenes typically picture the Roma. A non-Roma participant volunteered that some Roma women have monthly incomes "exceeding 2,000 euros without ever having worked a day in their lives," which they purportedly extract from the state by having many children. This claim is patently false.[22] The gendered stereotype of Roma as takers closely resembles the highly politicized "Welfare Queen" rhetoric used to describe poor Black women in America (Collins 1990; Hancock 2004), and is commonly used to accuse Roma of taking much from society, while contributing little.[23]

I use the public goods videogame mentioned in the previous section to capture the extent to which Roma behaviors mirror such a survival strategy, at least as perceived by non-Roma. In this game, everyone is better off if all players cooperate and contribute to the public good, from which everyone benefits; if a player defects by keeping his own endowment while others contribute theirs to the public good, however, the defector is better off—he receives a portion of the public good on top of his endowment. To non-Roma, not cooperating with the group while reaping the benefits of the public good is parallel to the survival strategy of relying on social assistance to make ends meet. Roma who defect (or rely on social assistance) are thus seen by many as cheaters and takers. Defecting is, of course, perfectly allowed in the context of the game, but it is nevertheless disliked and ethnicized by non-Roma participants.

Among randomly sampled Roma from Novo mesto, many indeed cooperate less in the videogame, when compared to non-Roma participants. Recall, however, that cooperating only works when others cooperate as well; as soon

[20] Based on the 2002 Census, there are about 3800 Roma in Slovenia. Data from 2007 indicate that 380,000 individuals received social assistance on the basis of having children, whereas 44,000 received social aid on the basis of short-term or, in rarer cases, long-term need (Lončar and Rabuza 2017).

[21] I use the word "ethnicized" in the same way as other scholars would use "racialized" when describing a similar occurrence in relation to race instead of ethnic group.

[22] The highest total amount of social assistance given to any family in 2016 was 1,294 euros per month; this is a family with 9 children and thus quite unusual (Lončar and Rabuza 2017).

[23] Recent investigations revealed that the woman originally described as a "Welfare Queen," Linda Taylor, might not have been Black at all, but instead a White woman pretending to be Black (Levin 2013).

as they stop, defecting becomes the better strategy. If Roma participants expect non-Roma players to discriminate and cooperate less when playing with Roma (which they did), it makes sense to defect. Defecting in the videogame is thus a parallel to real-life survival strategies that develop in an environment of constrained choices: an action that is perhaps not preferred, but one that is under the limiting circumstances (i.e. discrimination) the best available alternative. But not all Roma defect. Those who report expriencing discrimination cooperate significantly less than those who do not report experiencing the same. Personal experience of discrimination therefore appears tied to the expectation that non-Roma will discriminate in the context of the videogame, and to the subsequent decision to defect.

While defecting makes sense, it is nevertheless stereotype affirming. This is also the case for a number of everyday survival strategies, like collecting scrap metal, selling goods door to door, and, indeed, relying on social assistance. When non-Roma engage in these strategies—and they do—they are perceived as ways of making ends meet. When Roma do the same, however, they take on a different meaning altogether.

The attribution error

Humans commonly commit attribution errors. We follow a simple rule when we make these mistakes: we are nice to our own, and not nice to outsiders. For example, when an ingroup member does something good, we attribute that action to an inner quality—character, genetics, nature (Pettigrew 1979). This quality is often group-based. But when an outgroup member performs the same action, we attribute it to an outside circumstance (Pettigrew 1979). Suppose a non-smoker does well on a test. When asked why, fellow non-smokers say it's because he's smart (Gibson 1998). If a smoker does equally as well, however, they say it's because the test was easy (Gibson 1998). In the first case, they attribute success to an inner quality; in the second, to an outside circumstance. If actions are bad, we switch the attributions. When ingroup members behave poorly, we attribute the behavior to outside circumstances; when outgroup members do, we point to inner qualities.

Majorities often dislike survival strategies. And so, following this simple rule, non-Roma often attribute Roma uses of social assistance to "their nature as takers." In contrast, when non-Roma rely on social assistance to make ends meet, fellow non-Roma can point to a number of external circumstances that may have led to precarity—divorce, single parenting, loss of employment, chronic or debilitating illness, and long-term poverty. While those same reasons, among others, also lead to precarity among the Roma, they are rarely mentioned by non-Roma.

Instead, randomly sampled non-Roma from Novo mesto say the following. One participant said that "[the Roma] do nothing themselves, they expect to be entirely supported by the state;" another said that they are "[lazy and unwilling] to work because [they expect] the state to support them financially, pay their bills and take care of their dwellings". A third was bothered by "[Roma] refusal to work and [their] abuse of social assistance," and a fourth by the fact "that they steal, that they lie, that they receive social assistance instead of putting in some effort and working honestly." A number of participants spoke of Roma and social assistance with rancor, saying that they "abused the state" and "extorted rights" from it. According to these participants, the Roma from the very beginning intend to take from the state, refusing to work at all, whereas, the assumption goes, non-Roma would rather work, if they could. The very nature of the survival strategy changes based on who engages in it. When non-Roma rely on social assistance, they are persevering through hardship; when Roma do the same, they are extorting the state.

With this interpretation, non-Roma affirm the stereotype of Roma as cheaters, thieves, and takers. They erroneously attribute the use of the survival strategy to the Roma as such instead of recognizing discrimination—or any number of other, related hardships—as its cause. When attribution errors affirm stereotypes, they contribute to the already existing anti-Roma culture, completing the exclusion cycle.

To summarize, the exclusion cycle starts with anti-minority culture. For the Roma, this culture supports the prejudiced belief that they cannot be trusted. This culture provides space for non-Roma discrimination on numerous fronts, including employment. Coping with barriers to employment, Roma develop survival strategies that help them live and improve their lives. Such strategies include relying on social assistance, which is ethnicized despite the fact that many more non-Roma make their ends meet this way. When Roma rely on social assistance, non-Roma attribute the strategy to "their nature as takers," and not discrimination. Such attribution errors affirm stereotypes and feed anti-minority culture. Exclusion continues.

Breaking the exclusion cycle: Positive intergroup contact

In the summer of 2000, a number of teenage students enrolled in a wilderness survival course that involved a "physically rigorous camping expedition"

(Green and Wong 2009, p.4). Some of them were randomly placed in courses that consisted of only non-Latinx White students and instructors. Others were randomly placed in courses that included both White and Black, and at times, Latinx students and instructors. The students spent either two or three weeks together in the wild. A month after the course finished, the White participants were interviewed over the phone and probed about their feelings of hostility toward outgroups. White participants who had been in a racially heterogeneous group expressed significantly higher levels of tolerance than their peers who took the course only with other Whites (Green and Wong 2009).

Scholarship in social psychology, sociology, and political science shows that intergroup contact can affect prejudice as well as discriminatory behavior (Allport 1954; Enos 2014; Mutz 2016; Pettigrew and Tropp 2011; Scacco and Warren 2018; Sidanius et al. 2008). The vast majority of research focuses on the effects of positive intergroup contact, which tend to be predominantly positive for members of the majority (but are far more subdued for the minority).[24] The effects of positive intergroup contact can generalize quite broadly. Scholars have shown that lower levels of prejudice observed after a contact situation can generalize beyond the context of that particular situation (Cook 1984), and beyond the individuals involved in it—not only to members of the entire outgroup (Van Oudenhoven et al. 1996) but even to members of completely different outgroups (Sidanius et al. 2008).

Intergroup contact also need not be direct to work. People exhibit lower levels of prejudice when one of their ingroup friends has outgroup friends (Wright et al. 1997). They also exhibit lower prejudice if they read a book or watch a television show that features intergroup contact (Fujioka 1999; Vezzali et al. 2012), or if they imagine having a pleasant conversation with an outgroup member (Turner et al. 2007). Finally, positive intergroup contact can have effects beyond the individual; that is, if an individual lives in a neighborhood where other people engage in positive intergroup contact, that individual is likely to be less prejudiced even if she does not engage in contact herself (Christ et al. 2014). For members of the majority, then, benefits of positive contact can be direct, vicarious, or contextual. While research on intergroup contact has been expansive, a caveat is necessary—much of this scholarship relies on

---

[24] For members of the minority group, positive effects of contact are not nearly as pronounced and are often altogether absent. There is much less scholarship that studies the effect of intergroup contact on members of minority groups (Pettigrew and Tropp 2011). The effects of negative contact are also less explored, but tend to be negative.

non-experimental methods, and the research that does involve experiments does not focus on racial or ethnic prejudice (Paluck et al. 2018).

How could positive intergroup contact help interrupt the exclusion cycle? As it primarily affects members of the majority and as behavior tends to change first, while attitudes take longer to be affected (Pettigrew and Tropp 2011), positive intergroup contact is most likely to leave a mark on discriminatory behaviors of the majority. Scholars show that this happens when contact reduces levels of anxiety that the majority associates with intergroup contact (Page-Gould et al. 2008), increases empathy towards the minority outgroup (Galinsky and Moskowitz 2000), enables cultural learning (Triandis 1994), and changes norms on intergroup interaction (Tropp et al. 2014).

Once discriminatory behaviors change, the rest of the cycle should follow. If there is less discrimination, members of the minority should over time respond to that change by resorting to fewer survival strategies. However slowly, attitudes should respond to behavior, resulting in lower levels of prejudice and a weaker anti-minority culture. And, once anti-minority culture weakens, instances of attribution errors should also decrease—less prejudiced individuals living in an environment where anti-minority culture is not as pervasive should be less likely to interpret a survival strategy as an intrinsic trait of the minority. This may particularly hold if their levels of empathy towards the minority are higher.

Did positive intergroup contact work in Murska Sobota?

Murska Sobota, my second field site, closely resembles Novo mesto on a range of important factors, but differs from it in one crucial aspect. While the Roma NGO in Novo mesto provides services to the local Roma and typically does not involve non-Roma in its activities, the Roma NGO in Murska Sobota focuses on promoting intergroup contact and dialogue. Both organizations have been active for over 25 years. Romani Union in Murska Sobota organizes a number of low-stress, fun activities that include parties, concerts, theater productions, book launches, folklore workshops and performances, and a week-long summer camp; it also hosts a popular radio station. A number of relevant mechanisms may be at work as Roma and non-Roma attend these activities. The relaxed atmosphere of parties and concerts, where inter-group contact happens but need not be particularly intense, might reduce contact-based anxiety. The Roma radio station, providing an opportunity for vicarious contact, might do the same. Theater productions, book launches, folklore workshops and performances, and the summer camp provide transfer of cultural knowledge and likely encourage empathy as non-Roma learn about what life is like for Roma.

One of the chief organizers behind Romani Union, Monika Sandreli, explained that reaching across the ethnic divide has been a central part of the organization's mission since the beginning (Sandreli 2012). To assess their reach, I asked 100 randomly sampled non-Roma in Murska Sobota if they were able to name the local Roma NGO. Forty-six percent could. Among randomly sampled Roma participants there, everyone knew the organization. When I asked the same question in Novo mesto, regarding the service-providing Roma NGO, every Roma participant could name it, but only 2 percent of non-Roma were able to do the same. Compared to this, Romani Union's success in reaching non-Roma seems outstanding, but it makes sense: this is what they do.

To see whether reaching almost every other non-Roma leads to contact that helps break the exclusion cycle, I repeated data collection, including both experiments, in Murska Sobota. As posited above, possible effects of contact first manifest through behaviors. In the context of the cooperative games, randomly sampled non-Roma in Murska Sobota do not discriminate against the Roma. Correspondingly, randomly sampled Roma engage in far fewer survival strategies. This results in a meaningful balance of cooperation: in Murska Sobota, Roma are just as likely to cooperate as non-Roma. I did not observe the same in Novo mesto, where non-Roma discriminated against the Roma and Roma more often resorted to low cooperation. As levels of cooperation between members of both groups in Novo mesto differ, the potential for sustained cooperation never manifests. Taking a closer look at non-Roma participants from Murska Sobota, I find that participants who are able to name the Roma NGO or reported attending NGO events do not discriminate against the Roma; in fact, they cooperate *more* when partnered with Roma in the context of the game. I therefore have suggestive evidence that contact-promoting NGO action in Murska Sobota is related to lower levels of discrimination against the Roma.

Attitudes of non-Roma in Murska Sobota also reflect possible effects of contact, but to a lesser extent. While 28 percent of non-Roma there still believe that "the Roma cannot be trusted," this number is substantially lower than in Novo mesto, where 62 percent believe the same. Correspondingly, non-Roma in Murska Sobota still commit the attribution error, but do so less frequently. In another departure from Novo mesto, prejudiced non-Roma do not act on their prejudice in the context of the games. Even as they agree with the statement that "the Roma cannot be trusted," prejudiced non-Roma trust Roma just as much as they trust non-Roma when they play the games. Roma in Murska Sobota behave similarly to Roma from Novo mesto; those who report that they have personally experienced discrimination cooperate less than those who don't report experiencing the same. However, as fewer Roma from Murska Sobota report experiencing discrimination—when compared to Roma from Novo mesto—the overall level of Roma cooperation is higher there.

The evidence from these two Slovene towns thus suggests that positive intergroup contact can help break the exclusion cycle. Discrimination by the majority appears to have been affected first, followed by Roma uses of survival strategies. As non-Roma still commit attribution errors and express prejudice, the findings suggest that the non-behavioral parts of the exclusion cycle are slower to change.

A few caveats. First, contact-promoting NGO action was not randomly assigned to Murska Sobota, and non-Roma there were also not randomly assigned to become familiar with the NGO or attend its events. The link between Roma organizing and lower levels of discrimination in this town is thus merely suggestive. Second, just as the exclusion cycle I describe here revolves around individuals, so too does the contact-based solution I evaluate. Intergroup contact would be wholly insufficient if pitted against the larger, complex phenomenon of exclusion in which individual and systemic factors intersect and build on one another. Finally, while my exploration of intergroup contact and the exclusion cycle in the two towns is thorough, it does not extend beyond the two locations. Generalization of the findings beyond Novo mesto and Murska Sobota therefore requires considerable caution.

Development and prevalence

Exclusion cycles, while self-sustaining, require a series of steps to manifest. Before the cycle is in place, each part of the cycle could lead to the next—or not. Let's start with anti-minority culture. One would be hard-pressed to find a diverse society in which no one harbors prejudice. Anti-minority culture, however, is not ubiquitous. Where anti-minority culture exists, prejudice is a part of the social fabric. In such culture, stereotypes are quietly present in everyday life and find expression through art and music, in film, in literature, and on the street. In the United States, individuals might stereotype Germans as punctual and exacting, but there is no anti-German culture here. The same holds for anti-French, anti-Spanish, anti-Italian, anti-Russian and a number of other anti-minority cultures. In contrast, anti-Black culture in the United States and elsewhere, anti-Batwa culture in Uganda and neighboring states, and anti-Muslim culture in a number of countries all provide space for exclusion cycles to form.

Anti-minority culture need not be old, though it often is. Anti-Muslim culture in Denmark is a recent development; while anti-Muslim sentiment likely existed before, the European refugee crisis gave license to public expressions of racism and resulted in mainstream public discourse touting assimilation as the answer to diversity. As anti-minority culture is not static, changes in its salience or in its expression are likely an important source of variation in both the emergence or re-emergence of exclusion cycles as well as their prevalence.

Where anti-minority culture exists, the cost of discriminating against the minority is lower. In Slovenia, for example, providing the entire town with infrastructure required for electricity, but leaving out the area were the Italian minority lives, seems preposterous. And yet, doing so where the non-Roma houses stop and the Roma neighborhoods begin is in some localities done with impunity. Anti-Roma culture makes such impunity possible. Still, while anti-minority culture creates space for discrimination, maltreatment does not always follow. Although anti-Muslim and anti-immigrant cultures are alive and well in Britain, Germany, and Sweden, prejudiced citizens often do not vote as their anti-immigrant sentiment would dictate (Blinder et al. 2013; Harteveld and Ivarsflaten 2016). Where strong internal or contextual norms indicate that discriminatory behavior is harmful and inappropriate, voters who harbor prejudice but who are motivated to control it can refrain from discriminating (Blinder et al. 2013; Harteveld and Ivarsflaten 2016). And, in the United States, White Americans who live alongside Black Americans—whether as roommates in a college dorm (Sidanius et al. 2008) or as next door neighbors in housing projects (Deutsch and Collins 1951)—can curb their discriminatory behaviors, even as anti-Black culture permeates society at large. Anti-minority culture thus makes discrimination much easier, but not inevitable.

Suppose that discrimination does happen, however. For an exclusion cycle to manifest, survival strategies would have to follow. They often do, but not always. Consider the Balkans in the middle of the previous century. With rapid industrialization and state policies pushing for full employment, many Roma in Yugoslavia began abandoning traditional occupations to find standard wage jobs (Barany 2002). Some joined and worked in agricultural collectives, but many turned to industry (Barany 2002). The shift from traditional occupations to standard wage labor might look like assimilation (which is a survival strategy[25]), but that wasn't entirely the case in Yugoslavia. Its nationality and minority policy was one of "ethnic harmony" (Barany 2002, p.122)—natural or enforced—which led to measures promoting integration and not assimilation. After the 1974 constitution granted more autonomy to the constituent republics, the political visibility of the smaller minorities, including the Roma, was relatively high such that Roma were able to establish cultural and social organizations "relatively free of state control" (Barany 2002, p.122). Many Roma thus found industry jobs not because of discrimination, which is how survival strategies develop, but as a response to state policies on industrialization and mandatory employment. While discrimination and anti-Roma culture nonetheless persisted, this shift likely resulted in fewer exclusion cycles.

Finally, a complete exclusion cycle requires an attribution error. Members of the majority do not consistently commit these errors. For example, when Black Americans face barriers to employment, they often substantially widen their job searches (Pager and Pedulla 2015). White Americans are likely completely unaware of this survival strategy, which is thus neither ethnicized nor disliked. The attribution error does not follow, at least for this particular strategy.

Reacting to traditional Roma occupations, Slovene non-Roma in the past likewise did not consistently commit attribution errors. Unlike the example of widening job searches mentioned just above, making kettles, sharpening knives, making bricks, and other similar occupations were quite visible and very much associated with their respective Roma subgroups. Although some of these occupations might not have historically developed in response to discrimination, many Roma of more recent generations were confined to engaging in them for that reason. For them, traditional occupations were survival strategies. Non-Roma, however, respected many, though not all of these trades, and routinely sought out Roma expertise. While the link between Roma and their occupations was explicit, non-Roma did not dislike some

---

[25] Defining survival strategies as actions that individuals pursue because discrimination curtails their options—actions that they might otherwise avoid—results in a wide repertoire of potential strategies. Under this definition, voluntary assimilation is a survival strategy. While many might consider assimilation a desired end and would balk at the idea of equating it with survival strategies that are disliked, seeing assimilation as a solution to the problem of social exclusion is deeply problematic. This view reproduces the preferences of the majority, lending them legitimacy, without giving much consideration to those of the minority. In order to assimilate, members of the minority are variously expected to sacrifice parts of their identities or altogether leave their communities behind. Members of the majority, meanwhile, sacrifice nothing.

of the occupations. As a result, the typical error attributing engagement in these particular trades to a negative Roma trait did not manifest and did not contribute to anti-Roma culture.

Survival strategies that lead to assimilation also typically don't elicit attribution errors. Suppose a hijab-wearing Muslim woman in France is looking for work. Facing religious discrimination in hiring (Adida et al. 2016), she decides to go against a tenet of her faith to interview and work without a hijab. This is precisely the survival strategy those French who are prejudiced would have her choose. As a partial erasure of her identity suits their radical interpretations of laïcité,[26] they are unlikely to commit attribution errors in reaction to *this* survival strategy. Some might even commend her decision and encourage others to heed her example. If the job seeker instead chose a different strategy—applying only to jobs related to the Muslim community, which would welcome her hijab—the erring French might attribute her withdrawal to Muslim disinterest in integration. At the minimum, then, members of the majority are unlikely to commit attribution errors in response to survival strategies of which they are unaware, or of which they approve.

The examples I have listed here are few among many. Exclusion cycles could manifest in a number of different contexts, but they don't unless all four parts of the cycle fall into place. Anti-minority culture must be present and it must engender discrimination; survival strategies must follow, and attribution errors must be made in response. Still, while the examples above mention circumstances that derail a potential cycle, none of those circumstances result in a society completely free of exclusion cycles.

As I define them here, exclusion cycles happen at the level of individual behaviors. Regardless of context, if there is anti-minority culture, there will always be individuals who discriminate, individuals who resort to survival strategies, and individuals who commit attribution errors. Instead of asking whether exclusion cycles exist, we must therefore ask how common they are. If they are few and far between, with odd individuals discriminating and committing attribution errors, these cases, while harmful, do not dominate the social space and define group relations. If, however, more people discriminate and more people use survival strategies, the cycles gain visibility and over time become more and more entrenched.

---

[26] When they invoke the norm of laïcité, the rooted French refer to the 1905 law intended to allow each citizen to practice his or her religion. Many French, however, rely on a more radical interpretation, claiming that laïcité demands a complete absence of anything religious in the public life (see Adida et al. 2016).

This book does not provide answers to questions that naturally arise from the few paragraphs above. The conditions under which cycles might emerge are likely varied and context-specific; systematically exploring when cycles manifest and when they don't is a task for future work. Likewise, working out the dynamics under which exclusion cycles transition from the margins to take up a prominent role in group relations, eventually reaching a tipping point (Laitin 1995), is a question to revisit later. Here, I only offer an illustration of an exclusion cycle and an examination of one mechanism that might help break it.

Scope

Three conditions define the scope of this argument. First, exclusion cycles can only manifest in diverse societies. Second, they can only manifest in environments in which the minority is identifiable. And third, exclusion cycles require a power differential between the majority and minority where the majority is the more powerful of the two. Under these conditions exclusion cycles can form, but might not. Without these conditions, they cannot.

The first scope condition is rather obvious. Exclusion cycles cannot manifest where there is no one to exclude. While this book focuses on the exclusion of an ethnic minority, the cyclical dynamic can be observed in a context removed from ethnic or racial divisions. Consider homelessness.[27] Prejudice felt towards individuals who are experiencing homelessness is often associated with their appearance, the presumption that they are idle, and the presumption that they are criminal (De Las Nueces 2016). Subscribing to these stereotypes, healthcare professionals sometimes treat people experiencing homelessness with less respect than they typically afford other patients. Whether this results in a handshake that's conspicuously missing from an introduction, general rudeness, or a perfunctory inspection of symptoms, such discriminatory treatment is immediately harmful and can lead to a number of survival strategies (De Las Nueces 2016). Underusing healthcare services or avoiding them altogether is one such strategy (De Las Nueces 2016). And yet, when individuals experiencing homelessness die much younger than their housed counterparts and their deaths are attributed to a number of factors,

---

[27] While homelessness is closely associated with race in the United States, this association is less strong in a number of other countries. The added dimension of race, of course, further worsens exclusion.

mistreatment by healthcare professionals is rarely among them (Baggett et al. 2013; De Las Nueces 2016). This scenario presents a potential exclusion cycle and thus broadens the definition of a minority, as stipulated by the first scope condition, to include groups whose attributes are acquired—like homelessness, immigrant status, or some forms of disability—as well as those whose attributes are descent-based (Chandra 2012).

The second scope condition requires groups to be identifiable. Simply put, excluding a person on the basis of group membership is challenging if there is no way to tell to which group she belongs. Some descent-based attributes that signify group membership are among those most visible and most sticky: they can be easily observed and are difficult to change in the short term (Chandra 2012). The foremost among these attributes is skin color, closely followed by other physical features; among Batwa, for example, being of shorter stature easily identifies an individual as a group member. Wearing traditional or religious clothing and symbols; speaking a different language, a dialect or a vernacular; or having a name associated with a particular group are additional attributes that are commonly used to identify people as ingroup or outgroup members. While some of these attributes are less sticky than others—one can more easily abandon traditional dress than descent-based physical characteristics—merely having such attributes is insufficient to determine group membership. Socially constructed interpretations of the attributes are also required for such categorization (Chandra 2012), whether they are implicitly agreed upon or contested. While we might hope that an individual makes her own decision about who she is, this is not always so. Others can assign group membership as well, and so identity activation becomes a function both of self and of others, and is subject to power dynamics that guide social relations.

Power imbalance is the third scope condition. Disparity in power is not, of course, a matter of absolutes. While a minimal power differential might be sufficient, communities in which groups are profoundly unequal are likely at a higher risk of developing exclusion cycles. The more a group is pushed to the margins—politically, economically, or socially—the easier it is for a cycle is to emerge. Often, such a group is a numerical minority, but this need not be the case; any group whose members are treated differently and unequally on the basis of their group-based attributes might experience exclusion cycles. This argument can therefore also apply in the case of a society in which the powerful group is smaller in number and the numerical majority is disenfranchised (e.g. South Africa).

Horowitz's distinction between ranked and unranked groups provides a good starting point for thinking about power imbalance. In ranked groups, ethnicity and social class overlap such that one ethnic group is subordinate; unranked groups, in contrast, have no such overlap and no such hierarchy (Horowitz 1985). According to this logic, Osu and other Ibo in Nigeria, the Burakumin and other members of Japanese society, and the Rodiya and other Sinhalese in Sri Lanka are all in a ranked system, while Hausa, Ibo, and Yoruba in Nigeria are not, and neither are Malays and Malaysian Chinese in Malaysia (Horowitz 1985).

While Horowitz writes that "this distinction is as fundamental as it is neglected" (22), he also concedes that the line between ranked and unranked is not clear-cut. We might, therefore, think of the two as bookends on a continuum with a space of contestation in the middle. I contend that exclusion cycles are most likely to manifest at one end of this continuum: starting with ranked groups, but comfortably extending into the contested space. While there are a number of communities that might still place on the ranked end of the scale—including some in which Batwa and Roma live, in addition to those listed above—many that were ranked in the past are no longer ranked today. They are nominally unranked, but in fact often exist in the contested space, where the legacy of past hierarchies—slavery, Jim Crow, or apartheid—endures in power imbalances that are variously expressed in access to or control of resources, the design of political, legal, and social institutions, the ability to access and change those institutions, and more. Also in the contested space are groups entering environments in which they are, by definition, unequal; an immigrant, for example, typically has different, and fewer rights than a citizen possesses.

For exclusion cycles to manifest in a community, groups must exist, they must be identifiable, and at least one needs to have the power to exclude. While the first two conditions are fairly straightforward, I am only able to sketch the rough contours of the third. Further research is required to fully understand the role that power imbalances play in the emergence of cycles.

Roadmap

In conclusion, I offer brief descriptions of the coming chapters. Chapter 2, "Theory," elaborates on the exclusion cycle using the examples of Batwa in Uganda, Black and Latino boys in Oakland, Muslim immigrants in France, and Jews in Vienna at the turn of the previous century. I also briefly review the literature on intergroup contact and discuss how positive intergroup contact might help in breaking exclusion cycles.

In Chapter 3, "Roma," I first discuss Roma diversity, touching on language and dialect, customs, and traditional occupations. I also offer a few examples of how varying social, economic, and political circumstances might have differently affected Roma communities throughout Central and Eastern Europe. I then introduce Roma in Slovenia, and conclude with an illustration of a Roma exclusion cycle through the lens of a murder-suicide that happened in 2011, in Novo mesto, the first of my two field sites.

Chapters 4, 5, and 6 are the empirical chapters. Chapter 4, "The Rift," introduces two lab-in-field experiments, which form the core of my data-gathering strategy. The first uses the trust game and demonstrates that non-Roma from Novo mesto discriminate against the Roma in the context of single interactions. The second experiment uses the tower-building videogame and shows that non-Roma from Novo mesto discriminate against the Roma in repeated interactions, even when Roma (avatar) behaviors in the game are identical to non-Roma (avatar) behaviors. This experiment also demonstrates that Roma from Novo mesto use survival strategies, but to a much lesser degree than stereotyping would lead one to expect.

Chapter 5, "Contact," introduces my second research site, Murska Sobota, and explores the non-Roma parts of the exclusion cycle in more detail. In contrast to non-Roma from Novo mesto, non-Roma from Murska Sobota do not discriminate against the Roma. This is particularly true of non-Roma who are familiar with the contact-promoting Roma NGO or attend its events. In this chapter I also present evidence of the attribution error and anti-Roma sentiment in which non-Roma from both towns engage, though non-Roma from Novo mesto do so to a greater extent. In that town, I link anti-Roma sentiment to discrimination against the Roma in the videogame.

Chapter 6, "From the Other Side," explores Roma engagement in survival strategies, focusing on three factors that might affect it: deprivation, personal experience of discrimination, and perceptions of stereotype intractability. Linking Roma answers to an extensive survey to their game behaviors, I find that neither deprivation nor perceptions of stereotype intractability are linked to engagement in survival strategies. However, Roma who report personally experiencing discrimination are more likely to resort to survival strategies. By asking Roma about their experiences of discrimination, this chapter also provides independent corroboration of the experimental findings presented in Chapters 4 and 5, which directly captured non-Roma discriminatory behaviors.

Chapter 7, "Full Circle," underscores the central finding on Roma/non-Roma cooperation in the two towns (also presented in Chapters 4 and 6). In Novo mesto, non-Roma discriminate against the Roma and Roma engage in survival strategies; as a result, members of the two groups, on average, cannot sustain equal levels of cooperation in the repeated public goods game (videogame). By contrast, Roma and non-Roma from Murska Sobota cooperate at equal levels in the tower-building videogame, a finding that is only suggestively linked to the contact-promoting NGO there, but is nevertheless exciting. The chapter then cautions against generalizations, discusses open questions, and concludes.

2

Theory

Social exclusion starts with individuals. It is a dynamic process in which people engage in mutually reinforcing behaviors that incrementally contribute to its persistence. This chapter introduces the exclusion cycle through a narrative about Batwa, indigenous Forest People from Uganda. I then explain the four parts of the cycle in more detail, using examples of discrimination against Black and Latino American boys, Muslim immigrants in France, and Jews in Vienna at the turn of the previous century. These examples do not only show the structure of the cycle but also demonstrate that exclusion cycles can appear in different communities, in different spaces, and at different times. I then switch from illustrating the cycle with examples to a literature review of intergroup contact. I conclude by discussing how intergroup contact might help to break the cyclical dynamic.

Before I continue, three clarifications are in order. First, while exclusion cycles are sustained through individual behaviors, not all individuals in a society with such cycles participate in these behaviors. In some environments exclusion cycles happen on the margins, with a small subsection of a minority population actually being marginalized; in others, an entire minority is targeted. In some, few members of the majority engage in exclusionary behaviors; in others, such behaviors are routine. I do not endeavor here to systematically explore these variations.

Second, this book does not explore the conditions under which exclusion cycles develop. While there are plenty of situations in which exclusion cycles do not manifest themselves, I do not seek to answer *why* cycles develop in some situations and not in others. There are surely many sources of variation among factors that likely contribute to the onset of cycles, among them past or present economic conditions, local history of violence (or the lack thereof), and patterns of spatial segregation. I must pass over them here. Instead, I focus on describing *how* exclusion cycles work once they develop, rare or common as they may be.

Third, this book focuses on individuals, but exclusion cycles do not happen in a vacuum. Individual behaviors that contribute to cycles exist alongside institutions that in many cases either impede exclusion or, more likely, help

Breaking the Exclusion Cycle: How to Promote Cooperation between Majority and Minority Ethnic Groups.
Ana Bracic, Oxford University Press (2020). © Oxford University Press. DOI: 10.1093/oso/9780190050672.001.0001

cement it. In many contexts, exclusion cycles are a constituent part of systemic racism (Feagin 2000; Ture and Hamilton 1967) or über discrimination (Reskin 2012). However, exploring how the behaviors that fuel exclusion cycles interact with institutions and how that in turn affects exclusion cycles is beyond the scope of this book. The theory presented here, therefore, is necessarily limited, and it invites a multitude of extensions.

The Exclusion Cycle

Batwa: an example

Batwa are Forest People who live in south west Uganda and in Rwanda and the Democratic Republic of Congo across the border. Non-Batwa derogatively call them "pygmies" (Kidd 2008). Batwa identify themselves as the sole original inhabitants of the forests in this region. They are positioned by the West as a primitive people in need of civilizing—that is, the epitome of the Other. Outsiders initially saw them as savage, and then harmless (Guenther 1980); colonial depictions found them "more akin to monkeys than human beings" (Maquet 1970, p.111, in Kidd 2008). In 1904, six Batwa from the Belgian Congo were put on display at the St. Louis World's Fair; one of them, Ota Benga, later became a live exhibit at the Bronx Zoo, where he was placed in the monkey house next to an orangutan (Kidd 2008). Ota Benga ultimately took his own life (Anon 1912, in Kidd 2008).

Much as such treatment may seem a relic of the past, it is not so. In 2002, the town of Yvoir in southern Belgium held an exhibition, at its private zoo, of eight "pygmies" who were performing for tourists (Osborn 2002). The exhibit, which was purportedly raising money to "[h]elp these people who live at the start of the third millennium as we did 2,000 years ago" (Osborn 2002, p.1), was evaluated by the country's equality watchdog, which determined that the exhibit was "in extremely bad taste, but not racist" (Osborn 2002, 1). We might expect that depictions of Batwa today would be a far cry from those of the past, given the clear though insufficient progress from overt racism to covert intolerance. The example from Yvoir, however, suggests that anti-Batwa discourse and culture, in places, remains almost as extreme as it was a century ago.

In Uganda today, Batwa are stereotyped as dirty, lazy, backward (Kabananukye and Wily 1996, in Kidd 2008), "gluttonous, wasteful, ignorant, and stupid" (Kidd 2008, p.100). The forest is seen as "alien and uncivilized"

(Woodburn 1997, p.353), and so are the hunter-gatherers who came from it. Kidd reports having been warned by non-Batwa to avoid driving his motorcycle through the forest, as "that was where the animals belonged" (Kidd 2008, p.118). Tragically, Batwa in fact no longer live in their ancestral forests. Under colonial rule, Batwa were overtaken by agricultural development and displaced from their ancestral territories (Taylor 2004). Their last remaining rights to their land were removed through conservation efforts by government officials and global conservation groups in 1991 (Reed 1997). They remain landless and without legal access to the forests, which were their only source of subsistence and independence.

Discrimination against Batwa is widespread. They face enormous barriers to employment and education. A 2004 NGO survey of Batwa in Uganda reported that of the 2551 Batwa who were interviewed, only 38 men and 8 women—that is, 1.8 percent of the surveyed population—said they were employed full-time (Kidd 2008). As very few are able to secure a job, sending children to school is a hardship. Although education is free, the expenses of supplies, uniforms, and school lunches are too great (Kidd 2008). Children face peer discrimination in school and attrition is high. Coupled with financial challenges, this results in low overall levels of education; as of Kidd's writing, "no Batwa have completed secondary level education and none have attended University" (Kidd 2008, p.116). Low access to healthcare results in infant mortality rates that are twice as high as those of non-Batwa (Episcopal Medical Missions Foundation 2007); among Batwa who are landless and without medical aid an infant is more likely to die than to live (Kellermann and Kellermann 2004). Batwa are frequently turned away when they seek medical help as the nursing staff "claim that they are dirty and refuse to treat them" (Kidd 2008, p.126).

Abusive treatment of this sort extends to other spheres, most notably concerning food. Batwa are not allowed to drink using the same drinking straw as non-Batwa; if they drink from a cup, the cup must be broken afterwards (Kidd 2008). An interviewee explained: "We would be given some food and it would be poured into our hands and not into our plates or cups" (Kidd 2008, p.118). Such behavior by non-Batwa, paired with nearly complete exclusion of Batwa from the workforce, results in severe food insecurity. As Batwa are unable to freely hunt and forage, they engage in begging and depend on the charity of their neighbors and NGOs (Kidd 2008). Some are able to secure crops as payment for their work on their landlord's farm (Kidd 2008). Tellingly, Batwa conceive of "poverty as simply being without food, and conversely, if one has food to eat, one is wealthy" (Kabananukye and Wily 1996, p.132, in Kidd 2008).

The only other way to obtain food is to look for it in the forest anyway, which is now illegal (Kidd 2008). Nonetheless, 55 percent of all Batwa house- holds were estimated to engage in hunting and gathering in 1996 (African International Christian Ministry, 143 in Kidd 2008). The repercussions are severe, ranging from arbitrary imprisonment that can last weeks to outright murder. One of Kidd's respondents reported that his son was murdered by local neighbors because he was caught gathering food in the forest; afterwards, the family still went back to the forest to forage (Kidd 2008). Batwa are "terrified of entering the park" (Kidd 2008, p.121), and yet they keep returning as they simply have no other options. If this option were removed, it would result in "massive increases in fatalities though hunger and malnutrition" (Kidd 2008, p.128).

Begging and illegally looking for food in the forest are a clear result of marginalization. However, this is not how they are seen. Instead, they are "seen by most local people as qualities inherent in Batwa society" (Kidd 2008, p.118). Kidd writes that he was told by many that "if only Batwa stopped begging they would be able to integrate into 'normal' society" (Kidd 2008, p.118). Just as begging is seen as a "cultural trait" (Kidd 2008, p.130), returning to the forest feeds the stereotype of Batwa as "wild and savage people who are gluttonous" (Kidd 2008, p.117). Batwa are thus caught in a vicious cycle they cannot escape.

I call this phenomenon an exclusion cycle. Batwa live in a culture that sees them as alien, backward, and gluttonous. This culture motivates discrimina- tion, which begins before they are born and follows them for the remainder of their lives. Discrimination drastically reduces Batwa ability to secure food. To survive, Batwa beg and illegally look for food in the forest. These are their survival strategies, which the majority disdains. Although Batwa strategies of securing food clearly stem from discrimination and exclusion, the majority instead interprets them as cultural, quintessentially Batwa traits. This attribu- tion error, committed many times over, further feeds the damaging anti-Batwa culture and so starts the exclusion cycle over again.

A closer look at the exclusion cycle

Anti-minority culture and discrimination

We are constantly exposed to prejudiced beliefs, opinions, and depictions of stereotypes. Some are deliberate, others are not; some we actively perceive, and others fly under our radars. Research in psychology suggests that children can respond to social norms as early as the age of three (Olson and Spelke 2008; Vaish et al. 2010), but the manifestations of such norms and beliefs, of course, never stop appearing. We live in cultures that constantly remind us of the groups to which we belong and the groups to which we do not. Omnipresent in these reminders are value judgments attached to these groups, often bound to stereotypes, that reinforce our prejudices. In a kinder world, we might recognize these differences as quirks. But our world is not so kind. Our environments are quite often rich in histories of maltreatment and discrimination; those histories and their current realities create spaces in which prejudice and further discrimination are easily sustained. Anti-minority cultures and discrimination make up the first two parts of the exclusion cycle.

Back to the basics: ingroup, outgroup

Humans need to belong. By belonging to some groups but not others, we partly define who we are (Allport 1954). We form our *social identities*, a part of our self-image that we construct from social groups to which we see ourselves belonging. Writing about this phenomenon, Tajfel and Turner (1979) stated that (1) individuals endeavor to maintain or strengthen their self-esteem, (2) social groups either have positive or negative connotations which render social identity positive or negative, and (3) a person evaluates his or her group by comparing it to others. Individuals, then, strive to build and maintain a positive social identity, which they accomplish either through positive comparisons with distinct inferior groups, through altering their group so that it is more positively distinct, or through changing their group membership altogether. In search of a superior social identity that contributes to our self-esteem, we form ingroups to which we belong, and outgroups that consist of outsiders.

We require little to form an ingroup. Often, we do it on the basis of observable personal characteristics or meaningful lifestyle choices (Campbell 1958). The elderly, women of color, and police officers might form ingroups, for instance, as might evangelicals and vegans. Sometimes even less is required. In one study, researchers randomly distributed laboratory coats among small groups of participants. The groups were then instructed to do a group activity. Compared to others, participants who were a part of an all-coat-wearing group reported higher levels of group unity (Dovidio et al. 1995). There is no need for an identifying characteristic, such as a laboratory coat or a particular profession, either. The minimum required conditions for ingroup development are the mere perception that distinct groups exist and that we are members of one or the other. Groups endure even when formed completely at random and without any interaction between members (Tajfel and Turner 1979).

People tend to favor ingroup members, even when the basis for categorization is random group assignment (Billing and Tajfel 1973). This bias can manifest as ingroup favoritism, outgroup derogation, or both. Consider a college campus on gameday. University colors, commonly worn by fans, exhibit strong ingroup favoritism, as does the habit of sitting in a particular part of the stadium and singing the school's fight song. Booing the opposing team, in contrast, exhibits outgroup derogation. Placing a study in this environment, Gaertner et al. (1999) had student interviewers approach fans during a game, with a few questions about food preferences. When approached by a Black interviewer, White fans were significantly more likely to answer the questions if the interviewer wore a university baseball cap (Gaertner et al. 1999). Baseball caps had no effect when the interviewers were White. Disparate treatment, of course, does not only vary with type of ingroup or its particular categories, but also varies from one individual to another. Among Arab and Jewish populations in Israel, for example, those who feel more strongly Arab or Jewish also exhibit higher levels of ingroup favoritism (Montoya and Pittinsky 2016).

Ingroup favoritism and outgroup derogation extend to a variety of attitudes and behaviors, including those that are generally seen as benefitting other people or society as a whole (Hewstone et al. 2002). In the empirical section of this book, I focus on other-benefitting behaviors. Helping someone cross the street is other-benfitting, as is stopping at a stop sign. Volunteering at a homeless shelter, donating to a good cause, and participating in neighborhood cleanup are all other-benefitting. In a strict Darwinian sense, other-benefitting behaviors that exact a personal cost should not exist (Darwin 1859; Dunfield 2014). Subjected to natural selection, altruists, who bear the cost of their altruistic actions and are therefore not the fittest, would not come out on top (Silk and House 2011). Reflecting this logic, non-human primates limit other-benefitting behaviors to interactions with kin or reciprocating partners (Silk and House 2011).

Humans, however, often benefit complete strangers. By their first birthday, human children begin to exhibit helping and sharing behaviors towards strangers without being asked and without having been taught to do so (Warneken and Tomasello 2006). These behaviors come naturally (Tomasello 2009). Yet while one year-olds happily open a cabinet door for an adult stranger with full hands, three year-olds are somewhat more discerning. At around this age, children are more likely to help individuals who have helped others in the past (Vaish et al. 2010); they are also more likely to share if the recipient is from their ingroup and was previously nice to them (Olson and Spelke 2008). Ingroup favoritism and preferential treatment of those who reciprocate therefore develop quite early, in response to first-hand experience as well as social norms (Tomasello 2009). As adults, we might be more apt to clear our neighbor's sidewalk after a snowstorm, but not the sidewalk of the people down the street; we might be more willing to give spare change to a violinist performing on the street if we play the instrument ourselves; we might be more willing to help a mother carry her stroller up the stairs if she looks like us.

Adding context

Taken out of a real-world context, forming groups and favoring our own seems relatively harmless. Once we consider past and present imbalances in power, wealth, and other relevant factors, however, the consequences of ingroup favoritism become grave. The human need to belong, which demands exclusion as well as inclusion, has been harnessed time and time again to cement systemic inequalities at the individual level.

The stereotype of Black men as criminals, for example, is one of several sustained by anti-Black culture in the United States. When Gilliam and Iyengar (2000) showed study participants a televised news story that reported a murder, but presented no information of any kind on the perpetrator, 60 percent of participants falsely recalled a perpetrator. Seventy percent of those who did recalled a Black man. The mere presence of a violent crime can thus lead to beliefs that a Black man is responsible. Conversely, the mere presence of a Black man can lead one to think that he is a criminal (Eberhardt et al. 2004), even when he is in fact the victim and attacked by a White man (Allport and Postman 1947). Increasingly, Latinos in the United States have also been stereotyped as criminal, particularly in the context of anti-immigrant culture (Chavez 2008; Flores 2015). Perhaps the best recent example of such a portrayal is from the 2016 presidential campaign, when Donald Trump said, of undocumented Mexican immigrants, "[t]hey're bringing drugs. They're bringing crime. They're rapists" (Trump 2015).

While the histories of stereotyping Black and Latino men as criminals are obviously different, the two stereotypes are in practice sometimes linked. This is the case in some neighborhoods in Oakland, where a process of criminalization captures some Black and Latino boys well before they might commit a crime (Rios 2011). Criminalization, writes Rios, renders certain behaviors and styles deviant and risky, and treats them with "shame, exclusion, punishment, and incarceration" (Preface, 2011). The deviant behaviors often amount to very little, reflecting the bias of a teacher who feels "threatened" by a tall boy more than the boy's deviance, but the consequences are dire all the same. Reflecting criminal justice discourse and practice, some schools in Oakland have implemented a "three strikes" rule, where students are referred to the police after their third disciplinary infraction; this is more likely to happen to Black and Latino boys, as teachers send boys of color to the principal's office more often than they send other students, and for lesser infractions (Skiba et al. 2002). Although I do not discuss them here, it is important to note that Black girls, too, are more likely to experience exclusionary punishment than White girls (Skiba et al. 2002).

Entry into this system of punitive control, which is in large part sustained by individuals like teachers, police officers, probation officers, and parents, requires very little. Being recognized as a child "at risk" because a family member is incarcerated is sufficient, as is dressing in a fashion that evokes an offending aesthetic, or, counterintuitively, being a victim of a crime (Rios 2011). Black and Latino boys who are so profiled live their everyday lives with the expectation of being followed by store security as they shop; being told that they will amount to nothing by parents and teachers; being threatened with prison by police officers as they are stopped on the street on account of matching a gang member's description; and being ignored by school counselors "because they are not expected to make it to college" (Rios 2011, p.40). Anti-minority culture and discrimination in the context of criminality in the United States, of course, extend far beyond the case of Black and Latino boys in Oakland, and take many different forms. This disheartening case, however, illustrates how an exclusion cycle can marginalize a particularly vulnerable subpopulation.

Consider now the French controversy surrounding the hijab, a traditional Muslim headscarf. While many view wearing a hijab as a matter of personal choice and, indeed, a human right, the rooted French largely disagree (Adida et al. 2016).[1] They invoke the very same principle others may use in support of a hijab—freedom of religion—to restrict its use.[2] The widespread, and

---

[1] According to Adida et al. (2010), the rooted French are French citizens who have four grandparents who were born within the French hexagon.
[2] When they invoke on the norm of laïcité, the rooted French rely on an extreme interpretation. The 1905 law was intended to allow each citizen to practice his or her religion; the view that laïcité demands a complete absence of anything religious in the public life is therefore quite radical. Many

arguably erroneous, belief that the norm of laïcité requires one to hide any and all signs of religion lends license to disparate treatment. To capture the extent of religious discrimination in the labor market, Adida et al. (2010, 2016) conducted an experiment, sending two CVs in response to selected job announcements by the French national employment agency. They always sent out a CV of a reference candidate: Aurélie Ménard, who bore a typical republican French name and had worked only in secular firms. In the second CV they systematically varied between two candidates: Marie and Khadija Diouf. Both have a typical Senegalese last name, but one is Catholic and the other Muslim. To further prime their religions, they listed that each had worked for one religious entity and that each volunteered for a religious organization. In every other characteristic, their CVs were identical to that of Aurélie Ménard. French employers far preferred Marie over Khadija. The reference candidate, Aurélie, received a positive response 25 percent of the time; Marie, the Catholic, was successful 21 percent of the time, but Khadija only 8 percent of the time. French firms thus appear to engage in significant and substantial religious discrimination in hiring.[3]

As a third example, consider anti-Semitism and discrimination against Jews in Vienna in the late 19th and early 20th centuries. By that point in time, anti-Semitism of one kind or another had existed there for hundreds of years, having started nearly a millenium before (Paule 1992). However, the period between 1860 and 1880 was considered a golden era for Austrian Jews as all laws discriminating against them were removed, allowing them to buy land, pursue any occupation they wanted, and establish cultural and educational institutions (Paule 1992). Discrimination nevertheless remained—very few could obtain government jobs, for example—and full integration into Austrian society was unattainable for most. By the end of the 19th century the golden period was over. The ideas of Jews as "cunning, rootless, and conspiratorial" (Paule 1992, p.28) started to regain resonance; academics began making racial arguments regarding Jewish "shiftlessness in commerce and

---

French, however, rely on this view, which suggests that they may be using it to justify the exclusion of the Muslim population. For more, see Adida et al. (2016).

[3] One could argue that the hijab sends a strong signal that the potential employee might be more costly to employ than an employe with an identical skill set who is not Muslim. Adida et al. (2016) write that French employers who have canteens, for example, find that providing halal food adds to the expenses; in addition, devout Muslims require a space to pray during the day and many fast during the month of Ramadan, which would suggest that disparate treatment is due to statistical discrimination and not animus (statistical discrimination is discrimination based on rational optimizing behavior instead of hatred (Arrow 1973; Phelps 1972)). Adida et al. (2016) find that in this context, both statistical discrimination and animus-based discrimination are at work. I return to this in Chapter 7.

their ... cosmopolitan way of thinking" (32), while Catholic clergy and laity feared "Jewish domination" (40) and blamed them for "democracy, Marxism, and capitalism"(38).

When they live in environments where anti-minority culture and discrimination are a part of the social fabric, members of marginalized minorities are not passive. They develop survival strategies that help them live and improve their lives. The next section discusses a few of these strategies.

Survival strategies

I use the term *survival strategies* to refer to a broad set of behaviors that members of a minority develop in response to discrimination. While I call them survival strategies, the survival I have in mind is not limited to the physical aspect of surviving; instead, my understanding of survival strategies encompasses the human need to strive for dignity, humanity, acceptance, and a better life. Survival strategies are not thrust upon people; although those who are marginalized make decisions in a constrained environment, they have agency and choose their strategies. And while they are undoubtedly strategies, survival strategies are not necessarily strategic in a rational choice sense. Take traditional occupations. While some members of a marginalized minority might strategically decide to stick to a traditional occupation, others might simply turn to it because members of their families have done so for generations.

Members of a marginalized community turn to survival strategies because discrimination has severely curtailed their options. Criminalization of Black and Latino boys in Oakland, for example, leads to "blocked opportunities" (Rios 2011, p.94) that leave boys with limited options to improve their lives. Rios divides the common responses into two types, the first privileging dignity over freedom and the second doing the opposite. Choosing dignity over freedom—demanding to be treated as a fellow human being—often leads to strategies of resistance. Sometimes these strategies involve political mobilization against criminalization and mass incarceration; sometimes, instead, boys aim to discredit the punitive system with acts of defiance that typically result in harsher punishment. These acts of defiance are deliberate; when engaging in them, Rios writes, boys "knew they were facing very severe consequences but decided to break the rules in order to make a point" (Rios 2011, p.117). Such behaviors can verge on the absurd, like pointedly stealing a 25 cent bag of chips that one had fully intended to pay for until being accosted by a store manager as a potential thief.

Still, engaging in crime is not always entirely a matter of resistance. Rios relays an account by Tyrell, who, at the age of twelve, had been persistently stopped by police officers and asked "where [he] was hiding the drugs" (Rios 2011, p.50). For months, Tyrell insisted on his innocence, but the officers did not relent and the random checks continued. Eventually, Tyrell started selling marijuana. His survival strategy was a product of three factors. First, as all the other boys in Rios's study, Tyrell had internalized the school- and police-propagated belief that he was "inherently criminal" (Rios 2011, p.52). Second, given the financial struggles in his family and his lack of access to alternative job opportunities, selling drugs was one of the few viable options Tyrell could turn to for securing subsistence. And third, in the face of stereotype intractability—the stereotype of criminality pervading his everyday life and the concomitant belief, bolstered by police behaviors, that regardless of what he does, he will be treated as a criminal—Tyrell found something that he could control.[4] Thus, while he was operating in a limited space, he retained his agency when he made the conscious decision to engage in crime, having considered the risks. And although he might not have done it consciously, writes Rios, Tyrell was still resisting (Rios 2011).

While responses to criminalization that privilege dignity over freedom tend towards resistance, responses that place freedom above dignity typically involve evasion. Reacting to profiling, surveillance, and policing, some boys devise strategies aimed at avoiding punishment; this includes following school rules, complying with police officers, and avoiding situations in which they might even be suspected of having violated a law. To be clear, the nature of situations to avoid is far less serious than a reader unfamiliar with this context may expect; Rios observed boys receiving citations for not wearing a properly fitted bicycle helmet. Strategies of evasion, often called "acting lawful" (Rios 2011, p.146) by boys who prefer defiance, are not always successful. Boys who evade nonetheless remain targeted by school officials and the police, so following rules typically fails to lead to a break in harassment. Further, boys who evade are often seen as having bought into the punitive system by boys who resist, meaning they face pressures from parents, teachers, school officials, police officers in addition to their peers. While the examples from Oakland demonstrate why targeted boys might choose a survival strategy of defiance or of evasion, they also make clear that from a young person's point of view

---

[4] The concept of stereotype intractability, as I call it, is akin to stereotype threat (Steele 1997), but far more encompassing. While stereotype threat temporarily activates a stereotype—girls do poorly on a math test once they are told that women are bad at math, but perform better when they are not told the same (Shih et al. 1999)—stereotype intractability never relents.

neither strategy is desirable. The boys resort to survival strategies because their options are severely limited.

The repertoire of potential survival strategies is substantial. Members of a marginalized minority can thrive, or at least try to, by engaging in traditional occupations. Thus Jews in early modern Europe engaged in financial services; members of Midgaan and Tumal groups in Somalia engaged in leather- and metal-works, respectively (Laitin 1995); and Roma across Europe performed a wide range of occupations, from horse trading to kettle making, at least until the second half of the previous century (Štrukelj 1980). A new niche occupation can take the place of a traditional one. By the end of the 19th century, for example, numerous Jews in Vienna had abandoned traditional occupations in trade and became clerks, salesmen, and managers. According to Rozenblit (1983), these new occupations were just as identifiable as Jewish as the previous ones because Viennese non-Jews did not take them up at the same rate. While Jewish clerks in Vienna did not seek to completely assimilate into Vienesse society (Rozenblit 1983), many Jewish doctors, lawyers, and artists did, even going so far as converting to Christianity (Rozenblit 1983), and adopting Austro-German culture to the exclusion of all others (Rozenblit 1983; Silverman 2012). Although majority societies typically view assimilation as a desirable outcome, it is at root a survival strategy. Having to choose between defiance and evasion in Oakland for lack of better options is reprehensible, as is having to partially or completely abandon one's culture, traditions, or religion.

Discrimination in employment can lead to a number of survival strategies. To cope with having to search "twice as long as an equally qualified white candidate" (Pager et al. 2009, p.785) before obtaining a callback or a job offer, Black Americans substantially widen their job searches. A Muslim job-seeker in France might opt to interview without her hijab to significantly increase the odds of getting a job (Adida et al. 2010). Roma, meanwhile, turn to the informal economy and collect scrap metal, do seasonal agricultural work, and sell foraged wild mushrooms and blueberries at farmer's markets. Many Roma also rely on social assistance to make ends meet.

While the repertoire of potential survival strategies can be sizeable, it is often constrained. Some strategies may not be attainable, some too costly, and others avoided. Niche occupations that can be newly adopted, for example, are not always available, and even when they are they might not be universally accessible. While Jews in Vienna found jobs as clerks and managers, these occupations were typically not available to Roma. Indeed, even today formal employment remains elusive for many Roma, which is why they turn to the informal economy. Moreover, for a young Muslim woman in France who is in need of a job, the survival strategy of working without a hijab might be too costly. Instead of violating a tenet of her faith, she might prefer to look for jobs more accepting of her hijab. Absent a better way of discerning which jobs will be inclusive, jobs within or related to the Muslim community offer a safe bet. The strategy of retreat among Muslims is limited neither to France nor to work environments; in the United States, for example, Arab and Muslim Americans retreat from public spaces in response to hateful rhetoric and open discrimination (Hobbs and Lajevardi 2019). This includes withdrawing from social media, avoiding face-to-face interactions with members of other groups or political parties, and forgoing visits to parks, shopping malls, and restaurants (Hobbs and Lajevardi 2019).

Moreover, even if some survival strategies are nominally available, they might be avoided. Individuals who have experienced discrimination, for example, can shy away from strategies that require cooperating with others. Laboratory-based research on the effects of exclusion and ostracism offers some insight.[5] These studies often involve a game of Cyberball, a virtual ball-toss game played with three players (Gonsalkorale and Williams 2007). Cyberball simulates exclusion by having the two players who are not the participant play amongst each other, excluding the participant. Generally, when people are excluded in this context, they tend to be distressed, reporting lower levels of belonging, self-esteem, control, meaningful existence (Gonsalkorale and Williams 2007), and trust (Twenge et al. 2007). This happens even when they play with simulated players whom they despise, like KKK members, and for no longer than 15 minutes (Gonsalkorale and Williams 2007).[6] In addition, after a brief episode of exclusion, participants are substantially less likely to donate a part of their experiment pay to a student emergency fund; they are substantially less likely to volunteer to help with

---

[5] Within the confines of a laboratory experiment, treatments involving ostracism or exclusion tend to be short-term. Exclusion in a laboratory setting either lasts 15 minutes (Cyberball) or consists of participants being told, once, that they would either end up alone later in life (Baumeister and DeWall 2005; Catanese and Tice 2005; Twenge et al. 2007) or that other participants in the experiment had rejected them (Catanese and Tice 2005; Gaertner and Iuzzini 2005; Twenge et al. 2007). The control groups in these experiments are variously told that they would enjoy a future rich in personal relationships (future belonging), that they would be accident prone (misfortune control), or nothing (no-feedback control). Compared to decades of exclusion that span generations—as they certainly do in the case of Black Americans, Jews in early 20th century Europe, and Batwa—a 15-minute spell of exclusion seems rather short. Yet, the results of such laboratory experiments speak volumes.

[6] Further scholarship, conducted in a similar environment as the study just described, speaks to a wider set of outcomes. Exposure to short spells of rejection, ostracism, and exclusion leads to temporary feelings of abject misery, anger, sadness, and increased stress (Williams 2007). It results in eating unhealthy foods, giving up faster on a frustrating task, and an increased inability to screen out distractions (Baumeister and DeWall 2005). Excluded subjects exhibit lower levels of empathy (Twenge et al. 2007), and higher aggression towards innocent bystanders (Catanese and Tice 2005). They can become antisocial, hostile, socially susceptible to influence, and temporarily catatonic (Williams 2007).

another experiment or to help after a mishap; and they are substantially less likely to cooperate in a 10-round prisoner's dilemma game (Twenge et al. 2007). Experiencing discrimination therefore leaves a mark on a person's propensity to engage in other-benefitting behaviors, in particular leading to a tendency to avoid strategies that require cooperating with others. This may lead to survival strategies like dumpster diving or begging, which are not other-benefitting but bring harm to no one except potentially to people who engage in these strategies, as well as strategies that are not other-benefitting and are also generally harmful, like illegally tapping an electricity line.

Importantly, anyone can engage in behaviors that make up survival strategies. Members of the majority indeed often turn to the informal economy or rely on social assistance to make ends meet. However, when members of the majority engage in these behaviors, they are not survival strategies as I define them here: they are not turning to them because *discrimination* limits what they can do. And they typically don't face the attribution error when they do it.

Attribution error

So far, I have discussed how anti-minority culture sustains discrimination by the majority, and how members of marginalized minorities develop survival strategies in response to mistreatment. When members of the majority misinterpret these strategies and attribute them to the minority group as such—not an individual's experience of stereotyping, discrimination, or deprivation—they commit an attribution error. If we committed such errors invariably, without regard for group membership or identity, the attribution error would not pose a problem. But we don't. While we tend to assign undesirable behavior to the nature of the group when outsiders offend, we are forgiving of our own.

When Pettigrew (1979) termed this phenomenon the ultimate attribution error, he wrote that:

> (1) when prejudiced people perceive what they regard as a negative act by an outgroup member, they will more than others attribute it dispositionally, often as genetically determined, in comparison to the same act by an ingroup member; (2) when prejudiced people perceive what they regard as a positive act by an outgroup member, they will more than others attribute it in comparison to the same act by an ingroup member to one or more of the following: (a) "the exceptional case," (b) luck or special advantage, (c) high motivation and effort, and (d) manipulable social context.
>
> (Pettigrew 1979, p.461)

In an extreme form of the attribution error, positive acts by outgoup members might not be recognized at all, and interpreted instead as negative. Pettigrew (1979) calls this "[t]he most primitive defense," (465) and lists the following examples: "[a]n ambitious act becomes 'pushy,' an intelligent act becomes 'cunning'" (465). This difference in perceptions is largely attributed to our need for high self-esteem, which ingroup members can enhance by feeling superior to outgroup members (Coleman 2013; Tajfel and Turner 1979).

Indeed, individuals consistently tend to make ingroup favoring attributions, and to a somewhat lesser extent, outgroup derogating attributions as well (Coleman 2013; Hewstone 1990; Khan and Liu 2008). For example, non-smokers are more likely to attribute success on a test to the ability of a fellow non-smoker; but if a smoker does equally as well, they are more likely to say it was because the test was easy, or because he tried hard, got help, or was lucky (Gibson 1998). When failure takes the place of success, the attributions switch. Thus, if a fellow non-smoker fails the test, non-smokers are apt to conclude that the test was hard, or that he did not put in the effort, did not get the help, or was not lucky. Correspondingly, if a smoker fails, non-smokers are more likely to attribute the failure to his lack of ability (Gibson 1998). Similarly, Republican or Democrat undergraduates are more likely to say that outgroup politicians engage in bad spending practices because they are bad people; ingroup politicians instead do it because of outside circumstances (Coleman 2013). In contrast, undergraduates say that ingroup politicians engage in good spending practices because they are good people, while outgroup politicians do the same because of outside circumstances (Coleman 2013).

Members of the majority often dislike survival strategies, sometimes without cause. When Batwa beg for food, for example, they are not breaking a law or hurting anyone, and yet non-Batwa condemn the survival strategy. Following the attribution rule presented above, members of the majority mistakenly attribute the disliked survival strategy to the minority as such, and not the discrimination that in fact led to it. In the context of Batwa, begging is thus seen as a "cultural trait" (Kidd 2008, p.130) instead of stemming from extreme discrimination. Attributing a survival strategy to the nature of a group helps ethnicize it, such that in their society begging becomes automatically associated with Batwa.

Experimental research on attribution error speaks to Rios's case of Black and Latino boys in Oakland. In 1976, Birt Duncan showed White study participants a videotape of an interaction in which one man shoved another. The participants did not only describe the identical shove as more violent when perpetrated by a Black man, they also claimed—when asked why they thought the shove happened—that the aggressor was "given to violence"

(Duncan 1976, p.597) when the man was Black, but that "the situation" (Duncan 1976, p.596) was to blame when the man was White.

Years later, a group of scholars captured a similar bias. Study participants first listened to a 4-minute segment of violent rap music, non-violent rap music, or nothing (Johnson et al. 2000). They then read a passage about a White or Black defendant who, upon his fiancée leaving him, got inebriated, destroyed some property, and threatened to hurt her. Participants were asked to what extent his behavior can be attributed to the situation (alcohol, break-up) and to what extent to his disposition (violent personality). White participants were significantly more likely to attribute the violent behavior of the defendant to his disposition when the defendant was Black, regardless of the music they heard, if any (Johnson et al. 2000). They consistently committed attribution errors. In a similar vein, when a Black or Latino boy from Oakland defies the punitive system by engaging in crime, whether as frivolous as stealing a 25 cent bag of chips or as serious as selling drugs, White people from his community might attribute his strategy of survival to his purported criminal nature. This further racializes criminality, contributing to the American understanding of crime as a policy issue associated with race (Gilliam and Iyengar 2000; Hurwitz and Peffley 1997; Israel-Trummel 2015; Mendelberg 2001).

The study offers another powerful insight. By having participants listen to violent rap music, which is typically associated with "gangsta culture" (Alexander 2010, p.170), researchers primed them with the stereotype of Black criminality.[7] For White participants, this was of no importance; they made the attribution error regardless. But Black participants were significantly more likely to attribute the violent behavior of a Black, but not White, defendant to his personality when they received the violent rap treatment. Bringing to mind the same concept that undergirds the criminalization of Black and Latino boys in Oakland led Black participants to flip the rules of attribution error—instead of attributing the violence to the violent personality of the White man, the outgroup member, they were more likely to attribute it to one of their own.

This suggests a grim reality for Rios's group of Black and Latino boys. As some of the individuals who participate in the punitive system are people of color (if not the police officers or teachers, then at least some of the parents of targeted boys) the attribution error rules would suggest a reprieve: not

---

[7] While Black audiences consume this culture, it is important to note that the most damaging displays of gangsta culture, portraying Black people as "out-of-control, shameless, violent, over-sexed, and generally undeserving" (Alexander 2010, p.172), tend to be geared towards White audiences. For more, see Alexander (2010).

everyone should make this mistake. However, since the boys are constantly beleaguered—indeed Rios writes that "[o]ne only needs to spend a few hours with marginalized young people in their everyday settings to realize how much they are policed, stigmatized, and treated differently from other citizens" (Rios 2001, p.52)—the stigma of criminality is likely contextually salient most of the time. Their strategies of defiance are thus likely attributed to their disposition most of the time as well, by White and non-White people alike.

Consider now the job-seeking Muslim woman who decides to keep her hijab and only applies to jobs that would respect it, forgoing employment options that she would otherwise prefer to pursue. A rooted French person might react with disapproval upon finding out she works at an Islamic community center, attributing her occupation to a trait she supposedly shares with other Muslims: insularity. Adida et al. (2016) cite evidence of such a mindset among rooted French.[8] When asked whether people of Muslim origin were well integrated into French society, two-thirds of the respondents answered "no." When further asked whether French society was sufficiently open in welcoming Muslims, 69 percent answered "yes." And when asked about the reasons behind their (supposed) failure to integrate, 68 percent of respondents answered that "Muslims refuse to integrate themselves." The majority of the people polled thus blamed Muslims for their own exclusion, effectively saying that Muslims were excluded because they wanted to be.

But not all survival strategies lead to attribution error. Notably, strategies of which the majority approves typically don't, which can, over time, help exclusion cycles fade away. Assimilative survival strategies have likely led to countless cycle closures in the past. For example, when Italian and Bohemian immigrants in Brazos County, Texas, who were considered non-White at the time, spearheaded lynchings of Black Americans—literally "lynching to belong"—in order to move up in the societal hierarchy, they did indeed move up (Nevels 2007). Among a great number of other factors, this, too, might have contributed to the fact that in Brazos County today a White American of Czech descent is just as White as one of British descent.

Assimilation doesn't always work, though. By the early 20th century, Vienna's lawyers, doctors, psychologists, poets, writers, and journalists were disproportionately Jewish (Silverman 2012). As mentioned earlier, some among them sought complete assimilation; not only through conversion to Christianity—the belief being that conversion opened doors that rights

[8] The evidence is from a representative French population poll on "the image of Islam in France" conducted in 2012 by the newspaper *Le Figaro*. See Adida et al. (2016), 79.

on paper never could—but also by consuming, participating in, and creating modernist Viennese-German culture (Rozenblit 1983). Nonetheless, complete assimilation remained elusive. In their efforts to completely sever ties to their Jewish past, the assimilating Jews were drawn to other Jews who were doing the same, thus removing themselves even further (Bauman 1988).

Rising anti-Semitism, of course, put a decisive stop to complete assimilation. Seeing Jews as "visible defilers of the urban landscape" (Silverman 2012, p.23), anti-Semites referred to the phenomenon of Jews taking up occupations that were not traditionally Jewish as *Verjudung*, or jewification (Bauman 1988; Silverman 2012). *Verjudung* is a particularly troubling example of ethnicizing a survival strategy: assimilation, while deeply problematic, offered a means of escaping exclusion to many groups and individuals across time and space, but not to European Jews.

Attributing their rise in the social hierarchy and influence in Viennese society—not only in culture but also in business, industry, the professions,[9] and the financial sector—to the Jewish greed for power and "world domination" (Paule 1992, p.7) took little effort. This stereotype dates back to the French Revolution and was "[p]robably the most prevalent, notorious, and insidious of all anti-Semitic allegations, as well as one of the most universal" (Paule 1992, p.7). Assimilating Jews were particularly targeted because anti-Semites detested their social, political, and intellectual modernity; and just as modernity was morally corrupt and cosmopolitan instead of traditional and wholesome, so too were Jews who assimilated. In contrast, anti-Semites at the time "generally ignored Orthodox Jews" (Paule 1992, p.6), occasionally even expressing "admiration for them because [they] were among the most conservative and traditional people in Europe" (Paule 1992, p.6). The survival strategy of assimilation was thus disliked and ethnicized; *Verjudung* was attributed to the purported inner qualities of the Jewish disposition, like moral corruption and greed for power, and exclusion continued as damaging stereotypes were justified and further fed anti-Semitic culture. Eventually, a new kind of anti-Semitism—based on race, not religion—prevailed, ensuring that even conversion could not erase one's past and thus taking away the nominal option of completely assimilating from Jews who might attempt it (Bauman 1988; Paule 1992; Rozenblit 1983).

I have now discussed a number of different exclusion cycles. In all cycles, anti-minority culture paved the way for discrimination by members of the

---

[9] At the time, the professions included occupations in "medicine, law, education, engineering, journalism, and the arts" (Rozenblit 1983, p.49).

majority, to which members of the minority reacted with survival strategies, which members of the majority disliked, misattributed to the minority as such, and then ethnicized. These errors helped the majority sustain anti-minority culture, perpetuating the cycles.

Of course, the cycles I have described form only a small part of the dynamic between the majorities and the minorities in my examples. These feedback loops happen alongside other decisions, behaviors, reactions, and thoughts. I have thus neither intended nor attempted to provide exhaustive explanations of the complex relationships between members of different groups; I merely seek to illuminate one particularly damaging facet of those relationships.

Intergroup contact

In the middle of the twentieth century, Morton Deutsch and Mary Evans Collins interviewed several hundred people about their living arrangements. The participants, mostly housewives, were tenants in four biracial housing projects: two segregated, in New Jersey, and two integrated, in New York City. In New York, White and Black tenants lived in the same buildings and were in constant face-to-face contact with one another. In New Jersey, Whites lived in one building and Blacks in another; interracial social contact was rare. Deutsch and Collins found that in New York, Black and White tenants developed friendly relationships and built a vibrant social community. Among the White tenants there, stereotypes about Blacks broke down and the general atmosphere in the project welcomed interracial contact. But in New Jersey, the community encouraged segregation. This constrained social life, resulting in a divided community permeated by tension (Deutsch and Collins 1951).

Exploring the benefits of interracial housing half a century later, Sidanius et al. (2008) took advantage of random assignment of roommates at the beginning of freshman year at the University of California, Los Angeles (UCLA). By the end of freshman year, students who were randomly assigned outgroup roommates showed improved outgroup attitudes and behaviors. This was particularly the case for students who had Black roommates, where positive affect towards the outgroup even generalized to Latinxs. Complementing these findings, the longitudinal data from this 4-year study of interethnic contact show that voluntary interethnic rooming arrangements during sophomore and junior years were associated with increased intergroup competence and comfort, increased intergroup dating, and decreased symbolic racism (Sidanius et al. 2008, p.225). While the benefits of contact depend on who is involved in it, findings by Sidanius et al. (2008) suggest that positive contact, especially in the form of friendship, tends to reduce prejudice and curb anti-minority behaviors.

The idea that contact improves cross-group relationships has motivated scholars of attitudes and behaviors since the early 20th century, and motivates them still. Initially, contact was thought to invariably lead to conflict (Sumner 1906). As the events of World War II, and the Holocaust in particular, painted a stark picture of prejudice, a movement to eliminate it in United States gained some traction (Pettigrew and Tropp 2011). This movement, while overly ambitious and perhaps naive for the time, spurred interest by social psychologists and sociologists (Pettigrew and Tropp 2011). Their early investigations included expansive field research studies like the study by Deutsch and Collins (1951) mentioned above. By December 2000, scholars had conducted no fewer than 515 individual studies on intergroup contact, totaling 250,089 participants from 38 countries (Pettigrew and Tropp 2006). Interest among scholars continues to grow, resulting in increasingly impressive efforts like that by Sidanius et al. (2008), also above, which captured not only attitudes but also behaviors, in an experimental as well as a longitudinal setting.

While studies on intergroup contact initially focused on race relations, particularly those between American Whites and Blacks, by now scholarship extends far beyond questions of race and ethnicity. Scholars have examined the effects of contact with the disabled (Amsel and Fichten 1988), the elderly (Caspi 1984), the mentally ill (Desforges et al. 1991), people with AIDS (Knussen and Niven 1999; Werth and Lord 1992), immigrants (Vezzali and Giovannini 2012), homosexuals (Herek and Capitanio 1996), and imaginary groups put in place by the experimenters, like people in green or blue shirts (Wright et al. 1997), or Rattlers and Eagles (Sherif et al. 1961).[10] Contact has been studied in artificial laboratory set-ups as well as natural environments in the field, ranging from classrooms (Johnson and Johnson 1981, Rooney-Rebeck and Jason 1986, Scacco and Warren 2018) to summer camps (Green and Wong 2009; Sherif and Sherif 1953) to train station platforms (Enos 2014).

Scholarly opinions on the effects of contact remain divided. Some conclude that intergroup contact likely reduces prejudice and discriminatory intent, and that the effects of contact can generalize quite broadly; I will present their

---

[10] Rattlers and Eagles were the names of two groups of boys who participated in the Robbers Cave experiments (Sherif and Sherif 1953; Sherif et al. 1961).

side of the argument first. Others remain skeptical, pointing to a number of weaknesses among contact studies to date; I will turn to their thoughts second.

Contact works

Pettigrew and Tropp wrote that "over the last several decades, literally hundreds of studies have shown that intergroup contact can reduce prejudice" (Pettigrew and Tropp 2011, p.13). In their comprehensive meta-analysis of contact studies, they found that overall, greater levels of intergroup contact are associated with lower levels of prejudice (Pettigrew and Tropp 2011, p.17). They also found that these effects cannot be explained by participant selection, sampling biases, or publication biases. Finally, they found that recent research, which is more rigorously executed, "typically yields larger contact effects," (Pettigrew and Tropp 2011, p.201) as does research that is not recent, but is rigorous. Of course, not just any contact will do.

Negative contact does not tend to be associated with a reduction in prejudice; rather, the opposite (Barlow et al. 2012; Mazziotta et al. 2015; Paolini et al. 2010). While scholarship often simply refers to it as "contact," most research on intergroup contact has in fact focused on *positive contact*. The focus on negative contact and its effects has been relatively recent, suggesting, for example, that a person's history of positive intergroup contact can weaken or even eliminate the otherwise negative effects of an imagined negative and unenjoyable interaction with an outgroup stranger (Paolini et al. 2014). Future scholarship will undoubtedly grapple with the effects of negative contact further.

Other factors that affect whether and to what extent contact reduces prejudice are the quality of contact and the characteristics of those who engage in it. If, for example, someone engages in contact involuntarily, the negative effects of negative contact are particularly strong; voluntary contact, in turn, enhances the effect of positive contact (Pettigrew and Tropp 2011). Whether contact is superficial or substantive also matters, as substantive contact enhances the effects of positive contact and lessens those of negative contact (Pettigrew and Tropp 2011). The individuals who engage in contact are themselves a source of variation as well. Sidanius et al. (2008), mentioned above, found that contact has positive and generalizable effects on prejudice when outgroup members were Black or Latinx. When outgroup members were Asians, however, contact instead tended to result in an increase in prejudice. Sidanius et al. (2008) pointed to overall higher levels of prejudice among Asian students as a possible explanation (Sidanius et al. 2008, p.227), although they occasionally also observed the same with White students. Contact, then, is not particularly successful in reducing prejudice when the contact is involuntary, superficial, and/or negative.

On conditions that might enhance the effects of positive contact, Gordon Allport is by far the most influential authority. In his foundational book *The Nature of Prejudice*, he wrote:

> Prejudice (unless deeply rooted in the character structure of the individual) may be reduced by equal status contact between majority and minority groups in the pursuit of common goals. The effect is greatly enhanced if this contact is sanctioned by institutional supports (i.e., by law, custom, or local atmosphere), and provided it is of a sort that leads to the perception of common interests and common humanity between members of the two groups.   (Allport 1954, p.281)

Scholars have since explored the four conditions, later distilled by Pettigrew (1971) in consultation with Allport as "(1) equal status between the groups; (2) common goals; (3) cooperation between groups; and (4) institutional support for the contact" (Pettigrew and Tropp 2011, p.61). In their meta-analysis, Pettigrew and Tropp (2011) reported findings that are "consistent with much of the intergroup contact literature" (67). They found that while carefully structuring the contact situation such that it fulfilled Allport's conditions typically enhanced the effects of contact, often substantially so, Allport's conditions are not necessary for intergroup contact to reduce prejudice.

Positive effects of intergroup contact tend to generalize. They generalize to situations that are removed from the original contact situation, to entire outgroups, and even to outgroups that are not involved in the contact situation at all.

Formative imaginary railroad experiments by Stuart Cook speak to generalization beyond the immediate contact situation. In Cook's experiments, participants were tasked with operating an imaginary railroad system composed of 10 stations, 6 lines, and 500 freight cars (Cook 1971, p.48). The purpose of the task was to devise an optimal distribution of cars throughout the railroad such that when orders were placed with the railroad, cars were ready to travel. This exercise lasted 20 days and was completed in teams of three. All participants were young White women who had expressed vehement anti-Black attitudes. In addition to the treated participant, each team included two research associates, one White and one Black, who were presented as fellow participants. In the treated condition, the supervisor's assistant was also Black.

After 20 days of engaging in extended interracial contact that they otherwise would have avoided, participants, "with rare exceptions" (Cook 1971, 71), gave highly favorable reviews of the Black associate. Several months later, Cook measured prejudice levels of his participants again, in a non-laboratory setting that did not resemble the railroad set up. On a majority of the measures, the treated participants exhibited significantly less prejudice than their control counterparts. Cook's findings suggest that the effects generalized beyond the initial contact situation and lasted over time.

A person engaging in intergroup contact with members of one outgroup may not only find herself less prejudiced toward members of that outgroup in general (Van Oudenhoven et al. 1996), but also toward members of completely different outgroups. For example, in Cyprus, cross-group contact with Greek or Turkish Cypriots predicts attitudes towards mainland Greeks and Turks (Tausch et al. 2010); in Northern Ireland, cross-group contact with Catholics or Protestants predicts attitudes towards Black and Asian minorities (Tausch et al. 2010); and in France, Germany, Hungary, Italy, the Netherlands, Poland, and the United Kingdom, contact with immigrants is linked to positive attitudes towards gays and Jews (Schmid et al. 2012).

So far, I have mentioned only studies that focus on direct, first-hand contact. A person can, however, benefit from contact even if she doesn't experience it first hand. She can view an outgroup more favorably if one of her ingroup friends has a friend who is an outgroup member (Wright et al. 1997); she can benefit from imagined contact in the form of a mental visualization of a positive interaction with an outgroup member (Turner et al. 2007); and she can do the same by reading a book or watching a television show with intercultural content that vicariously exposes her to intergroup contact (Fujioka 1999; Vezzali et al. 2012). In fact, an entire generation of children may be somewhat less prejudiced because of the widely read and immensely popular Harry Potter series by J.K. Rowling (Vezzali et al. 2014), which aptly placed all readers in the marginalized "Muggle" outgroup, exposing them not only to extended vicarious intergroup contact but also to perspective taking (Batson 2010; Galinsky and Moskowitz 2000; Simonovitz et al. 2018).[11]

Finally, Christ et al. (2014) show that positive effects can spread from individuals to the neighborhoods in which they live. That does not mean that a more diverse neighborhood will necessarily foster better intergroup relations, however: mere exposure (Zajonc 1968) is insufficient. To benefit

---

[11] Perspective taking involves taking the perspective of an outgroup member and has beneficial effects for intergroup relations. See Galinsky and Moskowitz (2000).

from neighborhood effects, a person must live in the same neighborhood with people who engage in positive intergroup contact (Christ 2014). Christ et al. (2014) find this to be the case over several studies that include survey answers from Germans, South Africans, White Americans, and White British respondents. Using longitudinal data from Germany, they further show that this effect cannot be explained by self-selection. Their findings also suggest that over time, the neighborhood or contextual effects of contact are stronger than its individual-level effects. Remarkably, a prejudiced person can still benefit from the contact others have had, even if she herself assiduously avoids it. Indeed, "[p]rejudice is a function not only of whom you know but also of where you live"(Christ et al. 2014, p.4000).

The jury is still out

Scholars who remain skeptical about the effects of positive intergroup contact point to three main weaknesses in the scholarship to date. First, scholarship on intergroup contact predominantly examines attitudes, not behaviors. Second, most of the studies to date suffer from methodological shortcomings; specifically, there is a stark shortage of experimental studies of contact, in particular those that examine contact among adults of different races and ethnicities. And third, scholarship to date predominantly focuses on majority groups, leaving minority groups relatively unexplored.

Relatively few studies examine the effect of contact on behaviors. Among those that do is a recent study by Scacco and Warren (2018), which explored the effects of contact among 18 to 25 year-old Christian and Muslim men in Kaduna, Nigeria. They recruited participants to take part in a 15-week vocational training course that focused on computer literacy, randomly assigning participants to three conditions. First, participants were randomly assigned to a religiously homogeneous or mixed classroom. Within heterogeneous classrooms, participants were then randomly assigned to work with a co-religious or a non-co-religious learning partner. Altogether this resulted in co-religious partners in co-religious classrooms, co-religious partners in mixed classrooms, and mixed partners in mixed classrooms. While Scacco and Warren found no robustly significant changes in prejudice, they did find significant increases in generosity towards outgroup members as well as decreases in discriminatory behavior against them. Specifically, random assignment to a mixed classroom reduced discriminatory behavior of Muslim participants by nearly half, and that of Christian participants entirely

(Scacco and Warren 2018). Additional assignment to a mixed pair did not reduce discrimination further, but did increase generosity, especially by Christians. As participants were recruited from Kaduna's most conflict-prone neighborhoods, the results carry particularly powerful implications. A young Christian man, living in a city that has seen multiple deadly Christian-Muslim clashes over the past decade, can become substantially less likely to discriminate as a result of a 15-week computer literacy course during which he happened to be sitting with Muslim peers in a mixed classroom. Others have also found that contact affects behaviors, for example in the context of play and tutoring among third graders (Johnson and Johnson 1981; Rooney-Rebeck and Jason 1986), but more work is needed.

The second weakness of the contact literature lies in its focus on the attitudes and behaviors of the majority. Combing through their meta-analytic data, Pettigrew and Tropp (2011) found them to be quite out of balance. Of the 698 samples, only 142 or 20.3 percent examined the outcomes of contact among members of the minorities. In contrast, 72.4 percent examined outcomes among the majorities. The remaining 7.3 percent examined both. As 7 out of 10 studies on the effect of contact on prejudice do not examine minorities, our understanding of that particular relationship is suitably limited. The neglect, however, does not stop with the numbers. Perhaps expecting that minorities will respond to contact no differently than majorities do, scholars have yet to build a comprehensive theory of intergroup contact that looks first to the vulnerable.

The findings from the studies that do engage with the minority speak to just how far scholarship has to go. Splitting their meta-analytic data, Pettigrew and Tropp (2011) found that the effect of intergroup contact on prejudice is split as well: substantial for majorities, but quite weak for minorities. Probing further, they repeated the analysis with a subsample of contact situations that fulfilled all of the Allport conditions, and were thus more likely to successfully lead to lower levels of prejudice (Pettigrew and Tropp 2011). They did, but only for the majority. Allport's conditions did not enhance the effects of contact on prejudice for the minority.

Why might minorities react differently to contact? A simple, but unsatisfying, answer is that minorities approach contact situations quite differently. First and foremost, in an environment that sustains anti-minority sentiment, any interaction with a member of the majority outgroup is potentially threatening. The outgroup member might discriminate. If contact situations generate concern or apprehension a priori, an eventual positive interaction might not be sufficient to entirely overcome the initial worry. Indeed, if a member of a minority is exposed to prejudice within the contact situation, she may report more anxiety, more hostility, and less positive feelings about interacting with outgroup members in general (Tropp 2003). Exposure to a single instance of prejudice can have profoundly negative effects on how a minority participant feels about both contact and the majority outgroup (Pettigrew and Tropp 2011).

General perceptions of discrimination also matter. Using national survey data with White and Black respondents, Pettigrew and Tropp found that among respondents who perceive no, slight, or only some discrimination against their group, "interracial contact consistently predicted greater intergroup closeness" (136). In contrast, among Black respondents who perceived a great deal of discrimination against their racial group—and 56 percent did—contact failed to predict interracial closeness. This suggests that for the minority, the positive effect of intergroup contact would likely be quite limited.

Finally, contact situations that suit the majority might not work for the minority at all. What the majority might see as appropriate may look demeaning or patronizing to the minority (Pettigrew and Tropp 2011). Even a well-meaning effort may fall short of its purpose, as members of the majority tend not to reflect much on their privileged status (Leach et al. 2002), while members of the minority are often acutely aware of their own status (Jones et al. 1984).

Cross-group friendship, however, might work (Sidanius et al. 2008; Tredoux and Finchilescu 2010). Page-Gould et al. (2008) randomly paired White and Latinx participants either with an ingroup partner or an outgroup partner. Partners attended three friendship meetings and kept diaries for 10 days after each meeting. Before the first meeting, the participants took an Implicit Association Test; Page-Gould et al. also measured their levels of sensitivity to rejection on the basis of their ethnic group, and tracked their levels of stress (cortisol reactivity) after each meeting. Among the participants who were highly sensitive to rejection, those in the cross-group friendship condition exhibited high levels of stress following the first meeting. After the third, however, their levels of stress matched not only those of participants who were less sensitive to rejection but also those of participants who were paired with an ingroup partner. Further, participants who were initially high in prejudice but who were paired with a cross-group partner reported an increase in initiating cross-group interactions. These findings hold for both White and Latinx participants.

The third weakness of the contact literature comes in the form of methodological shortcomings. In my selected review, I mostly discussed studies that use laboratory or field experiments. This is not an accurate representation of the literature, however, as most works are not experimental. Numerous studies, for example, rely on survey methodology; the above-mentioned study by Christ et al. (2014) suggesting that contact effects can spread from individuals to their neighborhoods is one such study. Survey-based studies provide valuable information about interventions and are crucial for theory building, but also face a number of challenges. For example, intolerant participants might be inclined to lie on questions that probe for prejudice. Complicating the matter further, they might also be inclined to avoid contact with outgroups. Together, their possible reluctance to answer truthfully and their likely inclination to avoid intergroup contact might obscure our understanding of the link between contact and prejudice. In addition, survey-based studies do not conclusively demonstrate that a particular contact strategy is effective in the real world (Paluck and Green 2009). For that, an experiment is necessary.

Among the experiments I discussed, most were conducted in a laboratory. The laboratory environment offers control and precision, and so provides insight into mechanisms that might help reduce prejudice (Paluck and Green 2009). This approach does not test mechanisms in the real world, however, which tends to be more complicated. Field experiments, in contrast, do explore such mechanisms, but they are underutilized (Paluck and Green 2009).[12] In turn, they sacrifice some precision and control in exchange for testing an intervention in a real life setting. For better insight, field and laboratory experiments should be used together, but they rarely are (Paluck and Green 2009).

To assess how the findings in experimental studies of contact measure up against those in the review by Pettigrew and Tropp (2006), Paluck et al. (2018) conducted a meta-analysis of all intergroup contact studies that used random assignment and delayed outcome measures.[13] They found only 27 such studies, nearly two thirds of which were published after Pettigrew and Tropp's (2006) review; this pales in comparison to the sample in Pettigrew and Tropp, which included over 500. Overall, findings from these studies support Pettigrew and Tropp's conclusion: 24 of the 27 studies find positive effects of contact.

---

[12] Of the studies mentioned here and in the Introduction, a few use a field experiment: the two studies based on summer camps, both from the US, are conducted in the field (Green and Wong 2009; Sherif et al. 1961), as are some of the studies that take advantage of a classroom (Johnson and Johnson 1981, Rooney-Rebeck and Jason 1986, Scacco and Warren 2018) or a dormitory environment (Sidanius et al. 2008).

[13] This condition restricts the sample to studies in which measurement of outcomes happened at least one day after the contact intervention began. They limited their focus to such studies because measuring whether the effect of the intervention lasts for at least a day after the intervention is the "minimum policy standard of efficacy" (Paluck et al. 2018, p.4).

Paluck and her co-authors, however, identify several problems. First, most of these studies examine the attitudes and behaviors of children or young adults; in fact, there are no studies of racial or ethnic contact in which the participants are older than 25. Second, the effect of contact is contingent on the victim of prejudice; while contact appears to be particularly effective in reducing prejudice towards individuals with disabilities, it is much less effective in reducing prejudice towards immigrants, members of ethnic and racial minorities, members of religious outgroups, women, LGBTQ+ individuals, and the elderly. This differs substantially from findings in Pettigrew and Tropp (2006), who found no differences in the effects of contact on prejudice when they compared studies examining racial and ethnic contact to studies examining non-racial and non-ethnic types of contact. Third, Paluck et al. (2018) find that studies which estimate the effects of contact with greater precision reveal weaker effects. The same holds for studies that are analytically most transparent. Fourth, the studies do not record, in sufficient detail, what exactly happens during contact interventions; it is difficult to both recreate the contact experience and pinpoint why exactly contact was successful. Fifth and finally, no study in their sample has systematically varied any of Allport's facilitating conditions; as a result, when trying to account for inconsistent findings, "one can only speculate about whether divergent results reflect the treatments, subject pools or conditions of contact" (25). Paluck et al. (2018) thus conclude that the relationship between contact and prejudice is far from certain, and that further work is necessary to better understand the conditions under which contact reliably reduces prejudice.

Scholars across different fields have extensively explored the relationship between positive intergroup contact, prejudice, and, to a lesser extent, discrimination. While the promise of contact's beneficial effect remains high, more research is needed to pin down the conditions under which positive contact helps, what effects it might have on those who are the targets of prejudice and discrimination, and whether it can consistently result in a long-term reduction of discriminatory behaviors.

How intergroup contact might interrupt the exclusion cycle

Should positive intergroup contact affect the exclusion cycle, its effect is most likely to manifest itself in the context of discriminatory behavior by the majority. Since members of the majority tend to be more responsive to positive intergroup contact, they are necessarily the primary target in contact efforts.

While this takes the focus off of members of the minority and so repeats the mistake of privileging the majority, it also recognizes that the burden of exiting the exclusion cycle falls on the majority. Simply put, if discrimination does not cease, exclusion cycles will likely continue.

In exploring how positive intergroup contact affects prejudice, scholars have found that two major mediators help explain its effects.[14] The first is anxiety reduction, which happens at the early stages of contact. Compared to people who are used to cross-group interactions, people who have not interacted with outgroup members tend to feel higher levels of stress and anxiety during such interactions (Blascovich et al. 2001). Intergroup contact reduces the anxiety, which in turn leads to lower levels of prejudice (Page-Gould et al. 2008). Overcoming anxiety lets people engage in empathy, which is the second major mediator (Galinsky and Moskowitz 2000). Understanding and empathizing with the concerns of the outgroup, which happens in response to contact, also leads to lower levels of prejudice. Both anxiety reduction and an increase in empathy are affective processes, and together (but independently) explain almost two thirds of the effect of contact on prejudice (Pettigrew and Tropp 2011).

Cultural learning and perceptions of norms, which are among mediators that have been less explored, might also help in interrupting the exclusion cycle. While research has shown that knowledge of any sort about the outgroup is a significant mediator in explaining the effects of positive contact, it explains much less than anxiety reduction or empathy do (Pettigrew and Tropp 2011). However, a more specific type of learning related to culture might be a substantial mediator in and of itself (Triandis 1994). Thus, members of the majority who know more about a minority's culture may benefit from contact through that channel.

Perceptions of norms about group interaction could also lead to less prejudice. Plainly, intergroup contact will have a stronger effect on prejudice for a person who believes that her ingroup members support such contact (Tropp et al. 2014). Observing or engaging in behaviors that support the intergroup contact norm might further help explain the connection between contact and prejudice. A prejudiced individual can engage in behaviors that are in accordance with a new cross-group norm, and over time, such behaviors may

---

[14] A mediator is a variable or a process that is associated with both the treatment and the outcome. In the case at hand, mediators like anxiety or empathy are related to both contact and prejudice. An increase in intergroup contact, for example, contributes to a decrease in anxiety. The decrease in anxiety is, in turn, associated with a decrease in prejudice. Lower levels of anxiety can thus account for a portion of the relationship between contact and prejudice. According to Pettigrew and Tropp's (2011) meta-analysis, almost a third of the effect of contact on prejudice happens though the lowering of anxiety levels. Another third of the association between contact and prejudice is due to empathy.

help improve her outgroup attitudes (Olson and Stone 2005). As the effects of contact need not be direct, even vicarious contact under the norms that have made cross-group contact conventional may help reduce prejudice.

In the context of the exclusion cycle, contact is most likely to affect discrimination by the majority, eventually leading to the lessening of prejudice, which would be reflected in a less virulent anti-minority culture. Attribution error offers a tougher challenge. Lowering the incidence of attribution error requires understanding it, and that requires a level of introspection that may elude most members of the majority. An individual would first have to know why the minority may engage in survival strategies and have some understanding of or empathy for their position. Then, she would have to inspect her own reactions to survival strategies as potentially erroneous and, upon recognizing that she is committing an attribution error, adjust. Directly confronting attribution error is therefore cognitively challenging. In contrast to discrimination and anti-minority culture, which can be more productively targeted by affective processes that reduce anxiety and raise empathy, this challenge would be more difficult and time-consuming to resolve directly, at least partly because the effects of contact on prejudice are primarily governed by affective and not cognitive processes (Pettigrew and Tropp 2008, 2011). Nonetheless, the attribution error may be reduced indirectly as well, in response to lower levels of discrimination by the majority, a dampened anti-minority culture, and a decrease in the use of survival strategies by the minority. Finally, as scholarship so far shows that general positive contact does not tend to affect members of minority groups to the same extent, it is reasonable to expect fewer changes in minority behavior in response to mere contact.

Open questions that scholarship on intergroup contact has yet to answer cast doubt on the potential effects of positive intergroup contact. If one were to construct the most optimistic set of expectations based on scholarship to date, however, it might be as follows. The literature suggests that majority individuals who live in a place that promotes positive intergroup contact will both engage in fewer discriminatory behaviors and express lower levels of prejudice. Further, as effects of positive contact broadly generalize, a decrease in prejudice and discriminatory behavior will reach not only those who personally engage in positive intergroup contact, but also their ingroup friends, neighbors, and others who live in their communities. Eventually, members of the minority might adjust as well and reduce the use of survival strategies, but that is likely to happen in response to lower rates of discrimination rather than in response to intergroup contact itself. Chapters 5 and 6 explore this possibility in the context of Roma and non-Roma in Slovenia.

3

Roma

"Roma" is an umbrella term. It encompasses a number of heterogeneous and complex communities around the globe; many such communities use the term self-referentially and wish to be called Roma, while others—like the Sinti, Kaale, Yenish, Calé, Manuš, Dom, Egipćani, and Ashkalitë—retain separate identities but are nonetheless often placed by others under the bigger umbrella.[1] Over 12 million people from these diverse communities live in dozens of countries,[2] most in Europe, but many beyond, and they differ from one another on the basis of language, religion, traditional occupation, and more. Any description of "Roma" as a whole is therefore at best incomplete and capturing a quintessential "Roma identity" impossible. What it means to be Roma changes from one person to another, over time and over space.

In this chapter, I first offer a rough sketch of Roma diversity and then present Roma in Slovenia. I conclude with an example of a Roma exclusion cycle from my first field site, Novo mesto in Slovenia.

Before I continue, brief reminder. Marginality is an important dimension along which Roma experiences vary, and it delimits the argument in this book. As I exclude a significant segment of the Roma population—individuals and communities who are not marginalized—from my argument, it is important to keep in mind that they too represent what Roma lives are like. The experiences of Roma I write about here are not representative of all Roma experiences.

A brief sketch of diversity

Roma hail from northern and north-western India (Mendizabal et al. 2012). Their migration, which started about 1,500 years ago, took them to the Near or Middle East, and from there to the Balkans (Mendizabal et al. 2012). Traveling

---

[1] For a discussion of the problematic nature of defining and labelling these diverse communities, see the Introduction in Marushiakova and Popov (2016a). I use the term Roma in this book because the communities whose members participated in my study self-identify as Roma.

[2] European Union Agency for Fundamental Rights, Roma, URL: http://fra.europa.eu/en/theme/roma, accessed on July 2nd, 2017.

Breaking the Exclusion Cycle: How to Promote Cooperation between Majority and Minority Ethnic Groups.
Ana Bracic, Oxford University Press (2020). © Oxford University Press. DOI: 10.1093/oso/9780190050672.001.0001

through the Balkans, groups split off, some spreading to Northern and Eastern Europe and others west to the Iberian peninsula through Germany and France (Taylor 2014). While scholars have not yet determined when the original Romani identity began to form, they now accept that the Romani people formed after they left India, and not before (Taylor 2014).

While popular depictions of Roma tend to focus on their nomadic way of life, not all Roma travelled. Records from the city of Modon in the Peloponnese, for example, show a substantial settled Roma population in 1384; there are further records from this time period of settled Roma populations in Corfu, Dubrovnik, Zagreb, and Ljubljana (Marushiakova and Popov 2018). To be sure, Roma did migrate, but not because of an intrinsically nomadic identity (Barany 2002; McGarry 2017).[3] They migrated in search of a territory that would accept them, which was not an easy task. Indigenous populations tended to react negatively upon the arrival of differently-dressed, often darker-skinned Roma, and so persistent persecution as well as a lack of economic opportunities forced Roma to keep searching (Barany 2002; McGarry 2017).[4] Although the image of Roma as nomads persists and is often romanticized and stereotyped, most Roma are no longer peripatetic.[5]

As diverse Romani communities migrated to and settled in all corners of Europe, they influenced and were in turn influenced by the new communities surrounding them. This led to a rich array of cultural practices, occupations, and traditions among both. The numerous dialects of the Romani language attest to this diversity (Matras 2002).[6] Romani has six major dialect branches— Balkan, Vlax, Central, Northern, Iberian, and British—as well as a number of other dialects, which are not categorized within any of these six branches. Each of the major branches consists of numerous dialects. Romani dialects in the Balkan branch are divided in two groups and characterized by a strong Greek

[3] Constructing the Roma identity as nomadic proved eminently useful to the early modern states in Europe (McGarry 2017; Taylor 2014). "Belonging to a specific national or ethnic group determines access to the rights and services the modern state is supposed to guarantee" (Wimmer 2002, p.1); *not* belonging, in contrast, absolves the state of providing that access and, in addition, legitimizes systematic exclusion (Taylor 2014).

[4] Labeling Roma as the non-White "Other" can be traced back to these initial encounters, which roughly coincided with Marco Polo's travels east and European voyages to the American continents and the Carribean, and the concomitant debates over differences between different peoples (Taylor 2014). As early colonial constructions of race branded Blacks and non-Whites as savage and backward, White Europeans were able to trace a clear line of division that placed Roma on the other side of it (Taylor 2014).

[5] Commercial nomadism is increasingly rare, even among English Romanies and French Gens du Voyage (Law and Kovats 2018). Irish and Scots Travellers, who are nomadic, do not identify as having Romani heritage; some, however, have family ties to English and Welsh Romanies who do claim that heritage (Taylor 2014).

[6] All details regarding dialects are from Matras (2002).

and Turkish influence. The first group includes Arlije, one of the major dialects spoken in Greece, Albania, Macedonia and Kosovo; the Erli dialect of Sofia; the Ursari dialect of Romania; a number of related dialects spoken in northern Iran; and at least 12 others. The second Balkan group includes the Drindari dialect from Kotel and Varna in northeastern Bulgaria, and 3 more. Having originated in Romanian-speaking territory, the Vlax branch of dialects is also split into two groups. The first includes Kalpazea, Filipidzía, and Xandurja, all in Greece, spoken by Christian immigrants resettled from Turkey in the 1920s, and at least 3 more. The second Vlax group includes more than 5 affiliated dialects, some of which have numerous varieties; for example, Kalderaš, widely spoken in Romania, has sub-divisions with "names usually reflecting the very intact clan structure that exists among the group" (Matras 2002, p.8) and is also spoken in Sweden and in the United States. Lovari, also in the second Vlax group, originated in Transylvania and is influenced by Hungarian; it is spoken in Hungary, Norway, Poland, Austria, and elsewhere. The Northern group of the Central branch includes 3 dialects spoken in Czech Republic, Slovakia, Poland, and Transcarpathian Ukraine, while the Southern Central group includes Romungro and Vend dialects. The dialect spoken by Roma in Murska Sobota, one of my field sites, is a Vend dialect.

The Northern branch is divided into the Northwestern and Northeastern groups. The former includes the Manuš dialect, which has a strong German influence and is predominantly spoken in France, the Finnish Kaale dialect, and more. The Northeastern group includes the north Russian Xaladitka dialect, dialect of the Polska Roma, and the Lotfiko/Loftiko spoken by Roma in Lithuania, Latvia, and Estonia. The Iberian Romani branch is extinct, though it exists as "a special lexicon" (Matras 2002, p.10) in Errumantxela, which is Basque-based, and in the Spanish-based Caló. The British dialect branch is likewise considered extinct and survives as a special lexicon.[7] Two isolated groups of dialects exist in addition to the six big branches. The first consists of 3 dialects spoken in southern Italy that are related to the Balkan dialects and strongly influenced by Italian. The second is the Croatian dialect, which is in fact spoken in Italy and Slovenia. Roma from Novo mesto, my other field site, speak this Croatian dialect.

While this whirlwind of dialect variants aptly illustrates both the heterogeneity and the complexity of Romani communities—Roma in Hungary, for instance, speak Lovari, Romungro, a variety of Vend dialects, and the Gurvari dialect—it is incomplete and only covers the principal dialects of

---

[7] Matras 2002, but see Le Bas 2018.

Romani. Moreover, not all Roma speak a dialect of Romani; notable exceptions include the Beash Roma from Hungary and Croatia, who speak a variant of archaic Romanian, and sizable Romani communities in Hungary that speak Hungarian (Barany 2002). It is important to clarify that speakers of Romani, aside from young children, are rarely monolingual due to the necessity of communicating with non-Roma communities (Law and Kovats 2018);[8] in fact, the tremendous diversity of Romani leads to varying degrees of mutual intelligibility between different dialects and can result in cross-subgroup communication in a mainstream language.

As Romani communities are widely dispersed, they are often culturally closer to the communities that surround them than to Romani communities further away. This is the case with religion; while religious practice among Roma is not static, Romani communities typically practice the religion that is prevalent in their local environment (Law and Kovats 2018). Many Roma in Macedonia, Albania, and Kosovo are thus Muslim; many in Russia are Christian Orthodox; and most in the Czech Republic are Catholic. Recent decades, however, have seen increases in Roma conversions to Pentecostalism, with congregations forming across Europe (Law and Kovats 2018). Wide dispersion of Romani communities has also led to differences in ethnic significance of particular cultural practices. For example, when celebrated among Mačvaja in the United States, *Slava*, a patron saint celebration, is seen as a specifically Roma custom; in the Balkans, however, *Slava* is celebrated by several non-Roma communities as well, which also see it as an important part of their ethnic identity (Marushiakova and Popov 2016b). Similarly, the sacral opposition of 'clean-unclean'[9] is practiced among both Roma and non-Roma in the Balkans. Thus, the associated rituals and beliefs do not have an ethnic character among either. Outside the Balkans, however, where many Romani communities have retained and enriched these practices but where the surrounding population does not engage in them, the practices have evolved into a "specific [Roma] ethnic trait" (Marushiakova and Popov 2016b, p.44). *Pomana/pomen/pominki*, a set of traditions commemorating the dead, is another such custom; it is considered a Roma custom when

---

[8] Since Romani has traditionally not been a language included in formal education, Romani children are often at a disadvantage when they begin formal education. As states emphasize acquiring proficiency in the mainstream language instead of investing in Romani language instruction, however, Roma children quickly catch up (Law and Kovats 2018).

[9] Practices relating to this opposition include "isolating the women and a baby after the birth for 40 days among Roma Orthodox Christians and 52 days among Roma Muslims, and beliefs that women in this period of time and also in their monthly period should not deal with food" (Marushiakova and Popov 2016b, p.44).

practiced by Roma in Central and Western Europe and in the United States, but is widely practiced among both Roma and Orthodox Christian Slavs in the Balkans and in Eastern Europe (Marushiakova and Popov 2016b).

Although few Roma currently engage in traditional Roma occupations, they remain meaningful and for some communities serve as an ingroup-defining marker (Marushiakova and Popov 2013). This is particularly common for Roma in the Balkans as well as for their descendants who have settled elsewhere, but much less so for other Roma communities. Examples of the former include Čurari (sieve makers, Romania), Lovari (horse dealers, Hungary), Kalderaš (cauldron makers, Bulgaria), Bajaši (miners, Croatia), Rudari/Ludari (miners, Greece), Korytári (wooden bowl makers, Slovakia), Kanaloš (spoon makers, Ukraine), Fusari (spindle makers, Bulgaria), Košničari (basket makers, Bulgaria), Lautari (musicians, Romania), Kovači (smiths, Montenegro), Bugurdži (gimlet makers, Bulgaria), Arabadži (cart makers, Kosovo), and Čokenarja (smiths, Moldova). As these and other professionyms largely originate from surrounding languages, not Romani, several of the groups listed have counterparts in other countries, under names that are different but have similar or identical meanings (Marushiakova and Popov 2013).[10] While professionyms certainly serve as group markers among some communities, traditional occupations themselves were not necessarily fixed; Kalderaši in Bulgaria, for example, engaged in horse trading, agricultural work, comb making, wool combing, as well as in smithing copper and iron (Marushiakova and Popov 2013). And while the popular imagination sees Roma traveling from town to town to enjoy a comparative advantage in the provision of their traditional goods and services (Law and Kovats 2018), some communities instead plied their trades in the localities where they settled (Marushiakova and Popov 2016b).

Another and altogether different source of variation among Roma communities are the likely legacies of the social, political, and economic circumstances of the environments in which they have lived. There are many—I will only mention five. First, in the Ottoman Empire, which used the millet system—allowing self-administration of religious communities—and focused on collecting taxes in the conquered lands while maintaining social peace, Roma communities were able to exist without persecution, even though they were in a position that was subordinate to other groups (Barany 2002). Meanwhile,

---

[10] Professionyms as well as Roma group names that originate elsewhere are subject to re-negotiation and re-definition. Čurari, for example, is derived from the Romanian word for 'sieve' but also sounds like the Romani word for 'knife' (čuri); as a result, the group name is today sometimes translated as 'knife-makers' instead of 'sieve-makers'. For more, see Marushiakova and Popov (2013).

Roma in Wallachia and Moldavia were enslaved, while the communities under the Habsburg Empire faced extermination, and later, forcible assimilation (Barany 2002). Although imperial pre-communist institutions may seem a thing of the past, their legacies endure. Present-day differences in attitudes have been traced to institutional differences between the Ottoman and Austro-Hungarian Empires—specifically, to the Ottoman tax system change in the late 17th century that encouraged predatory behaviors and rent extraction. Seemingly as a result of this change, individuals who live on historically Ottoman lands *today* express higher willingness to engage in bribery and lower levels of trust toward outsiders (Karaja 2013; Karaja and Rubin 2017). Imperial institutions relevant to Roma or minorities in general could similarly affect present-day attitudes and behaviors of Roma and non-Roma.

Second, the victimization of Roma during Porajmos (the Roma Holocaust during World War II) varied substantially; while Roma in German-occupied lands were either murdered en masse or deported (Lewy 2000), persecution of communities elsewhere depended on local elites, such that Roma in Croatia and Romania died by the thousands, while in Bulgaria they did not, as the government resisted German demands for deportation (Barany 2002). Research from a part of this region shows that violence against Jews in the Holocaust corresponded to state-sponsored levels of anti-Semitism before the war; while non-Jews in parts of Romania that lived under state-sponsored anti-Semitism betrayed their Jewish neighbors, non-Jews who had lived under the Soviet Union and were thus exposed to radically inclusive nationality policies were more likely to protect them (Dumitru and Johnson 2011). As policies and norms on inclusivity made a difference in the case of Jews in northern Romania, the variation in local involvement in Porajmos might likewise have had consequences for different Roma and non-Roma communities after the war.

Third, although state socialism broadly resulted in raising many Roma communities out of socioeconomic marginality, there was considerable variation in the degree of repression applied by different regimes. Bulgaria and Czechoslovakia, for example, engaged in coercive assimilation: forbidding the use of Romani; offering women money in exchange for sterilization or sometimes sterilizing them without their knowledge or consent (Czechoslovakia); forbidding dancing and playing unique Roma musical instruments in public (Bulgaria); and halting the publication of Roma newspapers (Bulgaria). Yugoslavia, by contrast, allowed Roma communities a large number of social and cultural organizations "relatively free of state control" (Barany 2002, p.122); some localities, particularly in Serbia, also included Roma in land distribution schemes. The presence of forcible assimilation in some states and its absence in others might have left a mark not only on Roma who themselves experienced these policies but also on their descendants (Elias et al. 2012).[11]

Fourth, as states in Central and Eastern Europe transitioned from state socialism to capitalism and numerous enterprises and factories closed, the devastating job losses were disproportionately felt among Roma, who were particularly vulnerable because many had been employed as low-skilled workers. While insufficient on the whole, state responses aimed at Roma recovery varied considerably. Hungary, for example, allocated substantial funds for Romani programs as early as 1992, such that the number of programs aimed at assisting Roma climbed from 40 in 1990 to more than 500 in 1996–97 (Barany 2002). Conversely, between 1993 and 1997, the Mečiar government in Slovakia made "major annual reductions" (Barany 2002, p.322) to the budget allocated to Roma and other minorities. While the effectiveness of labor market programs varies with program type, training programs and programs that include wage subsidies can significantly increase the chance that their beneficiaries will secure employment (Kluve 2010); the former are particularly effective when unemployment is high (Lechner and Wunsch 2009). It is thus possible that the presence of programming in Hungary and its relative absence in Slovakia may have contributed to further differences between the affected communities.

Fifth, though Roma certainly mobilized before (Vermeersch 2017), democratization in Central and Eastern Europe brought new political opportunities and resulted in a dramatic increase in the number of Roma organizations across the region. Compared to others, Roma in Hungary were particularly successful in establishing organizations early on, and had, by 1994, raised the number of organized groups from 18, in 1990, to 210 (Barany 2002). Activity in other states hardly measures up; by 1994, Romania had 25 organizations while a year later Slovakia and Poland had 36 and 5, respectively (Barany 2002). While the number of organized groups is at best an incomplete indicator of mobilizational activity, a difference by an order of magnitude is surely meaningful—whether it indicates that establishing organizations was easier in Hungary, that Roma activists in Hungary shied away from working together,

---

[11] Scholarship on long-term consequences of trauma among First Nations Indian Residential School System survivors in Canada shows that trauma experienced first hand is indeed transmitted across several generations (Elias et al. 2012). While obtained in a different context, these findings might carry implications for some Roma communities, as they lived under several assimilationist regimes, some of which included prohibitions on marriage and the abduction of approximately 18,000 children who were placed in state schools and non-Roma foster homes (Austro-Hungarian Empire under Maria Theresa; see Barany 2002).

that the resources for mobilizing were substantially higher there, or that Roma in Hungary were indeed better equipped or motivated to mobilize. Variation in both extent and type of Roma mobilization efforts is thus another factor that renders Roma communities different from one another, with implications for human rights practices (Murdie and Davis 2012), political participation, and voter turnout (Boulding 2010).

At the least, Roma communities vary from one another in language and dialect; in religion; in cultural practices, traditional occupations, and the ethnic salience of both; in having experienced imperial persecution; in having experienced wartime violence; in having experienced forcible assimilation; in having had better opportunities to recover from transition-based unemployment; and in having benefitted from vibrant post-socialist mobilization efforts. There are numerous other dimensions that I have not mentioned but which are also important, including institutional factors like electoral rules that effectively bar Roma opposition from challenging the government-backed incumbent in national elections[12] (Romania; Mark 2017) or regulations that enable mayors to personally allocate spots in public works programs to whomever they choose (Hungary; Mares and Young 2019). All of this underscores the fact that Roma communities are tremendously diverse and that the experiences of some communities might not necessarily generalize to the experiences of others.

Nevertheless, members of different Roma communities are often considered a part of a larger Roma "imagined community" (Anderson 1983, p.6), connected not because they all know one another, meet one another, or hear about one another but because they hold in their minds the idea of a larger collective whole. Therefore, while Roma might among themselves primarily refer to situationally salient subgroups, many assume the larger, superordinate identity in relation to non-Roma. Moreover, unlike most nations whose community is imagined by its members (Anderson 1983), the Roma imagined community is to a considerable extent also imagined by outsiders (Chandra 2012, Marushiakova and Popov 2016a). Indeed, in some cases communities that would prefer to go by a different identity cannot do so, as the non-Roma imagining is set in stone (Stolipinovo neighborhood in Plovdiv, Bulgaria; see Marushiakova

---

[12] In order to run in parliamentary elections, new Roma political organizations must obtain special approval from a government agency (National Agency for Roma). The president of this agency, who makes the decision to grant such approval, is a political appointee of the only Roma political organization that has been granted such approval thus far (i.e., the incumbent Roma political organization). The incumbent organization therefore can ensure that it runs unopposed by not giving any opposition groups special approval, an opportunity of which it takes full advantage.

and Popov 2016a). The Roma/non-Roma boundary is thus determined by both Roma and non-Roma, and in at least this respect, treating Roma as a larger but diverse collective whole makes sense.

Roma in present-day Slovenia

Slovenia is a small country of about 2 million people, bordered by Austria, Hungary, Croatia, and Italy. It is a new parliamentary democracy that became a member of the European Union in the first wave of the Eastern expansion in 2004. Slovenia has been an independent state since June 25 1991, when it seceded from Yugoslavia. Its declaration of independence was followed by the Ten Day War, which was the first of the Yugoslav Wars of the 1990s and the 2000s. Before Yugoslavia, most of present day Slovenia was a part of the Kingdom of Serbs, Croats and Slovenes; earlier still, large parts of the country, including the localities I examine, belonged to the Austro-Hungarian Empire.

According to the country's 2002 Census, ethnic Slovenes make up 83 percent of the population (Statistični urad Republike Slovenije 2002). The next largest group, at 1.98 percent, are Serbs, followed by Croats and Bosniaks. The two communities that are granted official recognition as national minorities, Hungarians and Italians, make up 0.32 and 0.11 percent of the population, respectively. While the Census reports that there are 3,246 Roma in Slovenia (0.19 percent of the population), estimates made by various other institutions place the real number somewhere between 7,000 and 12,000. Challenges to obtaining accurate counts of Roma are not new (Štrukelj 1980), but they are serious; the question of whether an identity is determined by oneself or by others plays an important role here (Marushiakova and Popov 2016a), as do a number of other issues, including distrust of state institutions. As a result, any sort of national statistics on Roma as a group must be interpreted with caution, particularly because individuals who withhold their ethnic identities from Census takers might differ in some systematic way from individuals who do not.[13]

Roma communities settled in two regions of Slovenia, in Prekmurje (the northeast) and in Dolenjska (the southeast).[14] Today, Roma communities

[13] Indeed, at 2.47, the percent of individuals who did not wish to answer the ethnicity question is higher than the percent of ethnic Serbs.

[14] The third and substantially smaller nomadic community are Sinti, who settled in the northwest region of Gorenjska. Sinti are sometimes grouped together with Roma by others, but they retain a separate identity.

live in localities outside those regions as well (particularly if they arrived as refugees during the Yugoslav Wars), but the vast majority remain in the regions of original settlement. The two studies presented in this book include participants from Novo mesto, which is the regional capital of Dolenjska, and from Murska Sobota, which is the regional capital of Prekmurje. The dialects spoken by the members of the two groups come from entirely different branches of dialects; Roma from Dolenjska speak a Croatian dialect which also includes a substantial number of words from the Dolenjska Slovene dialect group, while Roma from Prekmurje speak a number of different varieties of a Vend dialect from the Central branch, which include words from both Hungarian and the Prekmurje Slovene dialect (Matras 2002; Štrukelj 1980). The dialects are different enough to preclude the communities from creating a unified syllabus for teaching the language to children; indeed, members of these communities typically communicate with one another in Slovene (but avoid the exclusive use of their respective Slovene dialects, as they are also not completely mutually intelligible).[15]

The first record of Roma arriving in Slovenia comes from a 1387 court document from Zagreb that mentions Roma from Ljubljana (Štrukelj 1980). Slovene archival materials mention the name "Cigan" (Slovene eqivalent of "Gypsy") in 1452, while Luger's feudal book from 1453 refers to a Romani blacksmith (Horvat-Muc 2011b; Štrukelj 1980). In the 14th century most of present-day Slovenia was taken over by the Habsburgs. While most Roma who were in Slovenia at the time were likely passing through on their travels west, Štrukelj (1980) writes that scholars nonetheless believe that this was the time period during which the first Roma families settled in Slovenia. Starting in the 17th century, Roma began to appear in archival documents from the region with more frequency. Many of these are court documents and include bills issued by executioners, which attest to the persecution of Roma in Slovenia at the time (Horvat-Muc 2011b; Štrukelj 1980).

Documents from the 18th century suggest that by then, Roma were known in numerous localities across the Slovene ethnic space; this was also the time when the first births of Roma children appeared in the official registers (Štrukelj 1980). Roma communities that resided in or moved around what is now Slovenia were subjected to the forcible assimilation policies developed by Maria Theresa and Joseph II in the second half of the 18th century

---

[15] The Slovene language has seven major dialect groups and forty dialects with varying degrees of mutual intelligibility; although it is spoken by only 2.4 million people, its dialectical diversity is very high, especially when compared to other Slavic languages (Bitenc 2013).

(Šiftar 1970). The Habsburg decrees included (1) forced settlement (1758); (2) compulsory military service (1761); (3) banning of traditional Romani authority over the communities, as well as the use of traditional Romani dress and Romani language (1767); and (4) banning of marriage between Roma men and Roma women, and abducting all Roma children older than five (about 18,000 children) from their families to place them into state schools or non-Roma foster families (1773) (Barany 2002). While Štrukelj (1980) writes that the policies were not particularly successful in reaching their goal, the cost to the Roma population was exorbitant (Elias et al. 2012).

Sources from the region suggest that by the end of the 18th century, Romani communities were already distinguished from one another by their traditional occupations; Štrukelj (1980) offers a detailed description of these occupations in Slovenia. The first Roma to settle in Slovenia were blacksmiths. In the Dolenjska region, blacksmiths made up the largest group of Roma; some families still travelled from village to village to ply their trade, especially in the summer. In Prekmurje, there were many families of knife sharpeners alongside blacksmiths. Knife sharpeners and umbrella menders also travelled from village to village to provide services; sometimes non-Roma brought their tools to them instead to have them sharpened and mended. Štrukelj writes that the services of knife sharpeners were in very high demand because it was known that no one else knew how to sharpen knives as well as Roma. Among trades related to construction, splitting rocks was a particular specialty of Roma in Dolenjska, at times performed by Roma who specialized only in this trade and at times also by blacksmiths. According to Štrukelj, local builders liked to employ Roma and paid them well; although rock splitting is not challenging, she writes, it requires a particular skill with a steel hammer that splits a rock without overly tiring the worker. This was a job that Roma men and women alike performed, as well as the older children. The nature of the work requires moving from place to place such that Roma families engaged in a job far away would leave their home for the duration and live in a tent nearby. Also in construction, Roma from Prekmurje were known as clay house or wattle and daub house builders. This, too, was a highly sought-after service; non-Roma typically did not engage in it and paid Roma well. While this was not the custom at the time, some peasant families even paid Roma builders in advance to secure their services. Roma men typically worked on inner and outer house walls and ceilings, while Roma women put clay on the insides of stoves and wood-fire ovens. In addition to these prominent occupations, there were also basket weavers, broom makers, pot menders, horse traders, horse healers, and musicians. From time to time Roma women would also walk from house to house seeking alms; typically, they'd offer a prayer and a blessing for the house in return. Lastly, telling fortunes—an occupation of Roma women—was quite widespread in both Prekmurje and Dolenjska.

Šiftar (1989) writes that as long as armies needed weapons made by black-smiths and their horses shod, Roma blacksmiths had work and were appreciated; this was also the case before farming became automated, as Roma smiths, basket wavers, and others made farming tools and offered repairs, and before horses, which Roma traders sold, were replaced by cars.

The economic marginalization of Roma began when automation started replacing artisans. When general economic hardship became acute toward the end of the 1920s, crime became prevalent and Roma were largely blamed for it (Šiftar 1970); at the same time (and somewhat inconsistently), Roma were also accused of taking jobs away from non-Roma (Štrukelj 1980). Reacting to the crisis, the authorities put into action a series of policies reminiscent of the Habsburg decrees.[16] The first, in 1928, demanded that Roma remain in the municipality in which they are settled, within which their movements were monitored, and present a permit to travel with details of the specific trip if caught outside of their municipality; this extended to travel that was related to traditional occupations (Šiftar 1984). The second, in 1935, authorized the police to conduct daytime and nighttime surprise checks in Roma settlements to verify that Roma were indeed there and to look for stolen property (Šiftar 1984). In response, local authorities in Murska Sobota and Novo mesto sent reports to the capital explaining that Roma neither wander from place to place nor engage in criminal acts attributed to them (Murska Sobota), and that they don't trade, but work in quarries, on roads, and on construction sites (Novo mesto) (Štrukelj 1980). The exchange of policies and reports that continued satisfied the authorities, but did not improve Roma lives (Štrukelj 1980).

In the beginning of World War II, many Slovene Roma joined the partisan movement; they founded a Roma partisan unit and rose through the ranks, particularly in Dolenjska. In Prekmurje, Roma were initially granted a reprieve from the worst, which changed rapidly once the Arrow Cross Party took over from the Germans and began to "cleanse the terrain" (Šiftar 1984, p.120), immediately targeting Roma. Across present-day Slovenia, many Roma were killed outright by occupying forces or by local collaborators; others were interred, some in Auschwitz, some in Jasenovac, and some possibly elsewhere (Šiftar 1970). Records as to where precisely Slovene Roma were taken

[16] These were not the first such attempts, however, as similar programs had been put into place in 1885 and in 1916 (Štrukelj 1980).

are poor, partly due to the Nazi practice of killing people "straight from the train" (Šiftar 1984, p.117) without noting their names; in addition, inaccurate census records of Roma before the war make estimating the number of Slovene Roma killed nearly impossible (this is the case in other states as well). After the war ended, no Slovene Roma were accused or convicted of collaborating with the occupying forces (Šiftar 1970). Roma communities that survived the war expressed enthusiasm for and commitment to building a better future together with others in the new homeland; this organization, stemming from a number of leading families, marked the first instance—however limited—of Roma inclusion in the development of policies that affected them (Šiftar 1970).

Yugoslavia's policy of enforced ethnic harmony, prizing integration instead of assimilation, was far ahead of those in other Central and Eastern European states. Within the Federation, however, there was considerable variation in the application of these principles, with Slovenia at one end of the scale and Macedonia on the other. For example, Slovene efforts for Roma inclusion in education stalled until the 1970s, when a substantial investment in Roma enrollment and retention led to dramatic increases in the numbers of children who attended school (Šiftar 1978). Nevertheless, other critical barriers to education were not removed; most notably, across all schools and kindergartens that Roma children attended, not a single teacher spoke Romani. Tellingly, Šiftar (1978) reports that teachers in one Novo mesto school relied on the help of a Roma janitor when running into language barriers. This differs substantially from inclusion efforts in Macedonia, where Romani was "integrated into the multicultural educational curricula" (Sardelić 2015, p.164). In Slovenia, a large number of Roma children were instead placed in schools for children with special needs, as Romani was considered too great a barrier for inclusion in mainstream schools (Sardelić 2015). Further, while this was not the case in Macedonia, Roma and non-Roma in Slovenia remained spatially segregated (Barany 2002), both by municipal administrative design and by non-Roma preference (Šiftar 1978). When Roma from Murska Sobota and Novo mesto were asked what they wished for most, home ownership in a desegregated neighborhood and education for their children took second and third place (Šiftar 1978). Formal employment was first.

In the first decades after the war, employment integration efforts were quite successful, with Roma finding jobs in various industries and sectors. Although this was certainly not the case for all Roma, their levels of education were typically low, and as a result most jobs held by Roma workers were low-skilled occupations including meat factory worker, road sweeper, laundry worker, factory seamstress, brick carrier, construction worker, and janitor

(Štrukelj 1980). The same survey of occupations, however, also mentions musicians, tailors, and a pilot instructor. Following the war, numerous Roma still engaged in their respective traditional occupations. By 1970, however, many families stopped providing their services and no longer taught their children how to do the same. According to Štrukelj (1980), this was at least partly due to the lack of interest among the younger generation, though much can also be attributed to low demand for artisanal work. If the lack of education was one reason behind predominantly low-skilled employment of Roma, employer distrust was another. In making this claim, Štrukelj (1980) points to Roma of younger generations who had secured better work across the border, where they were not asked who they were. As time passed, economic development further reduced the demand for low-skilled labor; as a result, Roma employment stagnated and began decreasing in the later decades of the Federation (Šiftar 1997).

Since independence, Slovenia has made a number of important strides in improving the status of Roma. The Constitution recognizes Roma as an "ethnic community" (Klopčič 2007, p.108) and accords them special rights; it bears mentioning, however, that Roma are not granted the same status as the two other, more prominently recognized "national minorities" (Hungarian and Italian), which have seats in the National Assembly and, in the localities where their members live, have their languages recognized as official. Two bodies charged with protecting Roma serve at the national level; one consists entirely of Roma representatives while the other includes state representatives, representatives of local communities, and members of the Roma community.[17] In localities with substantial Roma populations, the law requires that a Roma representative serve on the city or the municipal council; where such a representative is elected, a body responsible for keeping up with the Roma community is then formed. Currently, 20 localities are required to have a Roma representative in their councils; others in which Roma also live are encouraged to do the same.

The European Union (EU) accession process is arguably the strongest incentive-based mechanism for Roma rights change, as it requires candidate states not only to ratify human rights agreements but also to make appropriate changes to state policies and practices (Schimmelfennig et al. 2005). When undergoing accession negotiations, Slovenia thus adopted anti-discrimination

---

[17] Svet romske skupnosti Republike Slovenije and Komisija Vlade Republike Slovenije za zaščito romske skupnosti, respectively. For more, see http://www.un.gov.si/si/manjsine/romska_skupnost/organiziranost/.

legislation stemming from relevant international human rights agreements[18] and made a number of other improvements. For example, the Ministry of Education, Science, and Sport financed a project intended to include the Romani lanugage and Roma culture into educational programs; Roma teaching assistants now help Romani children bridge the gap between Romani and Slovene and provide other necessary types of support to schoolchildren (Klopčič 2007). Further, in response to concerns voiced by the European Commission, levels of police violence toward individuals in custody have decreased (European Commission 2001, 2002). And Slovene Roma activists point to the EU accession process as instrumental in allowing Roma to mobilize; two activists described it it as an "opening of space" in which Roma claims suddenly gained legitimacy (Balažek 2012; Tudija 2012). When the first umbrella Roma organization, *Zveza Romov Slovenije*, was founded in 1996, Roma were able to secure unprecedented levels of influence over policy decision-making (Klopčič 2007). Still, while the EU accession process has led to valuable steps in the right direction, the full implementation of the intended changes lags behind. This is typically the case as mere progress toward implementation is sufficient to secure EU membership and the situation on the ground is no longer scrutinized to the same degree once membership is granted (Bracic 2015, 2016).

Although Roma have made substantial political gains since Slovene independence, the end of socialism also brought a number of losses. First, as numerous factories and enterprises closed, Roma were "consistently among the first to lose jobs" (Klopčič 2007, p.104). While secondary or higher education was not a requirement for employment under state-socialism, it became increasingly important after; as a result, many Roma who only had primary school educations were locked out of job opportunities (Barany 2002). Since Roma unemployment had already been higher than that of non-Roma before the transition, the economic losses brought on by the neoliberal turn and exacerbated by discrimination in employment were more acutely felt among Roma. In the 1990s, the resulting poverty rates were reflected in alarming health disparities; compared to the mortality rate of non-Roma infants, that of their Roma counterparts was seven times as high (Barany 2002). Second, economic losses that accompanied the transition period, which were by no means limited to Roma, acted as accelerants of intolerance; as prejudice that had

---

[18] Among the required agreements are the European Convention on Human Rights and Fundamental Freedoms, the Framework Convention for the Protection of National Minorities, the European Charter for Regional and Minority Languages, and the UN Convention on Civil and Political Rights.

been kept relatively quiet during state socialism could now be freely expressed, Roma/non-Roma relations openly deteriorated. In a troubling example from 1997, non-Roma villagers from Maline staged multiple armed protests when a Roma family from a larger town, Grosuplje, bought a house in the village (Erjavec et al. 2000). The armed "village guard" (Erjavec et al. 2000, p.7) set up explosives around the house and patrolled the surroundings; the Roma family was unable to move in. Finally, soon after independence in 1991, the government secretly and illegally stripped hundreds of Roma of their permanent resident status and denied them citizenship, which led to formal exclusion from a wide range of state benefits (Dedić 2003a; Jalušič 2003).[19] While most of the "erased" Roma were able to again register permanent residence two decades after the erasures (Sardelić 2015), for many, the damage was done.

I collected the data I present in this book between the summers of 2010 and 2018, at a time when Roma had made political gains but suffered economic and social losses. Non-Roma likewise experienced economic losses, both during the transition, and during the economic downturn in the late 2000s and the early 2010s.

The final section of this chapter introduces a Roma exclusion cycle by drawing on a case of a murder-suicide that took place just outside Novo mesto, my first field site. The circumstances of the crime and the media coverage of it provide an example of an exclusion cycle as well as an opportunity to present Slovenia and Novo mesto in more detail. I supplement the murder-suicide with scholarship on Roma exclusion, both from Slovenia and from other Central/Eastern European countries. I reach across the border because Slovenia sees less systematic scholarship that covers various facets of Roma exclusion. In general, expansive policy-oriented studies of Roma and Roma rights in Central and Eastern Europe that aim to cover the most important countries where Roma live rarely include Slovenia.[20] Slovenia is perhaps excluded because of its size—in the EU, only Malta, Luxembourg, and Cyprus are smaller. Perhaps it is excluded because its proportion of the estimated

---

[19] These erasures did not target Roma exclusively, but they were ethnically motivated. The victims were Croats, Bosnians, Serbs, Montenegrins, Albanians, and Roma; some Slovenes with a mixed ethnic background and some who were born outside Slovenia were also included (Kogovšek 2010). The "erased" were not informed of their new status; they simply found themselves without the status of a permanent resident and without the fundamental socioeconomic rights attached to it: the right to work, the pension they had earned, social security, health care, protection from unemployment, and access to housing and education (Dedić 2003b). All their documents were rendered invalid (hole-punched); for some, this happened under the pretense of getting their papers in order, which they were invited to do—only to witness their invalidation. The "erased" individuals have also been subjected to police brutality, detention, and arbitrary expulsions from Slovenia (Zorn 2003).

[20] See, for example, the UNDP-World Bank-European Commission Regional Roma survey 2011, conducted in 12 states, but not in Slovenia (Ivanov et al. 2012), or the European Union Agency for

Roma population is lower than that in some other states—0.19 percent to Hungary's 1.9 percent or Slovakia's 5.4 percent.[21] Or perhaps because decades ago, it had an "image" (Jalušič 2003, p.16) as a Central European state with a commitment to human rights. Slovenia might be excluded from inquiry because of all three, but it shouldn't be.

A Roma exclusion cycle, through the lens of a murder-suicide

On February 8th, 2011, tragedy shook the community around the town of Novo mesto. There had been a shooting that left two people dead and a third wounded. Awaiting the official version of the events, which was not to come for a number of days, the rumor mill set out to reconstruct the crime. Olga Kovačič was shot and died immediately. Veljan Kovačič, Olga's son, was shot in the stomach and fled the scene. The shooter, Stane Vidic, turned the gun on himself. While the particulars of the crime were easy enough to string together, the motive remained elusive. Why would Stane, a well-known local businessman and by all accounts a peaceful man, resort to such violence?

A local newspaper relayed the town gossip:

> Two scenarios remain up in the air. According to the first, Vidic went to the Roma settlement... and offered the woman... a van full of iron, which he allegedly had in [a nearby village]. Olga, her son, and Vidic then allegedly went there. According to the second scenario, Vidic allegedly caught the woman and her son stealing his iron.   (Kastelic 2011).

Even though the two Roma, Olga and her son, were the *victims* of the crime, the reporter concluded that

> It is already clear that the state is partly responsible for this tragedy as it is unwilling, unskilled, or unable to resolve the Roma question... People are outraged, afraid of the Roma, while they [the Roma], as always, know nothing.

Fundamental Rights (FRA) Roma pilot survey, also conducted in 2011, which includes 11 states, but not Slovenia (FRA 2014a).

[21] The Slovene proportion is from the Slovene Statistical Office (Statistični urad Republike Slovenije 2002). I calculated the percent of Roma in Slovakia and Hungary using the Roma population data reported in Ivanov et al. (2012) and total population data from the 2011 Censuses conducted in both states (Juhaščíková 2015; Vukovich 2012).

The coming paragraphs will demonstrate that this take is far from unique.

First, a few words about Novo mesto, one of my research sites. Novo mesto is a large town in south-eastern Slovenia, about 10 miles away from the Slovene-Croat border. It is the regional capital of Dolenjska, and has the largest Roma population in the region. Roma have lived in Novo mesto for over 200 years, though some Roma have arrived more recently. Estimates of how many Roma live in the town, or rather in settlements on its outskirts, vary. The official estimate, according to the Statistical Office of Slovenia census conducted in 2002, is 1.2 percent; the unofficial estimate from a source in town is 2.8 percent. Most of the Roma live in settlements; the vast majority lives in Brezje-Žabjak, which is isolated from the main town center by fields and light woods. This is the settlement where Vidic had allegedly gone to offer Olga and her son some scrap metal.

Roma from Novo mesto have had a representative in the local government since 2002 (Dedić 2003b). A local Romani NGO, Romano Veseli, has been active since the early 1990s and predominantly engages in providing services to Roma. The local schools neither offer Romani nor teach the children about Roma history, culture, tradition, or past mistreatment—despite their long history in the town. The schools, do, however, employ one Romani assistant who helps Roma students with Slovene, which is their second language (Rajšek 2014).[22]

Anti-Roma culture

One can read anti-Roma sentiment straight out of the online Dictionary of the Slovenian Standard Language (SSKJ), a publication widely considered the language's authoritative source.[23] Searching for the words "Rom, Rominja, Romi" (male, female, and plural of Roma) brings up no results. Searching for "romski" returns "pertaining to the Roma: Roma language/the Roma question."[24] Searching for "cigan,"[25] the Slovene version of the ethnic slur "gypsy," however, returns 16 entries that explain the word and its permutations, and 28 more

[22] With 130 Romani students enrolled in one primary school, the single assistant is almost certainly overburdened (Rajšek 2014).

[23] Slovar slovenskega knjižnega jezika (Bajec et al. 2008), http://bos.zrc-sazu.si/sskj.html, accessed June 30th, 2017. The content of this online edition is equivalent to the 1997 and 2008 reprints of the Dictionary as well as the 1998 and 2000 digital editions.

[24] All translations from Slovene to English are my own (Slovene is my native language). In the original, "nanašajoč se na Rome: romski jezik/romsko vprašanje."

[25] The term is derived from the European term "Zingari," which originates from the Greek "athigganos" (Čupković 2015).

where the word or a version of it is used to explain something else. The first entry offers examples "they used to say that gypsies steal children; Hungarian gypsy; a gang of gypsies; black as a gypsy; lies like a gypsy."[26] The fifth entry explains "ciganíca" with "a *gypsy woman*: they accused a gypsy woman of stealing a chicken."[27] The fourteenth explains "ociganiti," or "gyp" with "to deceive, to cheat: the traffickers gypped him; gyp for money; they gypped them in cold blood, ruthlessly."[28] Of all the phrases on that page, only 4 are described as derogatory. None of the phrases I have listed here are among them. The Dictionary of the Slovene Standard Language thus reflects how deeply entrenched anti-Roma culture is in Slovenia. It not only normalizes anti-Roma language, but legitimizes it—to the point of offering no respectful and unbigoted alternative.

Few groups have been as extensively and universally stereotyped as the Roma. Not all stereotypes of Roma are explicitly bad—those that depict them as musicians of consummate skill, for example, might not be (McGarry 2017)—but most are, and *all* contribute to the construction of their identity as *the Other*. Here, I focus on one stereotype in particular, that of the Roma as cheaters, thieves, and takers. This stereotype is both universal and deeply intractable; so much so that it has become a part of everyday speech, used by many with nary a thought to what it signifies. When English speakers want to express indignation at being cheated at something, usually in sales or the service industry, some say "I was gypped." One of the entries in the dictionary above shows that Slovenes, too, use this word when they feel that they have been burned; they even have a popular song with that title that is broadcast over the radio every once in a while.[29] Slovaks, expressing the exact same thought, use the word "ociganil," while Croats say "*to nije posao nego ciganjenje*" (Čupković 2015, p.224) or "that isn't work, it's gypsying around," meaning that the job is not real work.

---

[26] In the original, "pravili so, da cigani kradejo otroke; ogrski cigani; tolpa ciganov; črn kot cigan; laže kot cigan."

[27] In the original, "*ciganka*: ciganico so obdolžili, da je ukradla kokoš."

[28] In the original, "ogoljufati, prevarati: prekupčevalci so ga ociganili; ociganiti za denar; hladnokrvno, nesramno so jih ociganili."

[29] The song, "Ociganil si me," is about a love affair with a non-Roma gone awry: "Ociganil si me, ti, ki nisi cigan, še najmanj po duši - ti moj mali meščan," or roughly translated as "you 'gypped me,' you, you are not a 'gypsy,' not in the least in your soul, you small city boy." The statement that "you are not a 'gypsy' and [yet] you 'gypped' me" seems to both imply that as a non-Roma, the man behaved reprehensibly and uncharacteristically, but that the same behavior would be understandable if he were Roma, as if cheating people is their prerogative or somehow in their nature. The addition of "not in the least in your soul" further suggests a deep, fundamental difference between non-Roma and Roma more generally, again speaking to some deterministic idea of Roma as soulful, romantic cheaters and of non-Roma as lacking in soul but, aside from this "city boy," having plenty of integrity. The song is by Romana Kranjčan, a non-Roma woman.

The stereotype of Roma as cheaters, thieves, and takers has changed so little that expressions of it today are nearly identical to those that were coined hundreds of years ago. Taylor (2014), for example, cites a reaction by a "Parisian Bourgeois," who, in a somewhat bewildered manner, records his reaction to a group of Roma who arrived in August 1472:

> . . . I must say I went there three or four times to talk to them and could never see that I lost a penny, nor did I see them looking into anyone's hands, but everyone said they did   (Taylor 2014, p.39).

Another account of Roma passing through northern Germany and Hanseatic towns in 1417 states

> [t]hey were, however, great thieves, especially their women, and several of them in various places were seized and put to death   (Taylor 2014, p.41).

The construction of this stereotype thus dates back to—at least—non-Roma retellings of early interactions between Roma and non-Roma in the European space.[30] Non-Roma privileging of coethnic accounts was likely due to prejudice, but also to the fact that some of these accounts were written and thus granted a certain legitimacy (in addition to being preserved for future generations). Roma retellings of these encounters, in contrast, were typically not written (Wogg 2019) and thus more easily ignored by non-Roma, if heard. Over time, this stereotype became worked into the very definition of the group, as seen in Diderot's Encyclopédie from the 18th century that describes Roma as

> vagabonds who profess to tell fortunes by examining hands. Their talent is to sing, dance, and steal   (Taylor 2014, p.98)

Having persisted and evolved, this stereotype is typically evoked in the following ways in present-day Slovenia. Non-Roma accuse Roma of refusing to work and preferring to take what they need instead of earning it. A former mayor of Novo mesto explained:

> We Dolenjci [non-Roma from the region] are hard working and enterprising, and we demand a lot from ourselves and our own. The Roma avoid work and prefer to party, unfortunately even with firearms.
>
> (Alojzij Muhič, 2011, cited in Rajšek (2011))

---

[30] This early account also reveals the often gendered nature of stereotyping against the Roma. The intersectional nature of stereotyping and mistreatment of Romani women is an important topic that has so far not received the attention it merits. For more, see Oprea (2004, 2012).

The reductive nature of the former mayor's statement betrays a narrow and stereotyped view of both communities—the non-Roma as excessively good and the Roma as excessively bad.[31] The erroneous belief that Roma refuse to work typically leads to two further accusations: that they exploit social assistance and/or engage in crime. A different article, from a regional radio station, reporting on the murder-suicide with which I began this section demonstrates both:

> This tragedy... reflects intolerance among people, but also a paradoxical relationship of the state toward its taxpayers and certain recipients of social assistance who are, in Slovene society, more protected than the Kočevje bear.
> (Radio Krka 2011)

While a reader might expect to hear details about the shooting itself, perhaps with a focus on the perpetrator, the reporting veers off track almost immediately, devolving into general discontent directed at Roma. The above statement sets up the dichotomy between taxpayers, meaning non-Roma, and certain recipients of social assistance, meaning Roma, who can get away with anything. Aside from the obvious insult, the comparison of Roma to an animal that is both beloved and protected in Slovenia also conveys a measure of indignation, suggesting that whatever social protection Roma experience is deeply unwarranted, unlike that given to bears. Having named the first facet of this Roma stereotype, the reporter then laments the lack of attention paid to "individuals who trade in weapons, drugs, 'colorful metals' and other things," (Radio Krka 2011) again meaning Roma, and ends the appeal with an unsubstantiated claim about the victim's finances:

> We ask again: have the responsible state authorities never asked themselves how an individual who has never worked has amassed such wealth[?] Wealth that an average person in Slovene society with a history of full employment obtains with difficulty, if at all. (Radio Krka 2011)

In the span of a few sentences, the reporter stereotypes Roma as cheaters, thieves, and takers—starting with Roma refusal to work, continuing with their exploitation of social assistance, and ending with their criminality. Alongside these accusations, the reporter pits Veljan, the purportedly criminal surviving victim, against the average hard-working Slovene non-Roma, highlighting the

---

[31] As this mayor helped a different Roma community modernize their settlement (Rajšek 2011) and was therefore a better ally to the Roma than many of his counterparts, his statement is all the more discouraging.

differences between Veljan and potential non-Roma readers and brushing aside his status as a victim. Concluding the article, the reporter takes a righteous stance:

> With this article we do not intend to support intolerance, but to say that we expect a serious attempt at resolving such problems ... by the authorities responsible. Similar matters ought not to be dealt with using weapons or violence.

To be clear, with "such problems" the reporter does not mean the murder-suicide; instead, Roma reliance on social assistance and their alleged criminality are considered the problems, and Vidic's murderous act an inappropriate attempt at a solution.

Stereotypical and prejudiced depictions of Roma in the media (Cahn 2007; Kanižaj 2004; Scicluna 2007), in speeches and statements by public officials (Scicluna 2007), in literature (Bardi 2006), in movies (Dobreva 2007),[32] in television shows (Beaudoin 2015)[33] and elsewhere, recreate the damaging perceptions of Roma over and over again. While such "practice is a coded nod to pre-existing anti-Romani sentiment" (Cahn 2007, p.6), public affirmations of intolerance strengthen anti-Roma culture of their own accord, creating an environment accepting of those who would turn their prejudice into action.

Taking a step back from the reporting on the murder-suicide, the next two sections provide some background on the phenomena relevant to this crime. The first addresses discrimination, particularly in employment, while the second discusses the resulting survival strategies, one of which is scrap metal collection. The section on the attribution error returns to the murder-suicide and concludes.

Discrimination

Discrimination against the Roma occurs in essentially all walks of life. Some of it is state-sanctioned, some even international,[34] and some local. Much

---

[32] See, for example, *Black Cat, White Cat* (*Crna mačka, beli mačor*) (1998) by Emir Kusturica (Dobreva 2007). Also see *Sherlock Holmes* (2009), *Snatch* (2000), *Thinner* (1996), and *Big* (1988); all mentioned in Beaudoin (2015).

[33] See, for example, *Criminal Minds* (2005–13), *House* (2004–12), *Law & Order: SVU* (1999–2013), and *Judging Amy* (1999–2005). However, *Buffy the Vampire Slayer* (1997–2003) developed "a dynamic and multifaceted Romani character, Jenny Calendar, who ... defied stereotype[s] and contributed to a positive Romani portrayal" (Beaudoin 2015, p.313).

[34] The UK practice of keeping Roma who bought airline tickets to the UK from boarding the flights at the Prague airport is one such example. For more, see European Roma Rights Centre (2001).

of it, however, happens at the hands of individuals. Based on the anti-discrimination legislation many Central European nations have passed,[35] such mistreatment is often illegal; and yet, discrimination is challenging to prove, and anti-discrimination laws are enforced only sporadically (Matache 2014). The case of the murder-suicide does not immediately call to mind discrimination in employment. But such discrimination plays an important role in this story: Veljan and his mother went with Stane to pick up the iron because scrap metal collection is one of the few ways of securing subsistence available to Roma.

While Kopčič writes that Slovene Roma were "by rule the first who were let go when companies were downsizing or went bankrupt" (Kopčič 2007, p.104), and remain victims of prejudice in employment, there is a lack of systematic in-depth research that explores Roma exclusion from employment in Slovenia. However, a comprehensive study by the European Roma Rights Centre (ERRC), based on 402 interviews conducted in Bulgaria, the Czech Republic, Hungary, Romania, and Slovakia found that employers in surrounding states appear unconcerned about anti-discrimination legislation and take no measures to ensure compliance (Hyde 2006). Further, enterprises in public and private sectors alike make very little effort to ensure equality in hiring by, for example, having an active equal opportunity policy (Hyde 2006).

While employment discrimination first and foremost happens at the hands of employers, others, such as individuals who work at state employment offices, are also involved. An anonymous ERRC interviewee explains:

> Emily's girlfriend works for the local labour office and she showed her on the labour office computer screen job offers where the employer did not want Roma people had an "R" flag to signify that no Roma were employed by the company. Joseph, from the same town, also reported that the local labour office only made placements to the locations where the "R" flag was missing from the name of the company.
>
> (ERRC interview, Hungary, August 2005, quoted in Hyde 2006, p.7)

Individuals who work at state employment offices can act as gatekeepers by respecting the wishes of employers who ask that no Roma job applicants be sent to them for job interviews. This practice ensures that the Roma are cut out of the process at the outset—they are not even notified that a job exists. Should a Roma nonetheless apply, some employers appear to have no compunction

---

[35] Passing such legislation is a requirement for EU accession (Schimmelfenig et al. 2005).

in rejecting Roma on the basis of ethnicity. An interviewee recalls such an experience:

> Before setting off to attend a job interview I called the potential employer to make sure that the position was still free. I was assured that nothing had changed and that they were looking forward to seeing me. As soon as I entered the office they told me that I had wasted my time as they do not employ Roma.
>
> (ERRC interview, Slovakia, July 2005, quoted in Hyde 2006, p.6)

Receiving such a response is not a rarity. When ERRC asked the interviewees how they knew that they were rejected because they were Roma, "almost one in two people said they had been openly told by the employer or someone in the company" (Hyde 2006, p.5). Some others were told the same by the employment office. In total, ERRC found that two out of three Roma they interviewed were unemployed, and that even Roma with university degrees had trouble finding jobs, unless they were in Roma-specific areas (Hyde 2006). Despite legislation that ought to ensure its demise, open discrimination against the Roma in employment appears to continue.

Individuals can, of course, discriminate against the Roma in other spheres as well. Police brutality remains a threat, and hate crimes are on the rise (ERRC 2013; Matache 2014). Teachers can discriminate against Roma students on a daily basis by placing them in the last row of the classroom (Matache 2014). Bureaucrats can mistreat Roma by refusing help or creating artificial barriers to obtaining documents or filing paperwork (Cahn 2003). Mail carriers, who tend to be state employees, can refuse to deliver letters to Romani settlements (ERRC 2013), and pubs can refuse to serve food and drink to Roma (BBC 2008). When a Roma enters a doctor's waiting room, non-Roma can conspicuously move away and sit on the other side of the room; when a Roma enters a bus, non-Roma passengers might secure their bags; when they see a Roma walking down the street, non-Roma pedestrians might cross the street just so they can avoid passing them face to face.

Survival strategies

Due to pervasive social exclusion, marginalized Roma operate within a severely constricted space in terms of employment. Jobs in the formal sector are often the least desirable and require a long commute; jobs on large construction projects, in mines, or in meat factories, for example, typically require low levels of expertise, pay the minimum wage or less, and leave workers vulnerable to exploitation (Messing and Molnár 2011). Many occupations that Roma turn to are in the informal sector: selling and re-selling various goods; used car sales; seasonal work in agriculture (gathering forest fruits and mushrooms, picking fruits at commercial farms); selling goods door to door; selling counterfeit goods; harvesting and selling wood; provision of musical entertainment at festivals; palm-reading; horse trading; and scrap-metal collection (Brazzabeni et al. 2015; Cofan 2016). In and of themselves, these occupations and activities are not survival strategies. I call them that, however, because they developed in light of severe exclusion from the formal employment market. That is, if Roma had access to the full market, formal and informal, they might have chosen to do something else. Since they are constrained, they either devise strategies that take advantage of the cracks in the formal market to informally provide goods and services which are in demand, or they create other solutions that let them improve their lives.

Consider the occupation of collecting scrap metal in more detail. Here I borrow heavily from an ethnographic study by Solimene (2015) on a group of Bosnian Roma who live and collect scrap metal around Rome. Briefly, scrap metal collection typically involves "collecting metal objects from dustbins and skips, the roadside and wasteland, or directly from people who want to get rid of old metal; after collection, the metals are extracted, sorted, and eventually sold to Italian metal dealers" (Solimene 2015, p.110). Unless they have appointments with regular customers, Roma collect scrap metal by canvassing a neighborhood with a truck that broadcasts a short message over a megaphone. The Bosnian Roma came to the area between 1960 and 1990, and have since meticulously developed scrap collection as a sustainable practice by both "gaining and maintaining familiarity with working territories and acceptance by those living therein" (Solimene 2015, p.113). Roma/non-Roma relations are good, as are those with the local police, ensuring "that [Roma] can work and not be subject to repeated spot checks or suspected of stealing from building sites" (Solimene 2015, p.114).

While collecting scrap metal is clearly other-benefitting—Roma provide a service to the community and protect the environment—its status as a desir-able activity is invariably put into question by episodes of theft, or of taking what looks like scrap without permission, even when those episodes are rare and the culprits unknown.[36] In the case of Rome, relatively recent arrivals of Roma from Romania have coincided with the "proliferation of [Roma] roaming the city in search of scrap and the increased frequency of theft from building sites and railways" (Solimene 2015, p.115). The Bosnian Roma attribute these activities mostly to Romanian Roma. Trying to hold on to the practice they've established, Bosnian Roma draw strict lines between themselves and the newcomers by appealing to non-Roma "collective imagery . . . that portrays Roma as inferior, dirty, and uncivilized" (Solimene 2015, p.120), saying, for example, that unlike them, the Romanian Roma " 'drive too fast and use megaphones too loudly, ask fees for their services and take scrap without permission' " (Solimene, 2015, p.115, quoting Bosnian Roma).[37] Whether or not members of the group of Romanian Roma were responsible for the thefts, the Bosnians defend their business, as non-Roma are quick to question their integrity, even in light of having worked with them for decades. Such questioning is not an anomaly. Media reporting on the case of the Novo mesto murder-suicide—with one scenario presenting the victims as scrap metal collectors and the other as thieves—recreates it perfectly.

Aside from taking up any available job that would pay, marginalized Roma also make ends meet by reducing their costs of living (Messing and Molnár 2011). A common way of cutting costs is to move into a slum, or to share a home with several families; in Hungary, some marginalized Roma live where they work, while others live in makeshift dwellings on the outskirts of towns (Messing and Molnár 2011). Also in Hungary, marginalized Roma often reduce costs of living by not heating their homes and by lowering their consumption of electricity and water. Some families thus use electricity to power their refrigerator, but not to provide light (Messing and Molnár 2011). Where electricity, water, and gas are provided, families may accrue unpaid bills, which results in having access cut off. When that happens, some families illegally tap the electricity line. Tapping the electricity line is also often the practice in neighborhoods where there is no provision of electricity at all (Messing and Molnár 2011). This is the case in the Žabjak settlement in Novo

---

[36] As some metal collectors store the scrap in their yards, or use their yards for sorting it, this practice can also result in a yard that looks untidy or dirty to an outsider; in addition to the stereotype of Roma as thieves and takers, this evokes the stereotype of Roma as dirty (recall the example of "black like a gypsy" in the Dictionary of the Slovene Standard Language—this example refers to both the darker skin of some, but not all, Roma and the belief that they are dirty).

[37] This points to a complex relationship between Bosnian and Romanian Roma, along with the dynamic and complicated relationship between the Roma and Italian non-Roma. As I cannot recreate Solimene's discussion of these relationships here, I urge interested readers to read his chapter in full.

mesto, where families either use a gas-fueled generator (which is expensive), tap the electricity line, or live without power (Pureber 2012). In the absence of proper infrastructure, the cables are often strung over trees and bound together, which is life-threatening; but as a viable alternative is not available, families continue the practice.

Relying on social assistance and child transfers to make ends meet is another common survival strategy among Roma who live in precarity—especially because they face higher barriers to employment than their non-Roma counterparts. Slovenia long maintained a level of social protection that kept beneficiaries from "slipping beneath the poverty line" (Leskošek 2012, p.108), but reforms in 2007 significantly curbed access to social assistance and the number of beneficiaries has been steadily declining ever since. Although the public often believes otherwise, the funds one can secure through social assistance are in fact insufficient to cover the daily cost of living and the needs of children (Messing and Molnár 2011). While social assistance pays less than the worst-paying jobs in the formal economy, the difference in returns is low; as the jobs are typically monotonous, require long hours, and leave workers vulnerable to exploitation, the incentives to forgo social assistance in favor of a low-paying job are sometimes insufficient. This is the case for anyone contemplating this particular trade-off, Roma or not (Messing and Molnár 2011). Coupling that with a high risk of experiencing discrimination on the job market makes social assistance an attractive option for marginalized Roma. Even so, relying on social assistance is typically not a survival strategy Roma would turn to first (Messing and Molnár 2011); the vast majority of the Roma who participated in my study, for example, sought formal employment instead.

While finding jobs in the informal sector, cutting costs of living, and relying on social assistance are common survival strategies among Roma, *none* of these strategies are quintessentially Roma. Even scrap metal collection, which for some Roma and traveller groups is an extension of their traditional occupation of working with metal (Le Bas 2013), is not a niche ethnic occupation; non-Roma engage in it as well (Messing and Molnár 2011). Instead of being an " 'ethnic' way of living" (Messing and Molnár 2011, p.73) these survival strategies are ways in which *people who are poor* make ends meet. Whether or not they are Roma, people of low socio-economic status in Hungary work jobs that pay too little; they rely on social assistance, and they cut living costs by not heating their homes or not paying for electricity (Messing and Molnár 2011). The same holds for Slovenia. These survival strategies are not ethnic but are *ethnicized*, and they lead to the attribution error when Roma engage in them.

Attribution error

Non-Roma often dislike Roma uses of survival strategies. When they attribute survival strategies to the Roma as such instead of holding discrimination responsible, non-Roma commit attribution errors. As non-Roma commit these errors, the survival strategies acquire an ethnic dimension; even though both Roma and non-Roma actually engage in them, these strategies become ethnicized and are often linked to Roma stereotypes. Media reports on the murder-suicide from Novo mesto demonstrate attribution errors in practice.

Non-Roma conversations on survival strategies aimed at subsistence often start with the notion that Roma refuse to work; Veljan, the surviving victim, is thus described as "a man of about 30 years of age ... with 0 years of work experience" (Radio Krka 2011). Before discussing scrap metal collection, the survival strategy that is actually relevant to the case, the article makes an offhand mention of "certain recipients of social assistance" (Radio Krka 2011); here, the reference to Roma is made without having to name them. In Slovenia, far more non-Roma than Roma rely on social assistance to make ends meet and yet this strategy is ethnicized (Lončar and Rabuza 2017; Messing and Molnár 2011), much like relying on welfare is racialized in the United States (Collins 1990; Hancock 2004).[38] When it finally mentions scrap metal collection, the article does not treat this trade as work; instead, it states that "among Roma there are many individuals who engage in unlawful acts ... trade in weapons, drugs, 'colorful metals,' and other things," (Radio Krka 2011) grouping scrap metal collection, which is not illegal, together with activities that are clearly criminal.[39]

Several other articles reporting on the murder-suicide impose the veneer of Roma criminality on the trade of scrap metal collection. Like relying on social assistance, scrap metal collection is ethnicized (Messing and Molnár 2011); so too is theft of virtually any sort of metal. When Barič, another reporter, writes that "[t]he businessman experienced several break-ins (according to the radio station at least four); the 'unknown' perpetrators took off with iron and other metals as well as the entire electrical installation," (2011) she does not have to mention Roma explicitly; the moment the theft of metal is mentioned, Roma are implicated. Her placement of quotation marks around "unknown" is a brazen nod to the idea that the authorities know who is responsible but

[38] The stereotype of the "Welfare Queen" in the United States also has gender and class dimensions; the extent to which this is also the case for Roma would be interesting to explore in future work.

[39] None of the statements made in the article, including those on Roma engagement in weapons and drug trade, are substantiated.

refuse to act, as Roma are somehow protected. With this statement, Barič sets the stage for a revision of responsibility, and demonstrates the flip side of the attribution error along the way. Recall that when ingroup members engage in bad behavior, other ingroup members attribute that behavior to outside circumstances. Following precisely this rule, Barič seeks outside circumstances that might explain why Stane murdered Olga and shot Veljan. Settling on Roma criminality as the explanation, she also follows the inverse of the rule, attributing a bad action (stealing metal) to an inner quality supposedly possessed by the outgroup. While Barič does not mention Roma explicitly, Kastelic spells out in the headline of his article what she merely implies: "Did he murder because Roma were stealing from him?"

The partial shift of responsibility onto Veljan or Roma in general, continues with these remarks: "[Stane] allegedly caught the woman and her son stealing his iron" (Kastelic 2011), "[s]omething must have been brewing in [Stane's] mind, to eventually boil over so unreasonably" (Kastelic 2011), and "[Stane] was under a lot of pressure, a contributing factor was apparently Roma extortion" (Kastelic 2011). Suggesting a different reason, the article by Radio Krka claims that "[a]pparently the businessman built a house and another building for the wounded man. Did he receive payment? According to our unofficial source, no. This was probably the last straw." The same article also reports that "[u]nofficially, the 32 year-old wounded Roma was apparently involved with numerous extortions" (Radio Krka 2011). Barič, too, writes that "[t]his Roma man [Veljan] . . . had allegedly (also) been extorting a priest" who "lives in fear of other Roma and expects to have to move away" (2011) from his parish. Upon having asked Veljan about the alleged extortion, Kastelic writes " 'Did you ever extort him,' we asked. 'No, never, truly never, that's not what we're like,' said Veljan with innocent eyes. All the Roma gathered there . . . nodded agreement" (2011). As Slovene reporting on issues pertaining to Roma has a troubling legacy of excluding Roma as sources (Erjavec et al. 2000), Kastelic's inclusion of Veljan's statements might seem commendable; however, his commentary on how Veljan answered the question with "innocent eyes" immediately casts doubt on the veracity of Veljan's answer.

Finding outside circumstances to which to attribute Stane's murderous act, these articles have stated that Veljan extorted a priest, that Veljan extorted Stane, that Veljan extorted other people, that Veljan did not pay Stane for his house, that Veljan and his mother stole from Stane, that Roma extorted Stane, and that Roma stole from Stane. With this litany of new, unrelated, and unsubstantiated crimes, the reporters accomplish four things. First, they taint Veljan's character, presenting him as a man who is by no means innocent and who, perhaps, deserves less compassion than a truly innocent victim. Second, by accusing Veljan of reprehensible behaviors toward Stane the reporters intimate that Veljan might be partly responsible for Stane's crime. Third, the reporters correspondingly absolve Stane of some of the responsibility by attributing his action to outside circumstances—Veljan's character, his behaviors, and the behaviors of other Roma—and so commit the first attribution error. Fourth, the reporters also commit a set of secondary attribution errors, as the unsubstantiated crimes they mention are ethnicized and linked to the stereotype of Roma as cheaters (not paying for house), thieves (metal theft), and takers (extortion, metal theft). While the unsubstantiated crimes are already ethnicized, the reporters further blur the line between Veljan and the Roma as a group when they at times attribute these crimes to Veljan and at times to Roma. Eroding the individuality of Veljan Kovačič even further, they often refer to him as "Rom" (Roma man), but call the shooter "businessman," or "businessman Vidic".

In Slovene media, reducing a minority individual to his or her ethnic identity is a fairly common practice, particularly when that individual is Roma. Erjavec et al. (2000) performed a comprehensive study of Slovene media reporting on Roma and found that in a total of 131 pieces, Roma are included as sources only 32 times, while non-Roma appear 226 times. Whenever Roma sources are mentioned, their statements are countered with (mostly intolerant) ones from non-Roma; they are rarely named and are only referred to as members of their ethnic group. Further, of those 131 pieces, only one reports positive news pertaining to Roma. The rest cover "the Roma question or Roma problem" (15), meaning "crime," "exploitation of social benefits," "cultural differences," or other ways in which Roma are bothersome to non-Roma. Erjavec et al. (2000) quote perhaps the most blatant example of an attribution error committed by the media. It comes from an interview with a prominent Roma activist and organizer, who was asked "Do you think that with you Roma, your refusal to work and your higher levels of aggression are genetically determined?" (POP TV, October 19, 1997, cited in Erjavec et al. 2000, p.20).

Almost two decades later, a substantial portion of reporting on Roma in Slovenia retains a derogatory tone, affirms common stereotypes, and commits attribution errors (Glücks 2016; Levanič 2018; Šuljić 2017). Reporting on the case of the murder-suicide is thus not an aberration but is rather representative of one common way the Slovene press writes about Roma—not only in Novo mesto, but also in Murska Sobota, and elsewhere. A recent headline, also from Novo mesto, reads "When the Roma from Dolenjska go shopping: how and what the Roma steal from shops in Novo mesto" (Glücks 2016); another headline, in reference to Murska Sobota, promised "Gypsy squabbles among the Roma" (Svet24 2010); and a third article, from Ormož, reported "[a] fence destroyed, electronic equipment shattered, everything that is metal taken away . . . This is the sort of devastation Roma leave behind" (Levanič 2018).

Days after the murder-suicide the police investigation concluded the following. On the day of the crime, Stane Vidic drove into the Roma settlement (Gazvoda 2011). After a short conversation, Vidic, Veljan Kovačič, and Olga Kovačič left the settlement and drove to Vidic's business building in Zalog. In the building, Stane attempted to murder Veljan, who escaped after shots were fired. Stane then murdered Olga with the same gun. After shooting her, Stane drove to Drgančevje and within the hour used the same gun to commit suicide. The investigation did not reveal a motive behind the attempted murder of Veljan and the murder of Olga. The police mentioned, however, that Stane's complaints regarding thefts—the most recent pertaining to his property in Drgančevje and not his business building—had been investigated and that two unrelated individuals had been charged.

The numerous allegations the reporters had made against Stane, Olga, and nameless Roma remain unsubstantiated. However, one would be remiss to think that they were without effect. When crimes that may have been committed by a Roma person are routinely presented as "acts[s] of specific ethnic nature" (Galia Lazarova, quoted in Scicluna 2007, p.49), "all Roma [are reduced] to negative attributes and characteristics simply because they are Roma" (McGarry 2017, p.95). The responsibility for the transgression is made collective and the agency of an individual—*if the individual committed that crime at all*—is erased: it is not only the one Roma who might be responsible for a crime; instead, all Roma are responsible. Affirming stereotypes about the Roma, such reporting feeds anti-minority culture and helps exclusion cycles persist.

4

The Rift

They are cunning; you can't trust everything they say.
Anonymous, about Roma.
Novo mesto 2015

We tend to interact with others in two ways. Some interactions last only for a moment; they happen once and never again. Others we repeat. The distinction between the two matters because in the first, we need not worry how we behave for the sake of another exchange in the near future. In the second, our early behavior matters. If we behave well in the beginning, our subsequent exchanges might go well, too. In this chapter I begin to empirically explore the exclusion cycle in Novo mesto through these two types of interactions.

The chapter proceeds as follows. I first discuss some of the challenges behind measuring discriminatory behavior, and explain my use of games as a measurement strategy. I then discuss single interactions and present results from the trust game, which I primarily use to capture the behavior of non-Roma in a one-off setting. I show that non-Roma from Novo mesto discriminate against the Roma. The findings in this section, while not designed to speak to Roma behavior, nevertheless provide a grim picture of how Roma uses of survival strategies might be misperceived and misinterpreted.

I then turn to repeated interactions. There, I present findings from the combination of the public goods game with indirect reciprocity, which I delivered in the form of a videogame. Again, non-Roma discriminate against the Roma. They do this regardless of how Roma behave. The common excuse behind disparate treatment—that if only Roma changed, discrimination would stop—finds no support here; when Roma behave no differently than non-Roma, they are still mistreated. I also show that Roma use survival strategies. This chapter presents a few central findings; I discuss the remaining results from the two games in Chapters 5 and 6, which focus on non-Roma and Roma, respectively.

Breaking the Exclusion Cycle: How to Promote Cooperation between Majority and Minority Ethnic Groups.
Ana Bracic, Oxford University Press (2020). © Oxford University Press. DOI: 10.1093/oso/9780190050672.001.0001

Quantifying mistreatment

Capturing discriminatory behavior is difficult, for three reasons in particular. First, scholars often measure discrimination in specific and limited real-life contexts. In a society where racism is systemic, mistreatment is pervasive. It exists in numerous spheres at the same time, which makes capturing all of it extremely challenging. People simply have different opportunities to engage in discriminatory behavior; a doctor may do so in a hospital, a potential employer at a job interview, a bureaucrat at the town hall, and a police officer on the street. One member of a minority group may thus experience discrimination as a patient, while another may experience it while interviewing for a job. To provide a complete picture of mistreatment, both encounters should be considered, yet our most insightful studies of discriminatory behavior tend to be limited to one sphere or another.

Scholars typically consider discrimination in hiring, education, consumer markets, housing, access to mortgages, and access to healthcare separately. Paper audit studies, for example, tend to be used predominantly in research on hiring. In these studies, scholars send otherwise identical resumes that signal different races, genders, socioeconomic classes, or sexualities to potential employers and track the interest expressed towards the candidates (Adida et al. 2016; Moss-Racusin et al. 2012; Pager et al. 2009; Rivera and Tilcsik 2016; Tilcsik 2011). As expected, scholars have found that Black men get fewer interviews than White men (Pager et al. 2009), as do women (Moss-Racusin et al. 2012), people from poorer socioeconomic classes (Rivera and Tilcsik 2016), and openly gay men (Tilcsik 2011). This approach, while methodologically highly valuable, has limitations. For instance, only those pursuing jobs experience employment discrimination. If barriers to employment are so high that they prevent people from looking for work, this phenomenon, too, is likely a result of discrimination and yet remains unseen in an exploration of discrimination in hiring. Other outstanding studies exploring discrimination in consumer markets (Ayres and Siegelman 1995), health care (Goyal et al. 2015), and police stops (Horrace and Rohlin 2016) face similar setting-based challenges.

Limiting insight to any one setting cuts the story short. Setbacks resulting from employment discrimination spill over to healthcare disparities, residential segregation, discrimination in credit and consumption markets, and unequal treatment in the criminal justice system; these are, in turn, also interconnected and together part of a feedback loop that perpetuates a veritable "race discrimination system" (Reskin 2012, p.22). Indeed, compared to his

White peers, a Black boy in the United States runs a higher risk of experiencing exclusionary punitive practices in school, which might lead to an increased likelihood of imprisonment later in life (Fenning and Rose 2007). As an adult, the same individual not only faces lower odds of getting a job, he is also less likely to secure a favorable loan (Pager and Shepherd 2008) and less likely to get pain medication should he find himself in a hospital in need of care (Hoffman et al. 2016). Capturing the full effect of such a wide-ranging system seems a nearly impossible task, particularly when access to any sort of data on discrimination is limited.

The second major challenge comes from the broader research context around the Roma. Systematic data on mistreatment of Roma are hard to come by. Cross-national or national surveys of Roma in various European states are fairly recent developments, and they tend not to focus on discrimination.[1] Looking to collect expansive data on socio-economic conditions, these surveys ask basic questions on access to electricity, health care, levels of education, and so on. The need for wide-ranging rudimentary information is acute as there is little we can systematically say about European Roma. Even the most basic tally, the census, is, in places, widely off the mark. For example, in the early 1990s in Romania, activists, who tend to overestimate, and the census, which tends to underestimate, differed in their respective estimates of the Roma population by 2.5 million (Barany 2002).

An anonymous source explained that in Romania, census takers often estimate the number of people living in a Roma household at a distance, without crossing the doorway to step into the residence, as an approximate number is deemed sufficient. Of course, many Roma prefer not to identify as Roma for census purposes because they fear discrimination (Barany 2002; Cahn 2007; but see Csata et al. 2019). Others might remember that pre-World War II registration efforts helped in identifying and rounding up their ancestors. Ironically, this exact reason—that the Nazis used census and registration data on minorities to exterminate them—today, at least officially, motivates the lack of transparency when it comes to government data with ethnic identifiers (Daniel 2010; Hojsik 2010; Ripka 2010; Tichy 2010). As I travelled from one government office to another across several Central European states, I was repeatedly told that ethnically identifiable data are either not collected or not shared outside the government, on account of what the Nazis did. Roma activist communities and NGOs do not appreciate this lack of transparency.

[1] See the UNDP/World Bank/EC Regional Roma Survey 2011 (Ivanov et al. 2012) and the EU Agency for Fundamental Rights 2011 Roma Pilot Survey (FRA 2014).

Not only would data be useful in devising and in subsequently testing the effectiveness of various interventions, they might also be useful in disproving claims regarding Roma criminality or their disinterest in pursuing formal employment, which are commonly made by anti-Roma politicians.

The third major challenge comes from the possibility of respondent biases. Due to past and current mistreatment and disrespect, Roma communities are often reserved with researchers and census takers. Research efforts by the government and academics alike are sometimes (seen as) exploitative. Members of the Romani community in Novo mesto have often expressed approval at the compensation they receive for participating in my studies, seeing it as a sign of respect. They typically do not receive anything in return for participating in other research efforts and often feel exploited. Keeping researchers at a distance sometimes results in respondent bias, be it based on general social desirability, a need to have the investigator satisfied and gone, or a guess at what the researcher or the sponsor of the research would like to hear (Barany 2002; Ripka 2010). This is particularly the case when the sponsoring agency has a say in resource allocation to Romani settlements or Roma populations in general. As a practical matter, this dynamic suggests caution in interpreting interview and survey answers. As a broader matter of research ethics, this calls for efforts that integrate interests of scholars with those of Romani communities, resulting in research that is not on or about Roma but research that is instead conducted together, with Roma (Bracic 2018). Native American standards for conducting research with (not on) Native communities offer a natural starting point (Harding et al. 2012).

Respondent bias is also likely among non-Roma, especially when they are asked directly if and how they discriminate. Even though Europeans may be open about their biases—recall the murder-suicide in Chapter 3—they may not all be equally honest. The high likelihood of individual variation in honesty is problematic and demands another approach entirely.[2]

My research design addresses these three challenges through games that capture other-regarding behavior. Instead of attempting to observe every potentially discriminatory interaction in every setting, I use games to evaluate individuals' underlying behaviors. This approach reduces incidences of respondent bias, and allows for quantitative data on discrimination in a field that lacks them.

---

[2] While I do not rely on self-reports by non-Roma about their own engagement in discrimination, I do use a measure of perceived discrimination by Roma. I discuss this measure and the benefits and limitations of its use in Chapter 6.

Games

Scholars in behavioral sciences commonly use games to capture other-regarding behavior.[3] As I aim to cast a wide net—capturing behaviors that in real-life contexts appear across a wide set of circumstances—I require a level of abstraction. Games provide just that, while still letting me examine behaviors (instead of, say, beliefs). A game offers study participants a stylized interaction that is real—most saliently, it involves real money—but nonetheless removed from any particular context. It gives participants an opportunity either to actively discriminate or to react to that discrimination in a scenario that simulates a real-life interaction. While, in an everyday context, a doctor is more likely to discriminate in the hospital and a police officer on the street, they can both play the game and, through their in-game actions, reveal their prejudiced behaviors. Likewise, those who are targets of discrimination can engage in survival strategies within the context of the game.

I use the games in an experimental setting. I assign participants to identical scenarios, but randomly vary the ethnicity of their game partners. This means, for example, that some non-Roma play a game with a Roma partner, while other non-Roma play the same game with a non-Roma partner. Games are typically administered in a laboratory or a laboratory-in-field; I use the lab-in-field approach here. In such an environment, a multitude of factors that may affect participants' behaviors can be held constant. A participant may, for example, act one way alone and another way in the presence of others; the laboratory approach addresses this concern by re-creating the same environment for all participants. The differences in the behaviors captured can therefore be attributed to the treatment (partner ethnicity) with much greater certainty: if the treatment is the only factor that systematically varies, it is likely responsible for the difference in behaviors observed, if any. Simply put, if participants behave substantially differently when their game partners are Roma, compared to how they behave when their game partners are non-Roma, I can be reasonably certain that the difference in the behaviors is due to the ethnic identities of their partners.

Finally, the game environment allows me to capture disparate treatment and survival strategies without asking participants directly about prejudice and discrimination. Avoiding direct questions and capturing actions instead should help reduce respondent bias.

Since the game does not capture discrimination happening on the street or in a doctor's office, one may argue that people's behaviors in the context of

---

[3] For a review, see Camerer (2003).

the game are not the same as those that they would exhibit in everyday life. This is true. It is the main weakness of the game approach. Yet making an actual decision, even if in the context of the game, goes a step further than simply expressing prejudice.[4] While concerns about the absence of a real-life context are quite valid and must be kept in mind when conclusions are drawn, they do not disqualify the approach out of hand. In my effort to generalize, the sacrifice of real-life specificity is necessary, and, as described above, focusing on such specificity brings its own limitations. To compensate, the games leverage stereotypical beliefs about the Roma and thus strike the very core of anti-Roma sentiment and behavior. I discuss this in the sections that follow.

The remainder of this chapter proceeds in two parts. I first address single interactions and then turn to repeated ones. Examining both types of interactions matters because we engage in both. They differ fundamentally in the extent to which building a reputation matters for a successful outcome. Single interactions are those that happen once and then conclude; there is no back and forth. As a result, reputational concerns are moot—that is, in a single interaction, an individual does not have to worry about establishing a reputation so that her future interactions will go favorably. A hypothetical scenario is illustrative here. Suppose a few tourists stop at a bakery in Paris. The owner can sneer at their pronunciation and send them off with their croissants without breaking her frown. Now suppose these croissant aficionados move in across the street. With the prospect of their repeated visits to the bakery, the owner might reconsider her sneer. Unlike single interactions, those of a repeated nature tend to take players' previous behaviors into account. As these types of interactions are so different, looking at both affords us a more comprehensive view of group relations. The section that follows explores the single interaction, using the trust game.

First study: single interaction and the trust game[5]

The trust game (Berg et al. 1995) has been used in a number of studies in behavioral sciences. Typically, scholars use it to explore trust and trustworthiness under a variety of conditions. Scholars have used the trust game to explore the way kinship ties within a community might influence trusting and reciprocating behavior (Barr 2004), the effects of wartime violence on

[4] Experimental (Dovidio et al. 2004) and longitudinal (Wagner et al. 2008) analyses demonstrate that prejudice and discriminatory intent are closely connected, and that prejudice is causally linked to discriminatory behavior.

[5] Parts of this section were published in Bracic (2016). This study was approved by the New York University IRB (HS11- 8405).

social cohesion (Gilligan et al. 2014), the comparative levels of trust expressed by patients with borderline personality disorder (Unoka et al. 2009), and variations in decision-making among identical and fraternal twins (Cesarini et al. 2008).[6] My use of the trust game contributes, broadly, to the literature that explores trust and reciprocity among ingroups and outgroups.[7]

Crucially, this game is primarily designed to capture the behavior of non-Roma. Discussion in this section therefore focuses on the non-Roma portion of the exclusion cycle. While this game speaks to survival strategies, it does so only in a limited way. I turn to this at the end of this section.

The game proceeds as follows. There are two players. Both know the rules of the game, and each makes one decision. One player is assigned the role of a sender and the other the role of a receiver. Both begin the game with an identical endowment. In this case, each receives 6 euros. The sender makes the first move. She can send some, all, or none of her endowment to her receiver. She knows that whatever amount she sends will be doubled, and that the receiver will have the chance to send a portion of his total amount back to her. Whatever she doesn't send, she keeps. The receiver then receives whatever the sender sent, but doubled. The receiver combines the doubled sum with his initial endowment and makes the second move. He takes the total pot and divides it, in any way he wants, between himself and the sender. He can send some, none, or all of it back to the sender. Whatever he doesn't send, he keeps. Whatever he decides to send to the sender is then delivered to the sender. The game ends.

To play this game, Roma and non-Roma from Novo mesto were randomly sampled and randomly and anonymously paired with a partner. This game is intended to capture discriminatory behavior by non-Roma; to that end, non-Roma participants far outnumbered Roma. Of the 202 trust game participants in Novo mesto, 151 were non-Roma, and 51 were Roma.[8] Of those, 101 non-Roma were assigned the role of the sender, while 50 non-Roma and 51 Roma were receivers.

The study was fielded in the following way. First, my research assistants and I recruited randomly sampled non-Roma participants from Novo mesto to

---

[6] For a general meta analysis, see Johnson and Mislin (2011).

[7] For a meta-analysis of scholarship that uses the trust game in this particular context, see Balliet et al. (2014).

[8] For a moderate effect size (around 0.25) and a power of 0.8, I required 50 subjects per treatment to find a statistically significant difference at the 5 percent level. This demanded 200 subjects per town: 100 non-Roma senders of which half were paired with 50 non-Roma receivers and half with 50 Roma receivers. See Cohen (1988).

participate in the study as senders. Potential participants were recruited face to face by a team of two enumerators, for both the ease of administering the games and to ensure safety of the enumerators. Each participant who agreed to take part in the study first read and signed the consent form, drew a unique identifier known only to them, participated in three games,[9] and filled out the exit questionnaire. All of their answers were recorded under their unique identifier and all decisions were made privately. Everyone participated alone, non-Roma in the privacy of their own home and Roma at a neutral location (an NGO office or someone's living room or backyard). We collected the data for senders first. After data collection from 101 senders was complete, we began recruiting the receivers, half randomly from the non-Roma part of town and half, also randomly, from the Romani settlement. Receivers first read and signed the consent form, then drew their unique identifier, participated in two games, and completed an exit questionnaire. Senders and receivers were matched to one another by drawing matching unique identifiers—each unique identifier for senders had a matching counterpart within those for receivers. After data completion for receivers was complete, we delivered whatever receivers intended for their trust game partners to the senders. See Online Appendix A for the full protocol.

The sequential nature of data collection—first collecting data from all senders and then from all receivers—is unusual. Typically, the trust game is administered in a group context, where all participants, senders and receivers, can see one another. In the context of Roma and non-Roma in Novo mesto, this option was untenable, as relations are quite contentious. Instead, subjects participated individually and anonymously. During the trust game, both senders and receivers were told that they would never meet their trust game partner (which they didn't). Each player received four facts about their partner: they were told that their partner was anonymous, randomly chosen, from their town, and either Roma or non-Roma. The experimental treatment—whether the receiver was Roma or non-Roma—was determined ahead of time, with a coin toss.

Typically, the decision made by the sender in the trust game is used as a measure of trust, while the decision made by the receiver is used as a measure of trustworthiness or reciprocity. The sender in the trust game has the chance to send some, all, or none of her endowment to the receiver. If the sender thinks that the receiver will not send anything or enough of the total pot

---

[9] The three games were the lottery, the dictator game, and the trust game. I describe the lottery and the dictator game in the pages that follow.

back, she should not send anything to the receiver. She should instead simply keep her own endowment. Trust, however, can make both players better off. Suppose, for example, that the sender trusts the receiver and sends him the entire endowment of 6 euros. The money is then doubled, to 12 euros. Together with the receiver's initial 6 euros, the total pot is 18 euros (see Tables 2 and 3 in Online Appendix A for a list of total pot possibilities). If the receiver is trustworthy and sends 7 or more euros back to the sender, the sender financially benefits from trusting her partner. Of course, the receiver could also keep the total pot. And that's the point.

This aspect of the trust game maps perfectly onto the stereotype that the Roma are cheaters and thieves.[10] If the sender thinks that her Roma partner is likely to keep the money, or, at least, to keep too much, she should be less inclined to share. If, however, the sender sees her partner as trustworthy, she would be better off sending her endowment to her partner. Importantly, there are no actual cheaters or thieves in the trust game; first, the game does not afford the players any opportunity to cheat or steal, and second, as far as returning money to the sender is concerned, anything goes. Someone who returns nothing exhibits very low levels of cooperation, but is not cheating or violating game rules in any way. While perfectly acceptable within the game, low cooperation might violate social expectations. And, in accordance with the damaging stereotype, low cooperation is interpreted as cheating when Roma engage in it. If non-Roma senders subscribe to the universal stereotype and thus expect that Roma receivers will be less likely to reciprocate, they should, on average, send less to their Roma partners than they do to their non-Roma partners.

As this game is played only once—the two players do not continue to play and thus have no need to build a reputation as cooperators—and since the sender moves first, the sender's decision is essentially a gut response. A sender only knows that her partner is anonymous, randomly chosen, from Novo mesto and either Roma or non-Roma. She has no other information about her partner and she knows that she will never find out who it was. The same holds for the receiver. The situation thus demands a rapid conclusion about how the receiver is likely to respond, and in the absence of more information about the receiver the sender's conclusion is likely shaped by the universal stereotype of the receiver.

Since the actions of a defecting (i.e. not cooperating) receiver can be interpreted as cheating and/or stealing, and as the stereotype that the Roma

---

[10] For more on this stereotype and how it translates to discrimination, see Chapter 3.

are cheaters and thieves motivates much discriminatory behavior, the trust game can reasonably be used as a measure of discrimination against the Roma. To confirm that this is indeed the case, I spoke to several Romani activist communities: two in Slovenia (in Novo mesto and Murska Sobota), one in Croatia (in Sitnice), and one in Romania (in Bucharest). Roma in these communities expressed overwhelming and enthusiastic support for the trust game. Specifically, they said that the game gets at the heart of the matter, and that it cleverly captures mistreatment that they experience on a daily basis. Several also thought it a resourceful way of capturing discriminatory behavior without openly asking people about it. Non-Roma, they thought, would not all own up to unequal treatment they practice, but may unwittingly engage in it in the context of the game. The trust game, while predominantly used to capture trust in other contexts, received a stamp of approval from four Roma activist communities as to its ability to capture discriminatory behavior.

To account for other factors that may influence participants' decision-making, the study included a few additional activities. The first two concern a sender's motivation behind sending her endowment to the receiver. She may send it because she trusts her partner, but she may also send it because she is altruistic or because she is risk-loving. To control for both of these possibilities, senders participated in two additional games. The first, intended to capture altruism, was the dictator game (Hoffman et al. 1994). In the dictator game, the participant is given an endowment (in this case, 6 euros) and told to divide that endowment in any way she chooses between herself and an anonymous local family in need. The proportion of the endowment sent to the family is used as a measure of altruism. The second possibility—that the sender is risk-loving—was controlled by a simple lottery game (Holt and Laury 2002). The lottery game captures a participant's risk preference by asking the participant to choose one of five lotteries, which all have the same expected value (4 euros) but which increase in risk—from no risk to high risk. The choice of the lottery is used as a measure of risk preference. The expected total payoff from the three games, for one subject, was approximately 60 percent of a net daily wage in Slovenia: 16 euros. In addition to participating in the lottery and the dictator game, participants filled out a short exit survey that asked for their age, gender, employment status, education level, and ethnic and national identities.

Finally, a few words on the implementation of the games and sampling are in order. I already mentioned that respondents participated individually and anonymously. To enable such participation, I created a portable experimental lab with equipment that my research assistants and I could carry from one randomly sampled house to another.

Ensuring complete confidentiality of decision-making was another necessary departure from the way these games are often administered in other environments. Several pilot studies with non-Roma revealed that non-Roma were unwilling to keep any of their endowments in the dictator and trust games if an enumerator was in the room. The location of the enumerator did not matter; if the enumerator stood in the corner of the room with her back turned so as not to face the participants, the participants still sent their entire endowments to the family in need and their trust game partner. Once the enumerator left the room, however, the participants exhibited a full range of decisions. Participation was therefore completely confidential; participants all received unique identifiers which were only known to them, and made the game decisions either in complete privacy (trust, altruism) or with the enumerators turning their backs (lottery, exit survey).[11] To avoid further bias, the enumerator pairs switched daily; no pair looked the same from one day to the next until we cycled through all combinations. In addition, the analyses controlled for both the gender of enumerators and my presence on the enumerator team; these variables were consistently not statistically significant.[12] To read about the protocol in detail, see Online Appendix A.

Potential participants were recruited using simple random sampling, from two strata: the non-Roma general population and the Roma general population. The Roma community was oversampled because it is substantially smaller than the non-Roma community. All the streets in the town and the Roma settlement were ordered alphabetically, and then reordered based on a random number sample. The streets on top of the new list were the sampled streets, starting with the top and moving down the list. Potential participants were recruited from all households on the sampled streets, with a systematic iteration on gender. Any individual over the age of 18 was eligible to participate. The response rate was 60 percent.[13]

[11] Enumerators turned their backs instead of leaving the room for the lottery and exit survey because they had already helped the participant with the lottery and so knew what the participant picked (head or tails) and because the questions on the survey were not sensitive. The only part of that process that enumerators were not allowed to see is the unique identifier that the participant wrote on the survey and the lottery slip, and for that turning their backs was sufficient.

[12] Results available upon request.

[13] Research teams attempted recruiting at a house on a selected street three times. The Statistical Office of the Republic of Slovenia reports response rates that range from 60 to 80 percent; rates vary with the topic of the survey (Lah et al. 2011; Remec 2005). I thank Matej Divjak from the Office for his consultation regarding response rates.

Findings

Non-Roma discriminated against the Roma. They sent a significantly smaller portion of their endowment to Roma partners. This suggests that compared to non-Roma from Novo mesto, Roma were not trusted to reciprocate as receivers in the trust game. The stereotype of Roma as cheaters and thieves, which fuels disparate treatment of Roma in other contexts, seemed to fuel the same treatment here.

I treat the dependent variable, the amount senders sent to the trust game partner, as a proportion. The values therefore range between 0 (nothing sent) and 1 (full endowment sent). Figure 4.1 presents the average proportion of the endowment sent to trust game partners, by partner ethnicity. It shows that non-Roma senders who were paired with Roma receivers sent, on average, 58 percent of their endowment to their partners. To non-Roma receivers, however, they sent more. Impressively, non-Roma senders who were paired with non-Roma receivers were willing to part with 78 percent of their endowment;

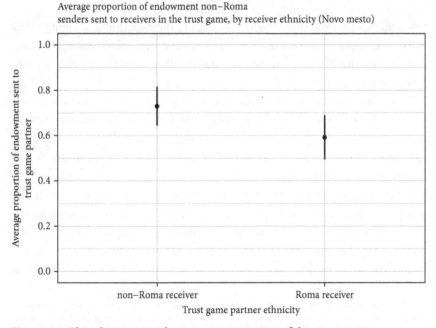

Figure 4.1 This plot presents the average proportion of the trust game endowment that non-Roma participants sent to their non-Roma and Roma receivers, respectively. The plot also shows 95 percent confidence intervals. The difference between the two means is statistically significant at the 5 percent level (p < 0.05).

Table 4.1 Effect of game partner ethnicity (Roma or non-Roma) on the amount sent in the trust game, pooled data analysis.

Independent variables	Murska Sobota and Novo mesto (inclusive NGO)
Roma dummy	1.546
	(1.031)
Novo mesto	0.642*
	(0.291)
Novo mesto x Roma	−1.133**
	(0.404)
Number of observations	189
conditional marginal effects (Murska Sobota)	−.081
	(.116)
conditional marginal effects (Novo mesto)	−.330**
	(.117)

*p < .05; ** p < .01.
Standard errors in parentheses.

this suggests a remarkably high level of trust in their coethnics. Although they are overall quite trusting, non-Roma are substantially more trusting of other non-Roma. The difference in means is statistically significant (p < 0.05). Non-Roma sent Roma less.

Regression analysis provides additional insight. The comparison of means presented above only looks at the average proportion of the endowment sent and ignores other potential factors, like the age of a participant or her risk preference. The regression analysis therefore includes the measures of age, gender, income bracket, education level, risk preference, and altruism.[14]

Table 4.1 presents partial results from the regression analysis.[15] Since the analysis included interaction terms between the control covariates and the treatment variable (ethnic identity of the receiver, labeled as Roma), which complicates the interpretation of the coefficients, I focus on the marginal effect. The effect of interest appears in the final row in this partial table. It

[14] The appropriate specification for a model in which the dependent variable is a proportion is a generalized linear model with the binomial variance and the logit link function (McDowell and Cox 2004; Papke and Wooldridge 1996); this was the primary model used for the regressions. The results are substantively unchanged using an ordinary least squared or a tobit regression. In addition to the listed covariates, all regressions included interaction terms between the covariates and the treatment variable (ethnicity of trust game partner) (Morton and Williams 2010). Numerous iterations of the model were run, with various numbers and combinations of control variables. The findings are robust to all additions. Results available upon request.
[15] For full results, see Online Appendix B.

denotes the change in the proportion of the endowment sent to the trust game receiver when the identity of that receiver changes from non-Roma to Roma. The −0.33 marginal effect (p < 0.01) shows that non-Roma from Novo mesto on average sent 33 percent less of their endowment to Roma receivers than they did to non-Roma receivers. Even when we control for education, gender, income bracket, risk preference, and people's willingness to donate money to an anonymous family in need, the findings stand. The regression results support the difference-in-means analysis.[16]

The behavior of non-Roma in Novo mesto in the context of the trust game demonstrates unequal treatment of Roma. Inasmuch as the trust game captures not only distrust but also discrimination, the results also show that non-Roma from Novo mesto discriminate against the Roma. While fielding this study, my enumerators and I encountered a fair amount of unsolicited commentary. Participants typically commented after they were finished with the study, although a few made comments during the exit survey. Thirty-six percent of senders from Novo mesto made comments about the Roma. Three percent were positive, 30 percent were neutral, and 67 percent were negative. A young woman, for example, exclaimed in relief "Thank God I wasn't paired with a Roma! Just, not a Roma, not a Roma. I really don't like Roma." A man half-jokingly threatened that "we will send a couple of bus-loads of our Roma to your hometown and you'll see what it's like." Another woman, having been paired with a Roma, wanted an assurance, saying "I won't have any trouble with those little Romas, will I?", while a man, remarking on having been paired with a Roma receiver, said, in reference to the trust game, "yeah, as if I'll get something back." These unsolicited comments speak to the general tenor of the atmosphere in Novo mesto. Almost one in four of the randomly sampled participants felt comfortable enough to make a negative comment about the Roma to a couple of complete strangers. While these field-based observations are not systematic, they do bolster the main finding of discrimination against the Roma. They also suggest that in this case, unequal treatment is not merely a matter of implicit bias, but also of comfortably expressed explicit bias.

The purpose of this first study was to capture disparate treatment of Roma by non-Roma in Novo mesto. With this goal in mind, the research design and the analysis focus on the actions of senders in the trust game. As the study was

[16] The results presented in Table 4.1 and in the main text are based on a regression that includes data from another town, Murska Sobota. This town and its comparison to Novo mesto will be discussed extensively in Chapter 5. I present the results from the common analysis for the sake of consistency. Results from a regression analysis of only Novo mesto, which confirm the findings presented here, are available upon request.

not designed to accurately and appropriately capture reciprocating behaviors of Roma and non-Roma, making general conclusions on the basis of receiver behavior would be inappropriate. Nonetheless, the actions of the receivers shed some light onto what survival strategies can look like, and how, when easily misinterpreted, they can cause further damage to the marginalized group.

In Chapter 2, I posited that some survival strategies would manifest as low cooperation. Should Roma engage in survival strategies in the context of the trust game, they might return less as receivers than their non-Roma counterparts. Indeed, as receivers, Roma and non-Roma in Novo mesto are starkly different. Figure 4.2 presents the average proportion of the total pot that receivers sent back in the trust game, by receiver ethnicity. The plot shows that non-Roma receivers sent back 62 percent of the total pot. Roma receivers, in contrast, sent back 9 percent of the total pot.

When superficially examined, this difference leads to the damaging conclusion that Roma reciprocate less and are therefore less trustworthy. It looks as if the plot could not be any clearer, and yet this conclusion is awfully premature. Two caveats, in particular, must be made. First, the plot shows the proportion

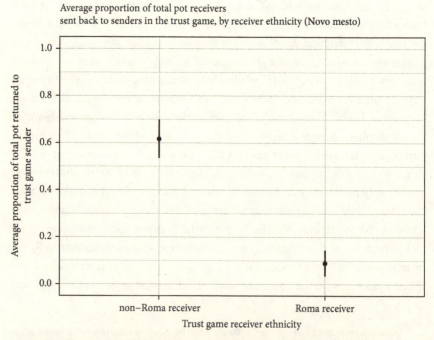

Average proportion of total pot receivers
sent back to senders in the trust game, by receiver ethnicity (Novo mesto)

Figure 4.2 This plot presents the average proportion of the total pot that non-Roma and Roma trust game receivers returned to their non-Roma senders. The plot also shows 95 percent confidence intervals.

of the total pot that receivers send back to their senders. Since senders sent substantially less to Roma receivers, Roma receivers had smaller total pots to begin with. Second, Roma and non-Roma receivers from Novo mesto likely perceived the value of the total pot quite differently.

As discussed in Chapter 3, Roma are predominantly quite poor and generally suffer from a lack of access to employment and often social services. All but two Roma participants from Novo mesto fell in the lowest income bracket on the exit survey; some insisted on circling just the "0" in the "0 to 600 euros per month" income bracket, to indicate that they earned nothing at all. That year, in 2011, the Slovene Statistical Office reported that the income threshold for people who were considered at risk for poverty was 600 euros.[17] In contrast, non-Roma receivers have substantially higher incomes; few occupy the lowest income bracket.[18] Therefore, an offer of 18 euros, which is the highest total pot one can collect as a receiver in the trust game, likely holds a different meaning for an average Roma person in Novo mesto than it does for an average non-Roma person. The same holds for any other sum.

The trust game is, then, stacked against Roma receivers as their socioeconomic status renders the decision of whether to send money back to a sender much more fraught. In this, the game perfectly illustrates a characteristic of the exclusion cycle: because of various barriers that discrimination sustains, a minority has fewer ways in which it can react to certain situations. While Roma and non-Roma receivers are ostensibly put in the same position, Roma receivers' overall low income and employment levels render them more likely to defect in the context of the game. Employing a survival strategy, they may decide to keep most of the money, and risk being incorrectly condemned as thieves as a result. Since the game does not provide Roma receivers with a fair opportunity to reciprocate—for them, reciprocation is far more costly than for non-Roma—interpreting the results in Figure 4.2 as indicative of Roma trustworthiness would be incorrect, ethically inappropriate, and, simply put, bad science.

And yet this is precisely what those who discriminate would do. Upon witnessing the survival strategy, they might brand the individual a cheater or a thief, assign that label to his ethnic identity, and carry on contributing to the anti-Roma culture that pervades Roma/non-Roma interactions in town. Few

[17] See Statistični Urad Republike Slovenije (2011c).
[18] According to the Slovene Statistical Office, the average gross monthly income in Slovenia in 2011 was 1524.65 euros, while the average net monthly income was 987.39 euros. See Statistični Urad Republike Slovenije (2011b).

would ask themselves if they, too, would keep 17 euros and return one, if that was the only sum they were going to earn that month.

With this example, a quick demonstration of the exclusion cycle comes full circle. Non-Roma discriminate and Roma engage in survival strategies. I do not demonstrate the attribution error with data; you likely committed it yourself when you first looked at Figure 4.2. If you did not, I commend you.

Either way, pressing questions remain. Did non-Roma discriminate because they expected Roma receivers not to reciprocate as much? If non-Roma discriminated because they expected Roma to defect, would they stop discriminating if Roma receivers reciprocated more? Would Roma receivers reciprocate more if the game weren't stacked against them? Or would they engage in survival strategies even if cooperation led to a better outcome? I turn to these questions next.

Second study: repeated interactions and the tower game[19]

The trust game I just presented demonstrates a one-off interaction. We call it a one-shot game because the players have no need to establish a reputation as they will not play with the same partner again. In such a situation, not cooperating comes at a low cost. We engage in many such interactions in our everyday lives. When in a hurry, we might cut off a stranger driving a car at an intersection, especially if we're driving in a big city with millions of people. We might be less inclined to do so if we know our neighbor is driving that car. We may be rude to a telemarketer over the phone, but we might think twice before we hang up on a volunteer firefighter soliciting donations for the local company. The one-shot trust game provides an easy test of low cooperation. As reputational concerns are irrelevant, the propensity to avoid cooperation is high and so we are apt to observe such behaviors with a relatively high frequency. Taken as indicative of all behaviors, this would likely underestimate the general degree of cooperation, because while some of our interactions are of a one-shot variety, many are not. The remainder of this chapter is therefore dedicated to the other type of common interaction: the repeated kind.

Just as before, I take advantage of games. I use the public goods game (Marwell and Ames 1979), which is another commonly used method of capturing other-regarding behavior. I couple this game with indirect reciprocity,

---

[19] This study was approved by the University of Oklahoma IRB (IRB #1: 5432, IRB #2: 7081) and pre-registered at EGAP (ID: 20160313AA).

as seen in Rockenbach and Milinski (2006). The public goods game has been widely used to study the dynamics of cooperation and defection in a group setting. It pits individual interest against that of a group. The public goods game presents a scenario where the group is best-off if everyone cooperates, but where incentives to free-ride without cooperating are high. Typically, participants are each given an endowment. They have the option of contributing that endowment to the total pot, but they can also keep it. Once all participants have made their decision, the total pot is multiplied by a factor, say 2, and is then evenly divided between all participants, regardless of who contributed. Having both their initial endowment and their portion of the total pot, the participants who defected and did not contribute are best off, but the group as a whole is best off if everyone contributes.

We encounter this dynamic all the time. Consider public goods like clean air, the public radio, or, at a local level, a voluntary neighborhood cleanup. These goods benefit everyone, regardless of whether they contribute resources to sustain them. Listening to NPR without donating money might not even be a matter of temptation; surely many people do just that. Not showing up for the neighborhood cleanup is likely more challenging, as neighborhoods tend to have boundaries, people talk, and moving is costly. If too few individuals contribute to sustaining a public good while many access it for free, the good may become exhausted. If too many entities pollute, if no one donates to NPR, and if no one shows up for the neighborhood cleanup, then everyone is deprived. In the context of common pool resources, like clean air, this phenomenon is the well-known "tragedy of the commons" (Ostrom 1990).

Much of scholarship on human cooperation stems from the goal of finding solutions to this tragedy (Ostrom 1990). Focusing specifically on the public goods game, scholars have extensively explored factors that may increase a participant's propensity to contribute to the common good. These include variations on punishing free riders monetarily (Fehr and Gächter 2002; Sigmund 2007), through expressions of disapproval (Masclet et al. 2003), or through expulsion of free riders by player consensus (Cinyabuguma et al. 2006); mechanisms that might spur cooperation also include face-to-face and chat-room communication (Bochet et al. 2006), advice from previous players (Chaudhuri et al. 2006), and rewarding cooperators monetarily (Andreoni et al. 2003; Sefton et al. 2007) or through social approval (Rege and Telle 2004).

The public goods game, much like the trust game, leverages the stereotype that the Roma are cheaters and thieves. Just like in the trust game, there is no actual cheating or stealing in the public goods game, but low cooperation, or free riding, might be interpreted as such by non-Roma. If one were to expect Roma to play as the stereotype dictates, one might suspect that they would defect relatively often, or at least at a greater rate than non-Roma. This is particularly so because Roma are often also seen as "takers." They are commonly accused of not contributing to society and therefore undeserving of social benefits, which they nonetheless receive. Numerous participants from Novo mesto have expressed frustration at the way Roma purportedly exploit the social benefits system. Calling to mind the "Welfare Queen" stereotype still applied to poor Black women in the United States (Collins 1990; Hancock 2004),[20] they spoke of how Roma are cunning and have many children in order to extract child benefits from the government. According to them, some Roma women, ostensibly, have monthly incomes "exceeding 2000 euros without ever having worked a day in their lives."[21]

The idea that Roma are not fit contributors to a thriving society is not abstract, nor is it limited to heated conversations. Claiming that Roma steal (Bilefsky 2010), and that they are loud (Barrie 1999) and dirty, communities in Romania (Estrin 2012), Slovakia (Bilefsky 2010), and the Czech Republic (Barrie 1999) have built walls to separate the resident Roma from the rest of town. Often, spatial segregation results in Roma living in isolated settlements that are not a part of the main town. This was not the case here; spatial inclusion was physically within reach in these Czech, Slovak, and Romanian towns, but non-Roma chose segregation instead of trying to build a community. The public goods game has a real-life equivalent in which a thriving mixed community rarely comes to pass.

An unexpected comment from a non-Roma participant confirms that low cooperation is ethnicized. Upon hearing the part of the game rules that describe free riding, an older participant loudly exclaimed "the Gypsies!" ("Ciganija!"), clearly upset at the idea that someone would not contribute to the common good. This occured *well before* the idea of particular ethnic identities was introduced, which happened as the participant was playing the game; the

---

[20] While the assumption had been that Linda Taylor, the woman originally described as a "Welfare Queen," was Black, recent investigations revealed that Linda Taylor might, in fact, have been a White woman pretending to be Black (Levin 2013).

[21] This claim is false. To lend it context, the average net monthly income in Slovenia in 2016 was 1.030,16 euros (gross monthly income was 1.584,66 euros) (Vrh 2017). The highest total amount of social assistance given to any family in 2016 was 1,294 euros per month; this is a family with 9 children and thus quite unusual (Lončar and Rabuza 2017).

participant reacted to the rules without knowing that Roma would be part of the study at all.[22]

Before I continue, a word on indirect reciprocity. Indirect reciprocity gives each player in the group an opportunity to award another, randomly chosen player, based on whether that player contributed to the common pool. When a player is rewarded she gets points or monetary units; when she is not rewarded, those points or monetary units are withheld. The indirect nature of this mechanism results in player A rewarding (or not) player B, player B rewarding (or not) player D, and so on. This differs from direct reciprocity in that players A and B are not mutually rewarding one another and not merely exchanging awards; instead player A's behavior as a player likely determines her chances of getting a reward. While indirect reciprocity can be quite effectively used to sustain cooperation in the public goods game, particularly when each round of the public goods game is followed by a round of indirect reciprocity (Rockenbach and Milinski 2006), I do not use it as a way of boosting cooperation. Instead, I use it to gauge rewarding behaviors toward coethnics and non-coethnics, and to capture behavioral changes in response to seeing a non-coethnic player either cooperate or defect.

My game scenario presents participants with an iteration of the public goods game and indirect reciprocity. Each decision about contributing to the common pot is followed by information about another player's decision and the option of rewarding that player; this process is repeated twelve times. Participants are not aware of that; they know that the game has a number of rounds, but not how many. The iterative (repeated) nature of the combination of public goods and indirect reciprocity allowed me to capture how non-Roma treat Roma in a repeated interaction setting. It also enabled me to more accurately capture the extent to which Roma rely on survival strategies because its incentive structure does not encourage consistent defection. That is, the players are not financially best off if they stick with a noncooperative strategy. This runs contrary to the single-shot trust game, in which it was very clear that receivers would be best off if they did not cooperate. Specifically, in the trust game a receiver would earn most if she kept the entire pot and returned nothing to her sender. Here, instead, a player can be better off if she cooperates.

If a group of eight players is playing the game for several rounds, defecting in the early rounds is likely to make other players defect as well, ending in a scenario where everyone defects in most, if not all, rounds. This does

---

[22] In the consent form, participants were told that they would participate in a study on relationships between people in their town.

not result in the highest payoff.[23] A "nice" strategy, to borrow a term from Axelrod (1984), in which a player cooperates, however, can keep the group better off, as long as other players do the same.[24] Such cooperation works as long as the players can sustain it by not defecting. In the iterated public goods game, then, a participant could ultimately earn more if she cooperates. In addition, indirect reciprocity affords another opportunity to increase one's payoff, again by cooperating, as other players are more likely to award cooperators than defectors. Participants may, of course, fail to identify the winning strategy in the iterated game. That's alright. Even if they play without intent and without thinking up a strategy, their decisions are still revealing, as they might reflect "standard operating procedures, rules of thumb, instincts, habits, or imitation" (Axelrod 1984, p.18).

Why does this matter? Frankly, it matters because marginalized Roma tend to be poor, while non-Roma are comparatively much better off. If, in a game scenario, non-Roma can more easily afford to cooperate because cooperation is not costly for them, while it is for Roma, the game scenario is not appropriate for comparing levels of cooperation across the two groups. In this case, Roma behavior would likely be disproportionately affected by financial need, and to mistake that for absence of cooperation would be incorrect. Put another way, it is unfair to compel Roma to free ride because they need the money, and then conclude that they are generally not cooperative. Instead, if Roma don't cooperate in a context that awards cooperation, we can make a stronger conclusion about the persistence of survival strategies. Iterated public goods and indirect reciprocity provide such a context, and with it a tougher test of survival strategies.

Expectations for Roma and non-Roma behaviors are as follows. Recall that cooperating can make participants better off, but only if everyone cooperates. If other players are not contributing to the common pot, it's better to defect. I expect non-Roma who subscribe to the sterotype of Roma as cheaters, thieves, and takers to systematically contribute less to the common pot when Roma are included in the game. Simply, if non-Roma expect Roma to free ride more, they will cooperate less when playing with Roma. In turn, I expect Roma participants to contribute less to the common pot when they antic-

---

[23] The stable equilibrium in which none of the players contribute to the common pot is not Pareto optimal (Rapoport and Guyer 1978).

[24] According to Hardin, "any analysis prescribing a solution for Prisoner's Dilemma must prescribe a similar solution for the game of collective action" (Hardin 1982, p.28). The public goods game is identical to Hardin's collective action game. And, a winning strategy in an iterated prisoner's dilemma game is a "nice" strategy which starts with cooperation and then follows a forgiving tit-for-tat logic, defecting only in response to the other player's defection (Axelrod 1984).

ipate discrimination from non-Roma. If Roma believe that non-Roma will cooperate less when playing with Roma, it makes sense for Roma to defect, for cooperation only works if everyone is cooperating. Free riding is thus a survival strategy: when non-Roma discriminate, defection becomes the best option for a Roma participant, even if she might otherwise wish to cooperate. As discussed in Chapter 3, real life parallels to free riding include tapping electricity lines when municipal infrastructure does not extend to Romani neighborhoods, and, when viewed uncharitably, relying on social assistance to make ends meet. And, as I discuss more fully in Chapter 6, my conversations with Roma from Novo mesto suggest that they would much rather avoid those strategies, if given the opportunity: having proper infrastructure for electricity is far preferable to tapping the line.

Delivery

Typically, the public goods game is played in a face-to-face group setting; participants can see one another, but either do not know who made what decision (Gilligan et al. 2014) or do know, but the identity of each person is obscured using a pseudonym so anonymity remains protected (Barclay 2004). In this case, face-to-face interactions were not possible. Just as the trust game does, the public goods game leverages the stereotype that the Roma are cheaters and thieves; additionally, this game brings out another, related, stereotypical characteristic of Roma as takers. To protect both the anonymity and physical integrity of my participants, I avoided the group setting. Indeed, when asked about a hypothetical mixed group component, Roma participants said that they would not be comfortable participating.

Another concern that significantly influenced my method of delivery is the comparatively low level of literacy among marginalized Roma. According to a 2014 study by the EU's Fundamental Rights Agency (FRA), Romani self-reported illiteracy rates range from 4 percent (Slovakia) to 52 percent (Greece); compared to the same among non-Roma, which is on average 1 percent, these rates are quite high (FRA 2014). There is considerable variation in illiteracy across both gender and age among Roma; older people are more likely to be unable to read, as are women. In Hungary, for example, self-reported illiteracy rate among 16 to 24 year-old Roma is zero; among Roma older than 45, it is 14 percent. In Portugal, the same among 16 to 24 year-olds is 10 percent, while among those who are 45 or older it is 60. Overall, 8 percent of Hungarian Roma women self-report as illiterate, while only 3 percent of Hungarian Roma men do. In Italy, 23 percent of Roma women do the same, compared to 12 percent of the men. Unfortunately, Slovenia was not included in the FRA study, so comparative numbers for Slovene Roma are not available. There is little reason to believe, however, that the general variation across age and gender is much different, even as overall rates of illiteracy are unclear. Therefore, to avoid disproportionally excluding the elderly and women from participating, I adjusted the game delivery such that anyone could participate without having to read.

In addition to the two challenges just described—that a face-to-face group setting is inappropriate and that not all Roma can read—there is also a third: simultaneous decision-making. Unlike in the trust game, in which the two players can make their decisions sequentially (the sender goes first, the receiver second), the decisions in the public goods game are typically simultaneous. If players can participate in a face-to-face group setting, making decisions at the same time is not challenging. If they cannot, one might be able to turn to technology and devise a game that can be played online, simultaneously, with each player in the privacy of their home (Egas and Riedl 2008). With financial and logistical difficulties that accompany fieldwork among a disadvantaged community (few Roma actually have computers, for example), the otherwise elegant online solution was not feasible.

Instead, I created a videogame. The objective of the videogame is to collect points, which translate into remuneration for participation at the end of the session. The game is played in groups of 8 players; the participant is the active player, while the other 7 are simulated (see Figure 4.3). As mentioned above, the public goods game presents a scenario where the group is best-off if everyone cooperates, but where incentives to free-ride without cooperating are high. The videogame presents it as a *tower building phase*. Each player gets a brick (10 points). Players can either keep their brick or put it into the tower (they have 4 seconds to decide). The value of the bricks added to the tower is multiplied by 1.6 and evenly divided among all participants (even those who chose to keep their bricks). An individual can earn the most points by keeping her own brick and getting a portion of the tower points in addition.

The indirect reciprocity game or *reward phase* gives players an opportunity to reward behavior in tower building. After each round of tower building, participants get 3 points. They can reward a member of their team for cooperating in tower building by giving them these points, which are then tripled. They can also choose not to reward and instead keep the 3 points. Each participant is randomly assigned one member of their team whom they can reward; when this happens, they receive information on how that player behaved in the preceding tower building phase, and, sometimes, information about the

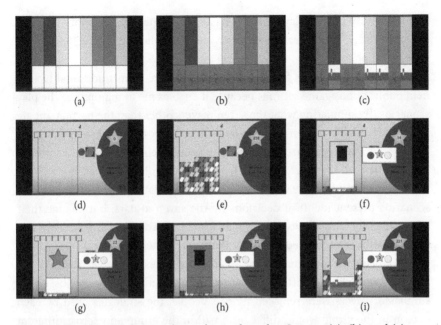

Figure 4.3 Videogame screenshots, absent the color. Screens (a), (b), and (c) show the presentation of players. This happens before each condition (once, before every 12-round combination). Ethnic ID of players is indicated by a Roma flag (wheel) for Roma, and a Slovene flag (shield) for ethnic Slovenes. (a) is the baseline screen in which no ethnic IDs are presented for the players; this condition is always played first. (b) is a coethnic condition, in which all players are Roma, and (c) is a mixed condition with players evenly split. The top half of the stripes are of different colors, each corresponding to a player. Bricks, also corresponding to these colors, are displayed in the tower as players contribute bricks to build it. The participant's color is always red. In (d), or the tower building phase, participants press blue (left button next to the brick) to contribute their brick to the tower and yellow (right button) to keep their brick. The star displays the points gained so far (points reset for every condition). Screen (e) shows a mostly built tower. The tower building phase is followed by either (f) or (g), both representing the reward phase (indirect reciprocity). If the partner presented contributed to the tower in the preceding round, the participant sees a black tower (f). If the partner presented kept the brick in the preceding round, the participant sees a grey star (g). The participant then decides whether to reward that player; if yes, the blue key (left button next to the star) sends 3 points (tripled) to that player; if no, the yellow key (right of the star) lets the participant keep the 3 points. Screens (f) and (g) present the reward phase of the baseline condition, without ethnic IDs. Screen (h) presents a Roma cooperator. Screen (i) presents a Slovene defector.

ethnic identity of that player. Both phases then repeat eleven more times in the same order - one iteration of tower building followed by one iteration of the reward phase.

The videogame allows for a significant departure from traditional lab-in-field public goods game settings because it enables me to manipulate the play scenarios. By simulating what the seven players other than the participant are playing, I am able not only to see how different people behave in the same setting, but also to capture how the same people behave in different settings. Each participant therefore participated in the control round (baseline) and in all treatment rounds. The chief feature of the simulation is that different play scenarios present identical decisions by the seven avatars, but change their ethnic identity. This allows me to gauge whether participants behave the same way in coethnic and mixed scenarios that are otherwise identical.

The videogame also enables me to conduct a clean test: because they are playing alone, all my participants are reacting to identical scenarios. If the simulated players were replaced by real people, the strategies used by each person in the group would differ both within the group and across different groups. Each player is reacting to her immediate situation; if one player happens to be surrounded by seven players who all happen to contribute to the public good, her behavior might differ from the behavior of a different player, who is surrounded by defectors. The videogame scenario, while forgoing the dynamic interactions of multiple unpredictable players, controls for this type of variation and truly allows me to compare the behavior of one player to another. Importantly, this means that the avatars in the game are not reacting to participant behaviors and continue to contribute to the tower with the same probability regardless. The game does react to participant behaviors in rewarding, however, such that cooperation is always rewarded and defection is consistently not.

Altogether, non-Roma participants played five games, while Roma played seven. Each game had 12 rounds, but the participants were not told how many rounds there were—they only knew that there were several. The first game is the baseline that presents a mix of cooperators and defectors, without ethnic identities. The second is identical to the baseline, except that all players are coethnic (non-Roma for non-Roma participants, and Roma for Roma partcipants). The third is identical to the baseline, except that half the players are non-Roma and half are Roma (defectors and cooperators are evenly distributed among the two groups). In the fourth game, all cooperators are non-coethnics (Roma for non-Roma and vice versa) and all defectors are coethnics. In the fifth, all cooperators are coethnics and all defectors non-coethnics.

The sixth, only played by Roma, has half Roma and half-non-Roma players, but all players are shown as cooperators. The seventh, also only played by Roma, also has half Roma and half-non-Roma players, but provides an ingroup rewarding scheme, such that Roma are only shown Roma avatars in the rewarding phase. The baseline game is always played first and the seventh (for Roma) last; the remaining games are randomized. The treatment—whether the game is coethnic or mixed—is administered before each game starts, when the participants are shown the roster of the players (see panels (a), (b), (c) of Figure 4.3).

While indirect reciprocity traditionally indicates whether a player contributed to the public good in the previous round, I selectively use it to provide information about the ethnic group of that player as well. In all but the baseline game, subjects are therefore deciding whether to reward Roma cooperators, non-Roma cooperators, Roma defectors, or non-Roma defectors. No deception was used in administering the protocols. Subjects were told that they were playing the videogame with a computer and that the other players were not real, but that the decisions of the simulated players were based on real decisions by people from their town; the decisions were taken from pilot rounds administered in June 2015. Even though they were told that they are playing the videogame with avatars and not real people in real time, participants became quite engaged with the game and played as if the other players were real.

As in the first study, I used simple random sampling to recruit 133 participants from two strata, the main town where non-Roma live and the Roma settlement. Streets in both were ordered alphabetically and then reordered based on a random number sample. We recruited participants from each house on the sampled street, starting at the top of the randomly ordered list, with a systematic iteration by gender. Anyone over 18 was eligible to participate. 66 Roma and 67 non-Roma from Novo mesto participated in this study. Using the same procedure as in the first study, my enumerators and I brought the lab-in-field to the potential participants: participants played the videogame on laptops we provided and then filled out a longer exit survey. Non-Roma participants participated outside in their backyards or in their living rooms. Roma participants also mostly participated outside, but more centrally, as a few volunteered their backyards. All decision-making was private and confidential.

The videogame resolves the three delivery-related concerns mentioned earlier. First, simulating seven of the eight players renders the concern about simultaneous decision-making moot. Second, as participants were able to participate confidentially and in private, their identities as well as their decision-making remained protected. Finally, as playing the videogame required no reading, participation was open to all potential participants. The tower-building visualization was quite intuitive and thus helpful in communicating the gist of the game. Enumerators explained the rules of the game while running a simulation of play on the laptop screen at the same time. Once they were sure that the participant understood the game, they started the practice session. During the practice session, the enumerators observed the participant; if the participant appeared confused, the enumerators stopped the practice session and explained again until the rules were clear. Participants were able to practice as many times as they wished. Once the games proper began, the enumerators stepped far enough away to ensure private participation (they remained within earshot). As with the trust game, the enumerator pairs switched daily in order to avoid bias; here, too, enumerator gender and my presence on the enumerator team were not statistically significant.[25]

Findings

The remainder of this chapter presents a few of the findings from the tower game. I discuss the remaining findings in Chapter 5, which focuses on non-Roma, and in Chapter 6, which focuses on Roma. Here, I present the findings that are most pertinent to the questions I posed earlier in this chapter. In the case of non-Roma, I asked whether non-Roma from Novo mesto treat Roma differently because they expect Roma not to reciprocate and whether, correspondingly, they would change their behavior if Roma were to reciprocate more. The short answer to this question is no. Of Roma, I asked whether they would reciprocate more if the game did not reward free-riding and instead rewarded cooperation. The short answer to this question is yes, but not enough. What follows will demonstrate and explain.

Figures 4.4 and 4.5 speak to the two findings summarized above, though in slightly different ways. The figures present the tower-building decisions that participants made in the game; that is, they demonstrate their willingness to contribute to the public good. They present participants' decisions from three games. These three games have identical play scenarios—meaning that the avatars make exactly the same decisions. The only variation between the three games is in the assignment of ethnic identities to those avatars.

---

[25] Results available upon request.

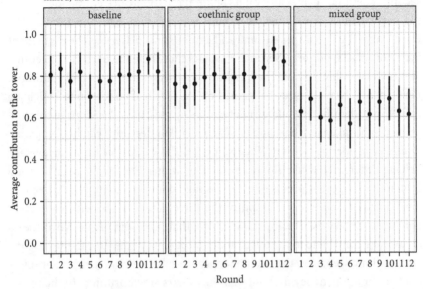

Non–Roma tower building behavior in identical baseline, mixed, and coethnic scenarios (Novo mesto)

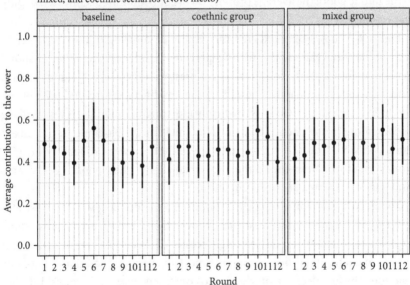

Roma tower building behavior in identical baseline, mixed, and coethnic scenarios (Novo mesto)

Figure 4.4 This figure presents the average contribution to the tower, along with 95 percent confidence intervals, that participants made in each round of the baseline, coethnic, and mixed games.

In the first "baseline" game, there is no ethnic identity assignment. In the second "coethnic" game, all avatars share the participant's ethnic identity (if the participant is non-Roma, all avatars are also shown as non-Roma). The third "mixed" game shows 4 Roma and 4 non-Roma players; as the participant is one of those 8 players, there are 3 avatars that share the participant's ethnic identity and 4 that do not. The baseline game serves as the control condition. Participants always played that game first. As they had no reason to anticipate that ethnic identifiers would be added to the games, their decisions in this first game can be taken as a baseline to which all other decisions can be compared.

First, consider non-Roma. The two figures show that non-Roma on average behave differently when Roma, even if fictitious, are involved in a group interaction. Figure 4.4 presents the average contribution to the tower that participants made in each round of the three games, along with 95 percent confidence intervals. The top panel shows that non-Roma from Novo mesto on average contribute to the tower about 80 percent of the time in the baseline and coethnic scenarios; they do not appear to substantially change their tower contributions once they find out that the avatars are non-Roma. In the mixed condition, however, non-Roma from Novo mesto contribute significantly less to the public good; the average proportion of contributions declines to roughly 65 percent.

Figure 4.5 shows the predicted probability of contributing to the tower in each of the three games, also with 95 percent confidence intervals.[26] It shows that a non-Roma participant from Novo mesto contributes to the public good with a predicted probability of 0.78 in the baseline scenario and 0.77 in the coethnic scenario; the two are statistically indistinguishable. She is just as likely to contribute in the coethnic scenario as she is in the baseline. In the mixed game she would do the same with a significantly lower probability of 0.59. Non-Roma from Novo mesto thus appear to change their public goods game strategies once Roma enter the equation.

The decrease in non-Roma contributions to the public good demonstrates two things. First, it shows that non-Roma instinctively react against Roma even in a repeated interaction setting. Second, it reveals that non-Roma do not appear to change their behavior over time. Consider the instinctive, gut-level reaction. The first decision of whether to contribute, marked as round 1 in Figure 4.4, happens right after the participant is told about the ethnic composition

---

[26] These are based on a logit model with individual clustered standard errors that included covariates for gender, age, employment, and education. The model also controlled for the order in which each participant played the randomized games. This model included data from both Novo mesto and Murska Sobota; results from a model that uses only data from Novo mesto are substantively unchanged.

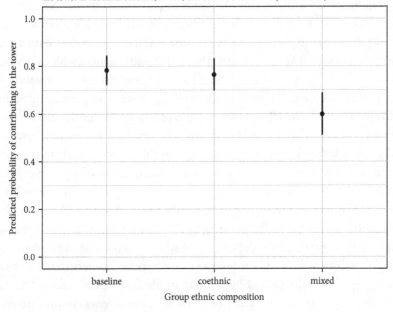

Non–Roma predicted probability of contributing to
the tower in identical baseline, mixed, and coethnic scenarios (Novo mesto)

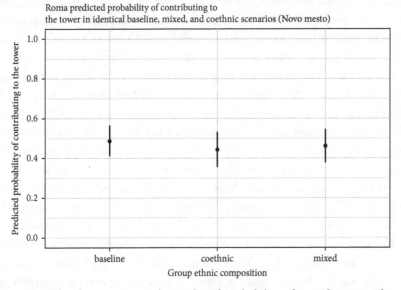

Roma predicted probability of contributing to
the tower in identical baseline, mixed, and coethnic scenarios (Novo mesto)

Figure 4.5 This figure presents the predicted probability of contributing to the tower in the baseline, coethnic, and mixed games. The predicted probabilities with their 95 percent confidence intervals are based on logit models with individual clustered standard errors that included covariates for gender, age, employment, and education. The model also controlled for the order in which each participant played the randomized games. The results presented in this figure are from models that included data from both Novo mesto and Murska Sobota. Results from a model that uses only data from Novo mesto are substantively unchanged.

of the group (see panels (a), (b), and (c) of Figure 4.3). As participants have 4 seconds to make the decision of whether or not to contribute, they have enough time to consider their choice, but just barely. Participants are given as much time as they wish to practice the videogame and the enumerators ensure that they fully understand the rules, so it is likely that participants decide in advance how they might act, at least to a degree. The sudden addition of information on the ethnic make-up of the group, then, is telling. Instinctively not contributing to the public good when Roma avatars are in play suggests that the stereotype of Roma as cheaters, thieves, and takers might be behind the quick first reaction. Indeed, if half the players in the group are considered more likely to free ride, the safer move is not to contribute. Such quick reactions happen every day. Upon seeing two Roma women in a doctor's waiting room, the non-Roma newcomer might, without giving the matter much thought, elect to sit next to non-Roma patients on the bench opposite. In a similar way, riders on a bus might pull their bags closer depending on who takes the adjacent seat.

Remarkable as the first, gut-level reaction may be, its persistence is most damaging. This is the second implication of the findings, also demonstrated by Figure 4.4. One might argue that given the pervasiveness of the universal stereotype about the Roma, the first gut reaction to not contribute may be inevitable. Not so its persistence. Keep in mind that behavior non-Roma observed was *not* less cooperation by Roma. Instead, each participant observed behaviors from avatars that behaved identically regardless of ethnicity. If non-Roma are cooperating less only because they expect Roma to free ride, they should adjust their behavior upon observing that Roma are not, in fact, all free-riding. This is precisely what we should expect to see in light of claims often said not only in the context of the Roma, but also that of the Batwa, Black Americans, and others: "If only they stopped [engaging in their respective stereotyped behaviors], we would accept them" (Kidd 2008). Non-Roma behavior, at least, did not heed that claim. Roma and non-Roma avatars behaved *identically*, and yet non-Roma participants kept contributing less in the mixed condition. I will discuss why in Chapter 5. Here, I now turn to Roma.

Unlike non-Roma, Roma from Novo mesto behaved quite consistently. The two figures show that their average behavior changed little across the three games. The bottom panel of Figure 4.4 shows the average contribution per round for each game for Roma; in all three games, Roma contributed almost half of their bricks. The bottom panel of Figure 4.5 shows predicted probabilities of contributing to the tower: a Roma participant would on average contribute with a predicted probability of 0.48 in the baseline scenario, 0.44 in the coethnic scenario, and 0.46 in the mixed scenario. The three predicted probabilities are essentially indistinguishable, an exceptional and unexpected finding.

Roma do not appear to favor their own. This finding runs contrary to expectations of social identity theory. Scholarship on ingroup favoritism demonstrates that ingroup members favor one another not only when ingroups are determined by clearly salient categories such as race or gender, but also when they are determined by something completely arbitrary, like a piece of clothing, or even at random. Moreover, this finding runs contrary to examples of members of marginalized communities helping one another, building their own institutions, and thriving against all odds. Why do Roma not contribute more to the public good when only Roma avatars are in play? Or, perhaps more saliently, why do they not contribute less when non-Roma, who discriminate against them, are involved? Fully understanding this unexpected finding will require future research.

The results also demonstrate that Roma indeed engage in higher levels of cooperation once the financial benefit of defecting is removed. While levels of cooperation in the one-shot trust game were low, Roma levels of cooperation in the tower game almost match those of non-Roma in the mixed scenario. Briefly, two points come to mind. First, Roma are not defectors extraordinaire. They contribute to the public good almost half of the time, regardless of who else is involved in the game. Universal as it is, the stereotype of Roma as consummate cheaters, thieves, and takers does not appear to match reality. Second, the difference between levels of cooperation in the two games speaks to the devastating misinterpretation of Roma behavior. As Roma often face barriers that severely constrain their options, they may sometimes be forced to resort to survival strategies. What non-Roma observe, then, is the survival strategy and not the behavior that Roma might prefer to engage in, if given the chance. As the survival strategy—say, free riding—fits the stereotype, the sweeping yet incorrect conclusion might be that Roma simply always defect. The findings presented above demonstrate that this is clearly not the case.

One might assume that the difference between Roma behaviors in the trust and tower games—not particularly cooperative in the first, but quite cooperative in the second—is due entirely to the different nature of the games. The first captures single interactions, and the second repeated; for receivers, it is therefore rational to defect in the trust game, while in the tower game, cooperation can lead to a superior outcome. While it is possible that Roma responded only to the single/repeated distinction, that seems unlikely. First, non-Roma participants behaved quite similarly in the two games. In the trust game, they cooperated about 78 percent of the time when paired with coethnics and 58 percent of the time when paired with Roma; in the tower game, they contributed with the predicted probability of 0.77 in the coethnic and with 0.59 probability in the mixed scenario. This suggests that although the two games elicit different expectations about how rational actors would behave, numerous participants in fact do not distinguish between single and repeated interactions and instead exhibit almost equivalent levels of cooperation in both.

Further, there are other reasons why Roma might behave differently in the two games. Most notably, cooperation is costly in the trust game, while in the tower game it isn't necessarily. Given that most Roma participants were officially at risk for poverty, it is possible that Roma reacted to the difference in the cost of cooperation, while for non-Roma, who are substantially better off, this difference was not salient. Indeed, the two Roma from Novo mesto who reported incomes that were above the "at risk" threshold (greater than 600 euros), both returned substantially more to their senders: they returned everything. While in my sample the number of Roma who are better off is very low, their behaviors suggest that material deprivation is linked to low engagement in costly cooperation, and they demonstrate that, unlike what stereotyping suggests, free riding among Roma is *not* a group-based characteristic in which all Roma naturally engage.

Finally, the findings reveal a rift between Roma and non-Roma levels of cooperation. Examining both panels of the two figures together shows that the Roma consistently contributed less to the tower than non-Roma did, even if not by much. Having the choice to either contribute their brick or keep it, Roma were slightly more likely to keep their bricks. Non-Roma were not; even in the mixed scenario in which they contributed notably less to the tower, they were still more likely to contribute their bricks than to keep them. Figure 4.4 depicts the average contribution to the tower by round; contributions by Roma participants consistently came in around the 50 percent mark, while non-Roma contributions tended to be between 60 (mixed) and 80 percent (baseline and coethnic). Figure 4.5 shows that a Roma participant would contribute to the tower a little under half the time, in all three games. The predicted probabilities estimated for non-Roma, in the top panel, are higher. On average non-Roma contributed more than Roma.

This small but significant difference plays an important role in sustaining the exclusion cycle in Novo mesto—as does consistent discrimination by non-Roma. Together, the two sketch a cyclical dynamic. Non-Roma persistently discriminate against the Roma by cooperating less when Roma are in play.

Anticipating discrimination, Roma resort to survival strategies. Indeed, free riding is the best response in the tower game for a player who expects other players to defect. Observing survival strategies, non-Roma double down on discrimination—though the findings suggest that whether or not Roma engage in survival strategies is actually irrelevant; non-Roma will discriminate regardless. This might, again, lead to survival strategies, and so on. Breaking this cycle would be no small task.

Conclusion

In this chapter, I discussed the first set of findings from my fieldwork in Novo mesto. First, I found that non-Roma consistently discriminated against the Roma. They discriminated against them in a single interaction setting, where participants interact once and never again. They also discriminated against the Roma in a repeated interaction setting, where 8 players interact several times as a group. They did that even when Roma players behaved identically to non-Roma players. Second, I also found that Roma used survival strategies. In a repeated interaction setting, where cooperation is not necessarily costly, Roma cooperated less than non-Roma—although not by much. This difference nonetheless plays a significant role in perpetuating exclusion, although non-Roma behaviors suggest that exclusion would continue even if this difference in Roma/non-Roma levels of cooperation disappeared.

Though I have answered some pressing questions, others still remain. Who among non-Roma discriminates against the Roma? Is it everyone? Are they all prejudiced? Or is it non-Roma who have had a bad personal experience, of some sort, with Roma? If prejudice drives discriminatory behavior, does it stem from anti-Roma culture or from general intolerance of minorities? And do non-Roma from Novo mesto commit attribution errors? As Chapter 5 will show, not everyone discriminates, but those who do are prejudiced against the Roma, specifically. Reporting a bad experience with Roma in the past is unrelated to discrimination, and non-Roma from Novo mesto do commit attribution errors.

I have shown that Roma from Novo mesto engage in survival strategies, but I have not yet explored which Roma are likely to free ride. Is it the Roma who are more materially deprived? Is it the Roma who have personally experienced discrimination? Or is it the Roma who believe that they, as Roma, will be seen as cheaters and thieves regardless of what they do? As Chapter 6 will show, material deprivation does not appear to be related to engaging in survival strategies, and neither are beliefs on stereotype intractability. Instead, Roma who report personally experiencing discrimination are less likely to cooperate in the tower videogame.

Finally, how do we break the cycle? Chapters 5 and 6 also present evidence from Murska Sobota, comparing behaviors of Roma and non-Roma there to the behaviors of Roma and non-Roma in Novo mesto. While findings from Novo mesto are grim, the comparison offers hope. NGO-led promotion of intergroup contact and dialogue might help break the cycle.

5

Contact

Our Roma are not civilized.
Non-Roma participant, Novo mesto 2015

And children mocked us, and they were afraid, and they held themselves apart
from us on account of us being "gypsies," up to 4th or 5th grade. Then, less. In
high school, later, we were friends.
Roma participant, Murska Sobota 2016

Non-Roma commonly claim that discrimination would stop if Roma behaved like the majority. The statement above, that "[o]ur Roma are not civilized," is a crude representation of this sentiment. Beyond illustrating how Roma can be seen as inferior to non-Roma, it shows that the perceived gap between the two groups can be substantial and that, according to non-Roma, the blame for this gap as well as the responsibility to close it rests solely with the minority. This statement suggests that Roma have quite a long way to go before they are seen as equal and contributing members of society. The unspoken but implied understanding, however, is that once they get there, Roma will be treated like anyone else. The findings from Chapter 4 suggest that this would not be the case. Non-Roma discriminated against the Roma when they interacted with them just once. They discriminated against them when they interacted with them repeatedly. And, importantly, they continued that discrimination even when Roma behaved no differently than non-Roma. What, then, would it take for non-Roma to stop discriminating? In this chapter, I argue that NGO-promoted intergroup contact might help.

To test the effectiveness of intergroup contact, this chapter introduces a second town, also from Slovenia: Murska Sobota. In many aspects, particularly those relevant to the treatment of Roma, Murska Sobota quite closely matches Novo mesto. It differs in one crucial way, however. Roma NGO action in Novo mesto centers on the Romani community and engages in service provision, providing educational aid as well as water to the remote parts of the Roma settlement that need it. In Murska Sobota, Roma NGO action focuses on

Breaking the Exclusion Cycle: How to Promote Cooperation between Majority and Minority Ethnic Groups.
Ana Bracic, Oxford University Press (2020). © Oxford University Press. DOI: 10.1093/oso/9780190050672.001.0001

Roma/non-Roma relations and dialogue. Both organizations are very well known among the Roma in their respective towns, but the NGO in Murska Sobota reaches across the ethnic divide, while the one in Novo mesto does not. The two towns, about 100 miles apart, are therefore suitable counterparts for this inquiry.

To carry out a comparison of behaviors in the two towns, I conducted the same studies in Murska Sobota as I did in Novo mesto. I looked first at single interactions with the trust game, and then at repeated interactions with the tower game that combines the public goods game and indirect reciprocity. This chapter only presents the findings on non-Roma behavior. Chapter 6 will present and discuss the behaviors of Roma.

While non-Roma from Novo mesto, which doesn't have a contact-promoting NGO, discriminated against the Roma, non-Roma from Murska Sobota, which has intergroup contact promotion, did not. Non-Roma from this town treated Roma no differently than they treated non-Roma. This was the case in the context of repeated interactions, where early decision-making matters for later success, as well as, remarkably, in the context of single interactions that require no reputation building.

In the study on repeated interactions I was able to isolate particular individuals who discriminated against the Roma to take a closer look at some of the factors they had in common. While they appeared to overwhelmingly believe that Roma cannot be trusted, and indeed were not swayed by the tower game that purposefully presented them with identical Roma and non-Roma avatars, those who discriminated did not appear do so because of their own bad personal experience with the Roma.

The findings lend support to the expectation that voluntary positive intergroup contact might help reduce discrimination. Non-Roma in Murska Sobota who have attended events organized by the intergroup contact NGO did not discriminate, and neither did those who were familiar with the organization. While the findings suggest that promotion of voluntary positive intergroup contact helps reduce discrimination, open ended answers that participants from both towns provided in one of the exit surveys show that stereotyping persists. While non-Roma from Murska Sobota did not appear to be swayed by the stereotype that the Roma are cheaters and thieves in the games, many still endorsed it.

This chapter proceeds as follows. I first briefly return to the discussion on intergroup contact and summarize the main reasons it might be beneficial in encouraging equal treatment. I then present the second location, Murska Sobota, first by discussing how it is similar to Novo mesto and then by discussing how it differs. The section presenting NGO action in both locations also addresses problems of endogeneity and omitted variable bias. The section that follows presents and discusses results, first from the repeated interaction tower game and second from the single interaction trust game. I conclude with open questions and possibilities for future research.

How might intergroup contact help interrupt the exclusion cycle?

Once more, the exclusion cycle consists of four parts: anti-minority culture, discriminatory behavior by the majority, survival strategies by the minority, and the attribution error, committed by the majority. Intergroup contact, if effective, would likely affect discriminatory behavior by the majority first, and anti-minority culture second, for two reasons. First, members of the majority are far more likely to respond to positive intergroup contact than are members of the minority (Enos 2014; Mutz 2016; Pettigrew and Tropp 2011; Sidanius et al. 2008; Scacco and Warren 2018). Second, as adjusting one's behavior tends to be easier than changing one's mind, effects of positive contact would probably manifest through behavioral changes first; changes in levels of prejudice might then follow (Pettigrew and Tropp 2011; Scacco and Warren 2018). Survival strategies are employed by members of the marginalized minority; since minority populations are less likely to respond to contact, we might only detect a decrease in the use of survival strategies later, once the majority has reduced its discrimination. Finally, the rates of committing the attribution error might decrease along with a decrease in prejudice, but they are also likely to present a tougher challenge, as a person might have to be aware of committing the error before they are able to stop (Stewart et al. 2010). Intergroup contact alone likely does not increase that knowledge, at least not in the short term.

Interrupting prejudice and discriminatory behavior by the majority could happen through several mechanisms. The first is a decrease in anxiety. People who have not interacted much with outgroup members tend to experience more anxiety in initial interactions (Blascovich et al. 2001). Positive intergroup contact can decrease this anxiety and thus lead to lower levels of prejudice (Page-Gould et al. 2008). Overcoming anxiety also enables empathy, which is the second mechanism through which contact might reduce prejudice and discriminatory behavior (Galinsky and Moskowitz 2000). Outgroup members can develop empathy as they learn to understand some of the concerns that marginalized individuals might have. Cultural learning is another mechanism that might help interrupt prejudice and discriminatory behavior (Triandis 1994). Lastly, intergroup contact might interrupt prejudice and discriminatory behavior through a change in the norms about cross-group interactions (Olson and Stone 2005, Tropp et al. 2014). If positive intergroup contact becomes the new norm, individuals will be more likely to engage in it, even if they hold prejudiced beliefs.

Academic opinions on the effects of positive intergroup contact are divided. Optimistic scholars suggest that the benefits of contact generalize beyond the individuals involved in the immediate contact situation (Cook 1984; Sidanius et al. 2008; Van Oudenhoven et al. 1996,). According to this view, ethnic Slovenes who have positive contact with a few Roma are likely to be less prejudiced towards Roma in general. This view further suggests that the effects of positive contact can extend beyond the individual who experiences it first-hand; her ingroup friends might exhibit lower levels of prejudice (Wright et al. 1997) as might her neighbors or people who live close by (Christ et al. 2014). Skeptics, in contrast, maintain that the jury is still out and that additional research is necessary, particularly regarding contact between adults of different ethnicities (Paluck et al. 2018).

Murska Sobota

To test whether sustained promotion of friendly intergroup contact and dialogue helps reduce discrimination and contributes to breaking the exclusion cycle, I carried out the two studies in a second town, Murska Sobota, also in Slovenia. Murska Sobota matches Novo mesto on a number of relevant factors, named below, but differs in a crucial characteristic. While Roma NGO action in Novo mesto primarily engages in service provision to the Romani settlements and tends to focus on Roma, Roma NGO action in Murska Sobota crosses the ethnic divide and actively promotes intergroup contact and dialogue.

How Murska Sobota and Novo mesto match

Murska Sobota and Novo mesto share a number of demographic and historical characteristics. As they are both in Slovenia, the towns match on all relevant present day state-level characteristics, as well as those that might have been historically relevant.

I selected the towns by performing nearest neighbor matching (Ho et al. 2007a, 2007b; Nielsen 2014)[1] on all towns in Slovenia that have a Roma population of at least 50. I excluded locations with fewer than 50 Roma because I needed 50 Roma participants from each location to participate in the trust game. As I determined the set of possible towns using the most recent Slovene Census (2002), this requirement restricted the number of possible locations to 14 towns.[2]

The matching procedure used five covariates. I included *town population, Roma inhabitants as proportion of total town population,* and *ethnic majority as proportion of total town population* to achieve balance in town sizes and their ethnic compositions. *Proximity to Slovene/Croatian border* controls for variation in potential exposure to other outgroups. This matters because people from borderlands more commonly interact with outgroups (Mirwaldt 2010), which can result in higher levels of ingroup favoritism. Ingroup favoritism can then result in disparate treatment of all outgroups, regardless of group-specific attitudes (Brewer 2007). Controlling for border proximity accounts for this type of potential variation in strength and saliency of ingroup sentiment. To control for institutional capabilities and resources at the municipal level, both general and those pertaining to Roma, I included a *regional capital* dummy variable among the covariates. Regional capitals tend to have more municipal resources. For example, among the twenty-four Slovene municipalities that have Romani inhabitants, as reported (and likely underreported) by the Census, only four have a municipal strategy for addressing the needs of their respective Roma communities (Vlada 2014). Yet, both regional capitals in the sample have such a strategy. Given a likely mismatch in resources, comparing a town that is a regional capital to a town that is not would be imprudent. The regional capital dummy variable is therefore the fifth and final matching covariate.

In the matching procedure, Murska Sobota was selected first.[3] It is the only town in Slovenia with a Roma NGO that focuses on intergroup relations. Of the

---

[1] The towns in my sample varied too much to merit exact matching; I therefore used the "greedy" matching method of nearest neighbor matching in MatchIt (Ho et al. 2011). This method finds the closest control match for each treated unit one at a time. As I was not looking to find a large number of matched pairs, this method was more appropriate than methods that seek to minimize average absolute distance across all pairs.

[2] There are quite likely over 14 locations with more than 50 Roma in Slovenia; as I mentioned earlier in Chapter 4, census estimates of Roma populations tend to be low. Since the 2002 Slovene Census was the only source that provided systematic data on all locations, however, I nonetheless opted to use it, erring on the side of caution.

[3] I selected Murska Sobota first because I had already done research there in the context of an earlier project on discrimination against the Roma. In that study, I compared Murska Sobota to Čakovec, a town across the border in Croatia (Bracic 2016).

13 other eligible towns, all without such organizing, Novo mesto was selected as the best match for Murska Sobota.

Murska Sobota and Novo mesto match quite closely on the five factors just named. The two towns also match on factors beyond those included in the matching procedure. The towns are from the two regions that boast the highest percent of Roma in Slovenia. Murska Sobota is the regional capital of Prekmurje, in the northeast, which has the highest proportion of Roma in the country; Novo mesto is the regional capital of Dolenjska, in the southeast, which ranks second. Both towns have the highest proportion of Romani inhabitants in their respective regions: in Murska Sobota, Roma make up 2.27 percent of the population; in Novo mesto, they make up between 1.2 and 2.8 percent.[4] The towns are of comparable sizes, having between 20,000 and 30,000 inhabitants (Statistični urad Republike Slovenije 2002). Both are about 10 miles away from the Slovene-Croat border (see Figure 5.1 for a map).

Roma have lived in the two towns for at least 200 years (Horvat-Muc 2011b). This is not always the case in the countries of former Yugoslavia; some Romani communities are in fact fairly new since they arrived as a result of displacement during the Yugoslav wars in the 1990s. Interestingly, in many locations the newly arrived refugee Roma have been able to integrate to a much greater degree (Klopčič 2012). It is therefore helpful that both towns chosen for the purpose of comparing Roma/non-Roma relations have Roma communities that have been around for a similar length of time. Although Roma are not originally from the two towns, they are considered autochthonous in both locations. Even so, they are not mentioned as such in primary school curricula used in the towns (Karba 2010). In fact, like in the vast majority of school curricula across Europe, Roma and their history are not mentioned at all.

As in many places throughout Central and Eastern Europe, the vast majority of Roma in the two towns live in segregated areas. Most live in one central Romani settlement, Pušča in Murska Sobota and Brezje-Žabjak in Novo mesto. The settlements are somewhat isolated, on the outskirts of town, and separated from the main town centers by a stretch of fields and some trees (Ajdiè 2008). In both towns, Roma are represented in the local governments (Horvat-Muc 2011a, Tudija 2012). The 2011 average regional monthly incomes were $1,927 for Murska Sobota and $2,176 for Novo mesto (Statistični urad Republike Slovenije 2011b). The similarity is useful since the trust and tower games both involve money.

---

[4] The percent for Murska Sobota and the lower percent for Novo mesto are based on the 2002 census (Statistični urad Republike Slovenije 2002). A local source in Novo mesto estimated the higher percent for that town (interview with author).

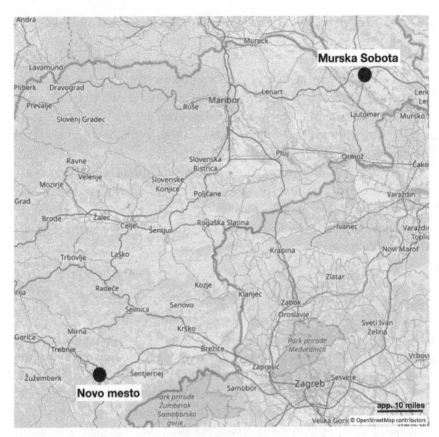

Figure 5.1 Map of the two towns. Murska Sobota, on the right, has an intergroup contact promotion NGO. Novo mesto, on the left, has a service provision NGO. (*Source*: OpenStreetMap contributors)

While the matching procedure did not include a number of relevant population characteristics at the town level, those that I collected from randomly sampled participants speak to the suitability of the match. First, the two populations should be approximately equivalent in general intolerance; that is, a match is inappropriate if people from Novo mesto are overall more intolerant than people from Murska Sobota. If this is the case, any difference in discrimination may be due to the higher level of intolerance in Novo mesto and not the promotion of intergroup contact in Murska Sobota. Figure 5.2 (top panel) shows how participants reacted to the possibility of same sex couples adopting children. The plots for the two towns are nearly identical, with two peaks at the extreme ends—participants are either "very bothered" or "not at all." Murska Sobota, then, is not a town without bigots. Next, a Roma-specific check is necessary, to ensure that some anti-Roma prejudice is present in both places.

To that end, I asked participants whether they would be bothered if children from their family were in kindergarten or school together with Roma children. The bottom panel of Figure 5.2 shows answers to this question. Non-Roma in both towns were most likely to indicate they were "not at all" bothered. There are some non-Roma in both towns, however, who would be "very" bothered by a mixed kindergarten or elementary school. While there is some imbalance between the two towns—there are more people in Murska Sobota who would not be bothered at all than in Novo mesto—the former certainly has non-Roma who harbor anti-Roma sentiment.

Overall, the samples are fairly balanced on gender, age, income, and education, and therefore comparable across locations.[5]

How Murska Sobota and Novo mesto differ

Importantly, Roma NGOs in Murska Sobota and Novo mesto differ in the mode of local Roma NGO action. Like many Roma NGOs throughout Central and Eastern Europe, the NGO in Novo mesto focuses on service provision. As its purpose is to help the resident Romani community, the NGO predominantly engages with Roma. The organization in Murska Sobota, in contrast, focuses on Roma and non-Roma alike, bridging the ethnic divide and promoting dialogue. Both NGOs developed in the early 1990s and both are led by Roma.

Service provision NGOs that serve Romani communities are relatively common among organizations that aim to assist Roma in Central and Eastern Europe. This is so because Roma need help, but also because such organizations tend to be more successful in obtaining funds (Anonymous 2013). Romano Veseli in Novo mesto is such an organization. This NGO provides socio-economic aid to the local Roma in need and focuses on education of Romani children and adults (Tudija 2012). Flexible and responsive to the needs

---

[5] The random sample of Roma in the tower game includes 54 and 47 percent women in Novo mesto and Murska Sobota, respectively. The mode for age in both is 18–24 years old, but the median age category is 18–30 in Novo mesto and 31–40 in Murska Sobota. In both locations, the mode for employment status is unemployed. The median category for education is some primary school in Novo mesto and primary school in Murska Sobota. The random sample of non-Roma in the tower game includes 59 and 62 percent women in Novo mesto and Murska Sobota, respectively. In both, the median age category is 41–50, and the employment status mode is fully employed. The median category for education is some college in Novo mesto and high school in Murska Sobota. In both, the monthly income median is 1200–1599 euros.

Reaction to same sex couples potentially adopting children

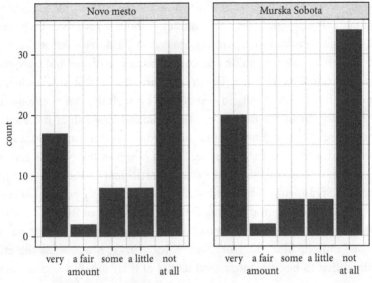

On a scale from 1 to 5, where 1 is very bothered at all and 5 is not at all bothered, how bothered are you by same sex couples being able to adopt children?

Reaction to having children go to school or kindergarten with Roma children

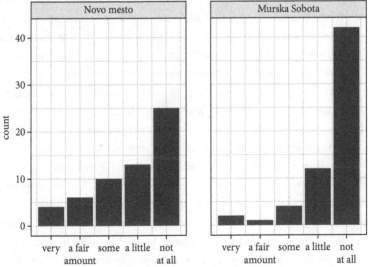

On a scale from 1 to 5, where 1 is very bothered at all and 5 is not at all bothered, how bothered are you with children from your family going to school or kindergarten with Roma children?

Figure 5.2 Capturing non-Roma participants' Roma-specific and unrelated prejudice.

of the community, Milena Tudija, the NGO leader, takes up issues that are pressing—from providing water tanks to a remote part of the settlement to arranging shipping containers for families without a roof over their heads. Its "Eko-etno romska moda" project, started in 2014, uses donated second-hand clothes to create fashionable contemporary clothing and accessories with a traditional Roma twist. The project provides local Roma, particularly women, with the opportunity to design and sew with the aim of empowering and preparing them for the job market. Romano Veseli does not focus on intergroup relations and non-Roma, aside from an occasional volunteer, are not involved in its activities.[6] Among Roma, however, the NGO is very well known. Every randomly sampled Romani participant in the trust game was able to identify Milena Tudija by name and many profusely praised her efforts.

Stepping in a different direction, Romani Union-Zveza Romov in Murska Sobota promotes intergroup contact and dialogue. In this telling passage, Monika Sandreli, who—together with Jožek Horvat-Muc—leads the effort, explained that to her, the intergroup nature of their organizing was obvious at the outset:

> ... [non-Roma] would ask me, "may we also come to this event?" and I thought the question was silly. It was silly because, as I told them, I go to your events. I don't know, and I said, you see here, everyone is invited, and the event is free, I don't see why coming would be a problem at all for you. It doesn't say just for the Roma. I really thought it funny. Mostly, the majority population thought that we were putting these events on just for ourselves [the Roma]. And then we started sending out invitations— we did before, but mostly to institutions with which we were collaborating, and not masses of people. But with "Gypsy night" we really drew people in. Because music is without borders and without prejudice. So. I can tell you that there was a period of time when more non-Roma than Roma came to our events. Roma took them as something that just happened to be happening, "someone is presenting a book," but non-Roma were more interested. And, predominantly, we did not host our events in Romani settlements, because then "this is the ghetto, just for the Roma." Instead we went to libraries, the cinema, the Sobota hall, the castle. You let people know that they should come, and then they stop asking if they may. And the way it happened, if you convinced someone, they brought someone else with them.
>
> (Monika Sandreli 2012, interview with author)

---

[6] A non-Roma designer for the Eko-etno project is the only non-Roma permanently involved; she is not from Novo mesto.

Here, Sandreli touches on several elements of positive intergroup contact. First, consider anxiety. The initial reluctance of non-Roma to attend NGO events might have been due to anxiety about how to behave or anxiety about how their presence would be perceived by Roma. The event that finally succeeded in breaching this barrier, the 1992 "Gypsy night" ("Ciganska noč"), is the paragon of a voluntary low-stress positive-contact situation with high entertainment value (Horvat-Muc 2010).[7] "Gypsy night" is a yearly concert of Romani music and dances that traditionally evolves into a lively party. The relaxed atmosphere promotes familiarity and likely reduces contact-based anxiety even if it does not lead to personal acquaintance or friendship. The event is quite popular; over the years, it has required a change of venues since well over 300 people attend (Sandreli 2012). As anxiety is one of the two strong mediators of intergroup contact (Blascovich et al. 2001),[8] it is quite likely that low-stress, fun events like "Gypsy night" contribute to lower levels of animus.

The NGO, however, does not stop there. Its other events—book launches, theater productions, folklore workshops and performances—also combine this relaxed atmosphere and its likely effect on contact anxiety with the transfer of cultural knowledge. In 2000, Romani Union started a small, independent publishing house, which publishes local Romani fiction and non-fiction, a newspaper, and proceedings from conferences, as well as recordings of music and Romani fairy tales. Book launches tend to be well attended. The Romani Union amateur theater group often stages plays written by Jožek Horvat-Muc and other Roma playwrights that speak to Roma life, while the amateur folklore group stages colorful performances. Starting in 1994, Romani Union has organized a yearly week-long international summer camp where Roma and non-Roma children, professionals, and activists can learn about Romani history, language, and culture, in addition to contemporary issues that affect Roma across the globe (Horvat-Muc 2010). While increasing general knowledge is a minor mediator of contact (Pettigrew and Tropp 2011), cultural knowledge in particular is hypothesized to explain a substantial portion of contact's effect on prejudice (Triandis 1994). The activities described—the music, the folklore, the summer camp, the literature published and available to the general public, and the plays performed—all offer cultural knowledge.

---

[7] The name of the event, chosen by Roma NGO leaders, uses a word that many Roma consider a racial slur. While most Roma activists in Eastern Europe no longer use this word and consistently use the term 'Roma,' exceptions are made in the case of music and dances. When music and dances are presented publicly, activists "frequently [use] the designation "Gypsy" considering it as more proper, generally accepted and even "traditional"." (Marushiakova and Popov 2016, p.46).

[8] An increase in intergroup contact might reduce anxiety and thereby lead to lower prejudice and, likely, less discrimination (Blascovich et al. 2001).

In fact, they offer cultural knowledge in different forms such that those who are interested can choose whatever suits them best.[9]

In addition to providing cultural knowledge, these activities likely encourage empathy. While anxiety is "crucially important" and its decrease is a likely "central initiator" (Pettigrew and Tropp 2011, p.94) of the process that leads from positive intergroup contact to lower prejudice, empathy is just as powerful. The camp, plays, and other publications offer a view of what life is like for Roma. Romani Union therefore does not only aim to reduce contact anxiety, it also encourages non-Roma to relate to their Roma neighbors. Thus, the NGO covers three important mediators of the relationship between contact and prejudice: anxiety, cultural knowledge, and empathy.

The final piece of the intergroup contact effort is Radio Romic, a Roma radio station run by a sister organization. The radio station is popular among Roma as well as non-Roma; recently, the number of non-Roma listeners has surpassed that of Roma. The radio station, requiring a lower level of engagement, provides an opportunity for vicarious contact even to those who might not seek it out. Aiming for a broader appeal, the station plays popular music, some Roma and some not. Romic also produces a daily hour-long show "Roma world," and a weekly one that airs on numerous other radio stations throughout Slovenia.

An interested non-Roma in Murska Sobota can easily engage with the local Roma, whether she prefers the low key option of tuning in from her car or the more involved one of attending a book launch. Indeed, Romani Union is quite well known among non-Roma in Murska Sobota. Of 100 randomly sampled non-Roma in town, 46 percent were able to name the organization. In contrast, while Romano Veseli is widely known among Roma in Novo mesto, only 2 percent of randomly sampled non-Roma there were able to name it.[10] This, of course, does not mean that Romano Veseli is an ineffective organization; it is merely indicative of the fact that their efforts center around the local Roma.

---

[9] To Roma, the NGO provides resources, entertainment, and numerous vehicles of artistic expression as well as a chance to engage in intergroup contact with non-Roma.

[10] Thirty-three percent of non-Roma in Novo mesto indicated that they knew of a Romani NGO; only eighteen percent were able to name any entity and only two percent in fact named a relevant organization. The municipal office for social benefits was the most commonly named "NGO" that dealt with Roma issues. I exclude the mentions of two organizations in reporting the data. The first is a volunteer work organization (Drustvo za razvoj prostovoljnega dela) that does work with the Roma but is neither staffed by Roma nor primarily concerned with Roma issues. Six percent of senders mentioned this organization. The second is Civilna iniciativa, which is an initiative formed by non-Roma that aims to resolve the "Roma question." It was clear that the senders who mentioned Civilna iniciativa understood it to be an organization that does not fight for Roma rights but rather aims to protect non-Roma from the (actual or perceived) negative consequences of living close to the Roma settlement. Two percent of senders named that organization.

If contact effects generalize broadly, beneficial effects of Romani Union's activities in Murska Sobota might not be limited to the 46 percent of non-Roma who could name it. Some non-Roma might attend cultural events organized by the NGO without realizing that the NGO organized them. Positive effects of contact on those who attend Romani Union events or listen to their radio have likely not only spread to their ingroup friends but also to the people who live in their neighborhoods.

To get a sense of contact between Roma and non-Roma in the two towns, I asked the randomly chosen non-Roma tower game participants how much they thought Roma and non-Roma in their town socialized together, as well as whether they, personally, had any Roma friends and acquaintances. The three plots in Figure 5.3 present their answers. In Novo mesto, the modal response to the question on how much Roma and non-Roma socialize was "not at all;" in Murska Sobota, the modal response was "some." Regarding Roma acquaintances, just under half of non-Roma from Novo mesto reported having none, while in Murska Sobota the modal response, with 28 percent of participants, was over 10. In both towns participants reported having few Roma friends; in Novo mesto, 85 percent reported having none, whereas in Murska Sobota, the mode was split between 0 and 1–2 friends, with 36 percent of participants in each category. Non-Roma from Murska Sobota therefore appear to have more Roma friends and acquaintances than their counterparts in Novo mesto. Non-Roma from the town with the intergroup contact NGO also believe that Roma and non-Roma socialize more.

Two caveats are in order here. The first concerns omitted variable bias and the second concerns endogeneity. Both are possible because neither type of organizing in the towns was randomly assigned. The difference in the two types of organizing as well as the difference in discrimination today could both be due to a difference in respect for Roma rights prior to NGO development in the early 1990s. In other words, even if we see a difference in discrimination against the Roma in the two towns, this difference might not be due to the fact that one town has organizing that focuses on intergroup contact and the other does not. In fact, it is possible that there is a third factor, such as levels of discrimination in the years before organizing started, that may be responsible for not only the type of organizing that developed in each town but also for the levels of discrimination today. This is omitted variable bias. If this is true, we may be mistakenly attributing an observed difference in discrimination to the organizing, while, in fact, both may be due to differences in how Roma were treated more than 20 years ago.

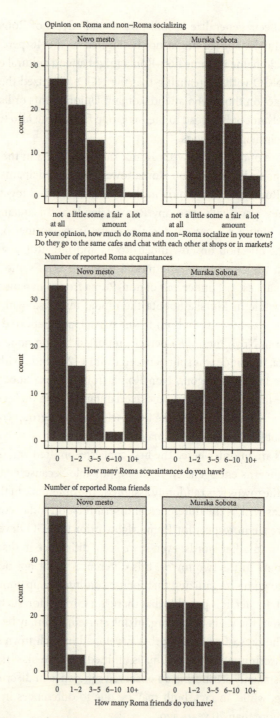

Figure 5.3 How much to Roma and non-Roma interact?

In fact, evidence suggests that Roma in Murska Sobota and Novo mesto received very similar treatment before organizing began in the early 1990s. Immediately before Slovenia declared its independence on June 25, 1991, relations between Roma and non-Roma in Murska Sobota and Novo mesto were as alike as they have ever been. This is largely due to inclusion efforts that stemmed from the strict and uniform Yugoslav policies on minorities, which had by then been in effect for several decades, not only across Slovenia but also across other Yugoslav republics (Šiftar 1989). These efforts sought not only formal but also socio-economic inclusion. While respect for minorities in Yugoslavia was emphasized, those identities gave way to unity; the people "were a colorful nation... but all, including Roma, Yugoslavians" (Baluh 2012). The insistence on a superordinate Yugoslavian identity may have reduced animus felt across ethnic and national lines. Indeed, scholarship in social psychology suggests that emphasizing the saliency of a common, superordinate identity shared by erstwhile outgroup members leads to an improvement in behaviors and attitudes of those members (Gaertner et al. 1993, 2000).

This was complemented by employment policies centered on equality, due to which Romani levels of employment in both towns were quite high during the 1980s (Balažek 2012; Klopčič 2012). Both settlements had Romani kindergartens (Balažek 2012; Horvat-Muc 2011b; Tancer 1997) and a similar level of primary school attendance: low, especially in the higher grades (Šiftar 1989; Tancer 1997). The lack of systematic variation in access to resources like employment and education, coupled with the cross-Yugoslav emphasis on a common identity suggests that Roma/non-Roma relations in Murska Sobota and Novo mesto did not differ considerably. As the transition to a market economy began, Roma were among the first to lose jobs (Balažek 2012; Klopčič 2012; Šiftar 1989), partly due to low levels of education which previously were less of an obstacle to employment (Klopčič 2012). In both towns, this happened particularly early (Šiftar 1989); general losses in employment followed, as did an increase in anti-Roma sentiment. It appears, then, that prior to the development of the NGOs, the Roma in both locations enjoyed a relatively high level of socio-economic security and lived in circumstances that encouraged the expression of a Yugoslav identity. Transition, roughly coinciding with early NGO efforts, brought socio-economic insecurity, freedom in identity expression, and anti-Roma sentiment. Several decades of unified policies on minorities and of equality in employment imposed upon all citizens do not guarantee that attitudes towards the Roma in the early 1990s were the same in Murska Sobota and Novo mesto. But they do weaken the threat of omitted variable bias.

Endogeneity, another peril that stems from non-random assignment of organizing, suggests that the activists in both towns chose to develop their particular types of NGOs because they thought that those would be effective in their respective towns, while any others would not be. Did Jožek Horvat-Muc and Monika Sandreli (Romani Union) focus on intergroup relations and dialogue because they thought that service provision would not work? Does Milena Tudija (Romano Veseli) think that service provision can be effective, but that intergroup contact activities would not help? Interviews with the activists suggest that this is not the case. Instead, the activists chose their respective foci because they are passionate about them. The activists from Murska Sobota, as seen in the quote by Sandreli reproduced above, have been passionate about cross-group activities from the beginning (Horvat-Muc 2011a; Sandreli 2012). Similarly, Milena Tudija engages in service provision because she believes it to be by far the most important cause for Roma (Tudija 2012). While my conversations with the activists suggest that leader idiosyncrasies, and not concerns of feasibility, are behind their choices of NGO types, they do not fully resolve endogeneity concerns. They do, however, alleviate them. Of course, in their choice of focus, the activists might have been influenced by factors of which they were not aware or which they were not deliberately taking into account. Such factors I unfortunately cannot fully guard against.

While non-random assignment of NGO types exposes the pair of towns to omitted variable bias and endogeneity concerns, it also offers an advantage. Instead of measuring discrimination after selectively exposing participants to artificial contact, as most experimental studies do, I capture discriminatory behavior in the wake of contact promotion that developed naturally, on the ground. This is not only a departure from laboratory-based studies that rely on short-term contact situations, but also from field-based studies that manipulate contact situations that last days or even weeks (Green and Wong 2009; Scacco and Warren 2018). In Murska Sobota, Romani Union has been promoting positive intergroup contact for 25 years.

Fully committed to voluntary intergroup contact, the effort by Romani Union is both more subtle and more sustained than experimental assignments. Non-Roma in Murska Sobota are not exposed to positive contact once or twice or for a period of weeks and then left alone. For them, the option of welcoming positive contact is always there. If they have not yet engaged in it themselves, their neighbors or their friends might have; after all, almost every other non-Roma in Murska Sobota knows the NGO well enough to name it. Having had over two decades to spread, the vicarious effects of positive contact may have even reached the more stubborn local non-Roma. In the next section I examine whether this is indeed the case.

Studying only two locations is another weakness of this design. Collecting data from hundreds of locations instead of just two would have been preferable. In this context, however, it was impossible. Although contact-promoting NGOs exist in many communities across the globe, I found very few that promote positive intergroup contact between Roma and non-Roma; those that do are quite different from the NGO in Murska Sobota. The Policy Center for Roma and Minorities in Ferentari, Romania, focuses on Roma and non-Roma children and promotes contact by alternative education activities and soccer. Vzájemné Soužití in Ostrava, Czech Republic, operates in the context of an artificially created Roma/non-Roma neighborhood. In addition to these two NGOs, a third was developing in Prague; when I tried to track it down in 2013, however, I found out that it had not secured the funds necessary to begin operations (Anonymous 2013). The lack of contact-promoting Roma NGOs does not mean that Roma organizing is stagnant—instead, most NGOs in this vibrant sector focus on service provision and rights advocacy. Coupled with a minimal research budget, however, the absence of contact-promoting NGOs did lead to a study design that is necessarily limited. There is no fix for this problem, short of establishing numerous contact-promoting programs for the purpose of more widely testing the contact hypothesis. As this option was not available to me, I urge the reader to exercise caution in drawing broader conclusions on the basis of the findings I present here.

Multiple interaction and the tower game

Unlike in Chapter 4, I will first examine multiple interactions, through the combination of the public goods game and indirect reciprocity. I turn to repeated interactions first because they nudge the participant towards cooper-ating, providing a somewhat easier test of discrimination. Recall the exchange with the rude Parisian baker and a group of tourists. Repeated interactions require us to think about the future early on, as our initial behavior likely affects how our next interactions will go. In the hypothetical example, the foreign pastry aficionados move in across the street from the Parisian baker, who is no longer brusque when she sells them croissants every morning. Likewise, in the tower building videogame, early behavior matters for later success; participants who cooperate early stand to benefit more in the end. Single interactions, in contrast, happen just once—in the hypothetical exchange, the

Parisian baker can be quite rude to tourists, expecting to never see them again. I will return to single interactions at the end of this chapter.

In Chapter 4 I discussed how Roma and non-Roma from Novo mesto played the tower-building videogame.[11] Here, I explore the behaviors of non-Roma from Novo mesto in more detail and compare them to the behaviors of non-Roma from Murska Sobota. As in Chapter 4, the main three games of interest are those in which the decisions made by all avatars are identical, but which assign those avatars different ethnic identifiers. The first is baseline, assigning nothing; the second is coethnic; and the third mixed. The figures I present here partly reproduce the figures from Chapter 4; I again show the behaviors of non-Roma from Novo mesto, but compare them to those of non-Roma from Murska Sobota.

Figure 5.4 shows the average contribution to the tower, along with a 95 percent confidence interval, in each round of the three games. Non-Roma from Novo mesto contributed significantly less in the mixed game than in either the baseline or the coethnic game. Non-Roma from Murska Sobota, however, contributed roughly the same in all three games. Figure 5.5 shows the predicted probabilities of contributing to the tower, again with 95 percent confidence intervals.[12] Non-Roma from Novo mesto contributed their brick with a predicted probability of 0.77 in the coethnic scenario and 0.78 in the baseline (the two are statistically indistinguishable), but with a significantly lower 0.59 in the mixed scenario. In Murska Sobota, there was hardly a difference. Non-Roma there contributed their bricks with a predicted probability of 0.68 in the baseline, and a predicted probability of 0.66 in both the coethnic and the mixed game (the three are statistically indistinguishable).

The evidence presented in Figures 5.4 and 5.5 is quite clear. In the context of the public goods game, non-Roma from Novo mesto discriminated against the Roma, while their counterparts from Murska Sobota did not.

The tower game set up allows me to capture discrimination in another, somewhat different context. This second measure comes from the indirect reciprocity phase, or the reward phase. The reward phase shows the participant one of the other avatars and the way this avatar behaved in the previous tower-building phase. In coethnic and mixed games, but not in the baseline, the reward phase also shows whether this player was Roma or non-Roma. Participants then receive 3 points and have the opportunity to reward this

---

[11] See Chapter 4 for game rules.
[12] These are based on a logit model with individual clustered standard errors that included covariates for gender, age, employment, and education. The model also controlled for the order in which each participant played the randomized games.

Non–Roma tower building behavior in identical baseline,
mixed, and coethnic scenarios (Novo mesto)

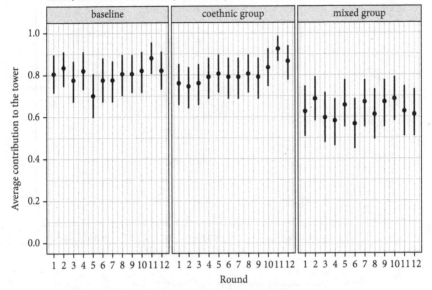

Non–Roma tower building behavior in identical baseline,
mixed, and coethnic scenarios (Murska Sobota)

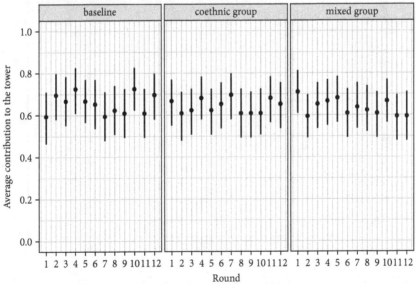

Figure 5.4 This figure presents the average contribution to the tower, along with the 95 percent confidence intervals, that participants made in each round of the three games.

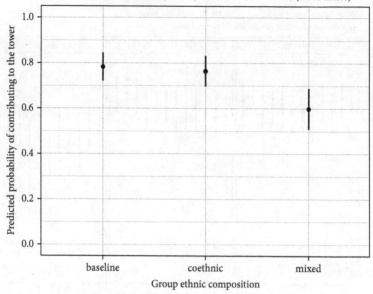

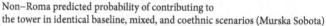

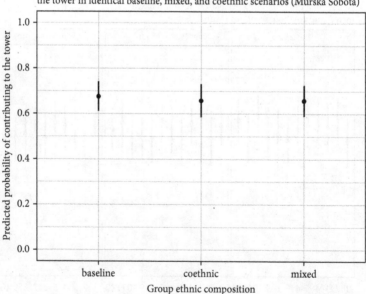

Figure 5.5 This figure presents the predicted probability of contributing to the tower in the first three games, for non-Roma from Novo mesto on the top and for non-Roma from Murska Sobota on the bottom. The predicted probabilities with their 95 percent confidence intervals are based on logit models with individual clustered standard errors that included covariates for gender, age, employment, and education. The model also controlled for the order in which each participant played the randomized games.

player; they can either send those points to the player, who receives 9, or they can keep them. Looking at how participants reward the avatars offers additional insight, as participants are reacting to individual players. Do Roma cooperators get rewarded as often as non-Roma cooperators do? Are Roma defectors denied a reward more often than non-Roma defectors? Figure 5.6 presents the answers to these questions.

In rewarding, non-Roma from Novo mesto discriminated, while non-Roma from Murska Sobota did not (see Figure 5.6). In all cases, rewards for baseline players (no ethnic identifier) were statistically indistinguishable from rewards for non-Roma players. Non-Roma from Novo mesto penalized Roma across the board. They rewarded them less for cooperating than they rewarded non-Roma (predicted probability of 0.64 vs 0.78), and denied them a reward more often than doing the same for non-Roma when they defected (predicted probability of rewarding 0.28 vs 0.41).[13] Non-Roma from Murska Sobota, in contrast, treated Roma and non-Roma the same, whether they cooperated (predicted probability of 0.64 vs 0.63) or defected (predicted probability of 0.48 vs 0.44).[14] While non-Roma from Murska Sobota rewarded impartially, those from Novo mesto rewarded Roma defectors *and* cooperators significantly less, compared to the baseline.

This is meaningful because rewarding is retrospective. When deciding whether to contribute to the tower, a participant may decide on a strategy based on group composition and based on what she and other players have done in the previous rounds. Ultimately, however, she does not know what the other players will do. She is making a guess. There are no guesses in rewarding; the reward phase shows how an avatar behaved in the previous round. When participants reward Roma cooperators less than they reward their non-Roma counterparts, they are not hedging their bets; they are choosing not to reward Roma who have *already* cooperated. This is what non-Roma from Novo mesto did. They also withheld rewards more often from Roma defectors (though this finding loses statistical significance when population covariates are included in the model). Inasmuch as we see withholding rewards as a form of punishment,

---

[13] These differences are all statistically significant in the basic regression ($p < 0.05$), but the difference between rewards to Roma defectors and non-Roma defectors loses significance when population controls are added. The difference between rewards to Roma and non-Roma cooperators remains statistically significant ($p < 0.05$).

[14] Rewarding defectors may seem a curious, and certainly an irrational, habit. For Slovene participants, however, such behavior was commonplace. While playing the game, numerous participants made comments suggesting that this was an act of grace, but also of judgment. Independently and on different occasions, two participants said "I will send this to him nonetheless, perhaps he's going to learn something." Ethnic Slovenes are sometimes stereotyped as holier-than-thou.

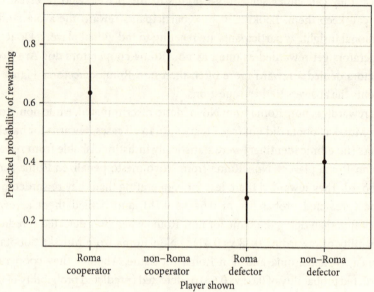

Non–Roma predicted probability of rewarding a
Roma cooperator, non–Roma cooperator, Roma defector,
and a non–Roma defector in the tower game (Novo mesto)

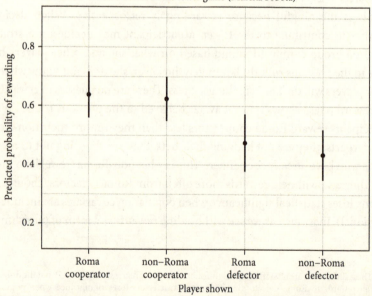

Non–Roma predicted probability of rewarding a
Roma cooperator, non–Roma cooperator, Roma defector,
and a non–Roma defector in the tower game (Murska Sobota)

Figure 5.6 This figure presents the predicted probability of rewarding the player whose avatar is shown in the reward phase. The predicted probabilities with their 95 percent confidence intervals are based on logit models with individual clustered standard errors.

this suggests that in Novo mesto, Roma are seen as more deserving of punishment than non-Roma if they are not cooperating.

This speaks to two crucial points. First, it underscores the presence of anti-Roma animus in Novo mesto. In Chapter 4, I raised this point in reference to the lack of adjustment in tower contributions by non-Roma from Novo mesto. If they were truly only treating Roma differently because they expected Roma to cooperate significantly less, they might have adjusted their behavior upon interacting with Roma who cooperated equally as often as non-Roma. They did not. That this behavior extends to rewarding, which carries no risk, is sobering. It demonstrates the depth of animus felt, dispelling any possibility that disparate treatment is due merely to legitimate expectations of Roma defection.

Second, inconsistent rewarding in Novo mesto speaks to the attribution error. Recall Pettigrew's (1979) explanation: when an ingroup member does something good, we attribute that to an inner quality, but when an outgroup member does the same thing, we attribute it to outside circumstances. With bad actions, we reverse the attributions. Following this logic, we can interpret rewarding behaviors by non-Roma from Novo mesto in the following way. When non-Roma cooperate by engaging in good behavior, non-Roma attribute their behavior to the nature of the group. As favorable behavior is seen as stemming from an inner quality, a reward seems appropriate. In contrast, when Roma cooperate, non-Roma attribute this behavior to an outside circumstance. As their behavior is attributed to the situation and not to a group-based quality, they do not seem as deserving of a reward. Then, when non-Roma defect, their defection is attributed to an outside circumstance; because the disliked behavior is a result of the situation, punishing the individual by withholding a reward seems unduly harsh. But when Roma engage in the same disliked behavior, their defection is attributed to the group as such, and as the group-based inner quality takes the blame, withholding a reward from an individual who supposedly possesses that quality seems deserved.

I have now demonstrated that non-Roma from Novo mesto discriminate in two different contexts, while non-Roma from Murska Sobota discriminate in neither. Two conclusions seem most likely. The first suggests that intergroup contact and dialogue, promoted for over 20 years in Murska Sobota, contributed to lower levels of discrimination against the Roma. The second suggests that ingroup favoritism, expressed by non-Roma from Novo mesto towards their own, is at the root of disparate treatment I have observed in that town.

The second conclusion is certainly possible. I have tried to account for this possibility by including the baseline in the game design; the underlying assumption I made is that the baseline records how a participant would play the game without thinking about the identities of the other players. Following this logic, non-Roma behavior in Novo mesto does not in fact privilege coethnics (baseline and coethnic behaviors are identical), but derogates the Roma. It is also possible, however, that participants played the baseline game with an attitude that unwittingly imagined the other players as coethnics. If an interaction with a coethnic is the default interaction they experience in daily life, it's possible that the baseline game did not truly serve its purpose. If participants assumed they were playing with ingroup members in the baseline, it makes sense that their behaviors in baseline and coethnic scenarios match. Adding another ethnic group to the game would have addressed this issue, but it was practically untenable.[15] It is something to consider in the future.

For all that, what I have observed in Novo mesto is without a doubt discrimination. Discriminatory behavior often manifests itself as a result of ingroup favoritism, and not outgroup hostility. Greenwald and Pettigrew (2014) understand "ingroup favoritism as not just *a* cause but as the *prime* cause of American discrimination" (670, emphasis in original). While Greenwald and Pettigrew ground their finding in research on racism in the US, Balliet et al. (2014) take a more expansive look. Performing a meta-analysis on 212 studies of costly cooperation with ingroup members, strangers, and/or outgroup members, they find that intergroup discrimination is indeed driven by ingroup favoritism. This means that discrimination tends not to be derived from hatred of the outgroup, but instead from favoring one's ingroup. The results from the videogame suggest that this is the case here as well, though participant answers to a few survey questions also offer evidence of outgroup derogation. I turn to those later in this chapter.

One might next point out that in the mixed game, non-Roma in both towns contribute bricks to the tower in at about the same rate and that therefore, Roma in Novo mesto and Murska Sobota are treated the same. Non-Roma contributions in the mixed game are indeed statistically indistinguishable from one another, but this does not mean that Roma were treated the same way in both towns. In Murska Sobota, Roma and non-Roma were treated *equally*, even if overall levels of non-Roma cooperation in the coethnic game were lower there than in Novo mesto. By contrast, in Novo mesto Roma and non-

---

[15] With a minimal research budget and a commitment to avoid deception I was unable to add another set of game scenarios (e.g., including ethnic Croatian players in addition to Slovene Roma and non-Roma) to the design as such an addition would have substantially increased the number of participants. Moreover, adding another set of games would have lengthened the time of participation, likely resulting in some participants quitting before finishing the games.

Roma were treated *differently*. As an illustration, think of two teachers, in classrooms where half of the students are White and half are Black, and they all performed identically on a test. The first teacher gives everyone a B. The second teachers gives the Black students a B and the White students an A. The second teacher is clearly discriminatory. Even if Roma got the same treatment regardless of where they lived, they were still discriminated against in Novo mesto, but not in Murska Sobota.

In the sections that follow, I further address the distinction between possible ingroup favoritism and outgroup derogation in Novo mesto, as well as the connection between NGO action in Murska Sobota and the lack of discrimination there. As this study did not randomly assign some participants to contact experiences while leaving others without, it is impossible to claim with certainty that contact caused the lack of disparate treatment to manifest in the case of Murska Sobota. Asking a few more questions of the participants, however, gives me an opportunity to gain more insight. I thus explore whether being familiar with the NGO in Murska Sobota is related to treating Roma equally, whether discriminatory behavior in Novo mesto is linked to open prejudice, and whether intolerance towards other groups there is linked to discrimination.

Taking a closer look

The first question I asked the participants is whether they are familiar with Roma NGOs in their respective towns, and whether they attend any events that these NGOs put on. Scholarship on intergroup contact and prejudice suggests that direct, vicarious, and even contextual positive intergroup contact might all decrease prejudice, at least for the majority. Still, direct positive intergroup contact is likely to result in stronger effects, which might appear sooner as there is no need for them to transfer from one individual to another. Asking participants a set of questions on local NGOs that address Roma issues resulted in varied answers, presented in Figures 5.7, 5.8 and 5.9.

The simplest question posed, whether they knew any such organizations in their respective towns, resulted in a fairly balanced answer as 64 percent of non-Roma from Novo mesto and 60 percent of non-Roma from Murska Sobota claimed that they did (top panel of Figure 5.7). Asking participants to name the NGOs clarifies the unusually high number of yeses given in response to the first question. In Novo mesto, where Romano Veseli engages in service provision, only 1.5 percent of participants were able to name it; in Murska

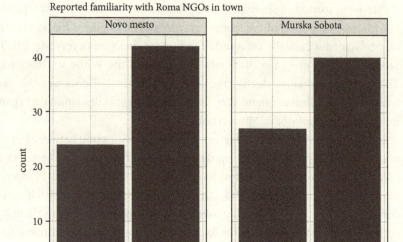

Reported familiarity with Roma NGOs in town

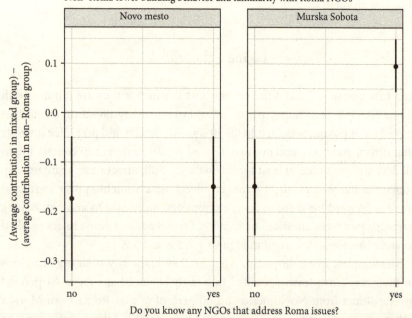

Non–Roma tower building behavior and familiarity with Roma NGOs

Figure 5.7 The top panel of this figure shows non-Roma familiarity with Roma NGOs in both towns. The answers from Novo mesto are not realistic (see the main text). The bottom panel plots claims of familiarity along with the mean difference in average participant contributions to the tower in the mixed and coethnic games.

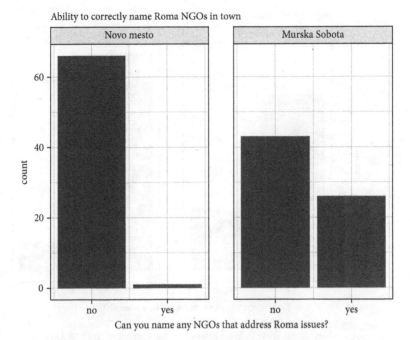

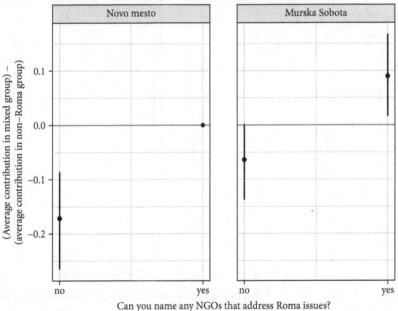

Figure 5.8 The top panel of this figure shows non-Roma ability to correctly name a Roma NGO in town. The bottom panel plots correct naming of the NGO along with the mean difference in average participant contributions to the tower in the mixed and coethnic games.

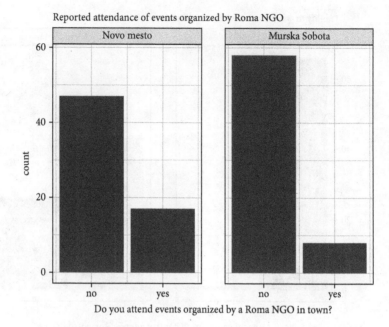

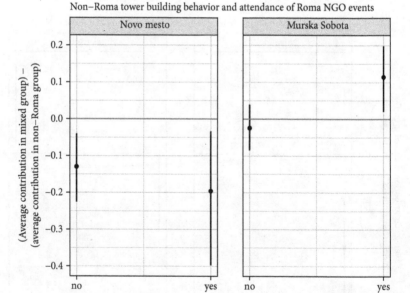

Figure 5.9 The top panel of this figure shows non-Roma reported attendance of Roma NGO events in town. The bottom panel plots reported attendance along with the mean difference in average participant contributions to the tower in the mixed and coethnic games.

Sobota, 38 percent could do the same (top panel of Figure 5.8). Finally, I asked participants whether they had attended any events organized by the organization they had in mind. In Murska Sobota, non-Roma can and do attend a range of events; the largest, "Gypsy night," draws over 300 people (Sandreli 2012). Among the participants in my sample, 12 percent said they had (top panel of Figure 5.9). While this number is not large, it is nonetheless substantial. I recruited participants using random sampling; if we were to generalize to the town population based on these answers, we could reasonably say that about 3000 people from Murska Sobota have been directly exposed to voluntary positive intergroup contact through the NGO.

Twenty-seven percent of Novo mesto participants reported attending an NGO event, a response I consider non-credible for several reasons, not least that Romano Veseli does not host intergroup contact events.[16] For reasons that will become clear in the coming paragraphs, the actual number for Novo mesto does not ultimately matter.

Did direct contact make a difference at the level of the individual? In the tower game, all participants played all the games. I therefore have information on how each individual played in the baseline, the coethnic, and the mixed scenario.[17] Since the avatars play identical strategies, I can capture whether individuals changed their strategies when the ethnic composition of the group changed. The bottom panels of Figures 5.7, 5.8, and 5.9 present this information. On their y-axes, these plots present the differences in the

---

[16] First, the NGO in Novo mesto chiefly operates in the settlement, where non-Roma do not go. Second, only one participant was actually able to name the NGO. During my interactions with non-Roma that included general and vague discussions of my work, a common question they asked me was whether I had ever been to a settlement. In Novo mesto, several asked this question with apprehension and looked quite shocked by my answer, which was always the same: "Of course I go to the settlements, but only with my consultant." Non-Roma in Novo mesto seldom venture into the settlement, except in the context of work or perhaps if visiting a friend, which is rare. Roma tend to be quite attentive and generally, upon spotting a stranger, inquire as to his purpose for the visit to the settlement. For a newcomer, this can be unnerving. In my visits to the settlement, we have often been spotted in a manner of seconds, not minutes, but I have always felt very welcome there. Because relations are contentious, non-Roma have little interest in visiting; Roma vigilance and reports of occasional violence only act as additional deterrents. If a non-Roma were to visit, it would likely be under the auspices of the NGO, but since only one participant in the Novo mesto sample was able to name it, this seems rather unlikely. Most participants who named an "NGO" referred to the municipal office, and a couple specifically mentioned the Romani representative who serves in municipal government. The other commonly identified "organization" was an NGO for volunteer work, which is not a Roma NGO and deals with volunteering more generally. A final NGO, identified by two participants, is a non-Roma NGO that aims to mobilize *against* the local Roma community, on account of alleged Roma crime and poor neighborly relations. As all participants who named an NGO, with the exception of one, named a different entity, they likely also took part in events organized by that different entity. Their answers, with the exception of one, can therefore not be considered valid.

[17] Recall that the mixed scenario is composed of 4 Roma and 4 non-Roma players. For non-Roma participants, the game therefore has 4 Roma avatars and 3 non-Roma avatars.

average amounts contributed to the tower in each game. The basic difference is calculated by subtracting the average amount contributed in the coethnic game from the average amount contributed in the mixed game for each participant. These averages of individual differences are then averaged again, based on the participant subgroup presented in the plot—Figure 5.7, for example, presents the means of average differences separately for non-Roma who said they knew a Roma NGO and for non-Roma who did not.

The values for the average differences in contributions range from −1 to 1. If a participant played the same way on average—that is, contributed the same number of bricks to the tower, on average, in both coethnic and mixed scenarios—the value of this variable is 0. This is intuitive: 0 means no difference. If participants, on average, contributed more in the mixed scenario, then the value of this variable is positive, between 0 and 1. Finally, if participants on average contributed less in the mixed scenario than they did in the coethnic scenario, the value of this variable is negative, between 0 and −1. The means for each subgroup are presented with 95 percent confidence intervals.

Before discussing the plots, a word of caution. Participant characteristics, as captured by the survey, are not randomly assigned. This holds for their knowledge and behaviors in the context of the contact-promoting NGO, as well as all of their other attributes. It is therefore impossible to infer any causality from the figures that plot game behaviors against participant covariates. These figures are suggestive.

The bottom panel of Figure 5.7 presents the means of average differences in contributions for non-Roma who indicated they knew a Roma NGO and for those who did not. Non-Roma from Novo mesto contributed significantly less in a mixed scenario than in a coethnic scenario, whether or not they reported a (dubious) familiarity with a Roma NGO. That non-Roma from Novo mesto misidentified the NGO is therefore interesting, but not problematic. They discriminated either way. In Murska Sobota, however, there was a difference between the two groups. Non-Roma who said they did not know a Roma NGO contributed less in the mixed scenario; again, the mean for this group is below 0. The mean for non-Roma who reported that they knew a Roma NGO, in contrast, is above 0, indicating that this group of non-Roma actually contributed more in the mixed scenario.

The difference between Novo mesto and Murska Sobota is already compelling, as non-Roma from Novo mesto discriminate across the board. Even more compelling, perhaps, is the gap between non-Roma in Murska Sobota. Plotting the relationship between the average difference in contributions to the tower and the ability to name the NGO, or reported attendance of NGO events, confirms this finding. Figure 5.8 shows the average difference in contributions between those who knew the NGO and those who did not; non-Roma in Murska Sobota who correctly named the NGO decidedly contributed more in the mixed game, while those who did not contributed equally. Participants from Murska Sobota who said they attended NGO events also contributed more in the mixed games; those who did not contributed equally in mixed and coethnic games (see Figure 5.9). Non-Roma in Novo mesto, again, discriminated across the board.

The behavior of non-Roma in Murska Sobota is noteworthy. For someone who strives to improve Roma/non-Roma relations, a result of equal treatment is a feat in itself. To find that non-Roma who are familiar with the NGO try harder to cooperate in a mixed setting than in a coethnic setting suggests remarkable success and offers support for the contact hypothesis. Yet because neither the knowledge of the NGO nor the attendance of its events were randomly assigned, excessive optimism is unwarranted. Those who choose to attend the events of a contact-promoting NGO might be prone to treat Roma as equals no matter what (though this seems less likely to hold for non-Roma who say they do not attend, but who know the NGO and were likely vicariously exposed to its efforts, and they, too, contributed more in the mixed game). While I cannot say for certain that contact-promoting NGO action is behind the difference in discriminatory behaviors of non-Roma in Novo mesto and Murska Sobota, these findings are promising—even if merely suggestive.

Looking at open prejudice

If non-Roma from Murska Sobota no longer discriminate against the Roma, does this mean their prejudice is gone as well? The problematic nature of questions that openly probe for prejudice limits my ability to get to the bottom of this. As I discussed in Chapter 4, some people may not answer such questions honestly, resulting in my failure to capture prejudice they may nonetheless harbor. I can, however, speak to the segment of the population that is willing to openly express prejudice—under the condition of anonymity. In fact, many Slovene non-Roma feel no compunction about speaking their minds when it comes to Roma. Numerous participants blatantly violated the norm of anonymity after they completed the survey to explain in more detail how they felt.

In brief, open prejudice persists in both towns, but there is more of it in Novo mesto. In what follows, I first discuss participants' answers to an open-ended question. I then discuss the relationship between open prejudice and discriminatory behavior, which offers insight into how intergroup contact might be taking effect in Murska Sobota.

What bothers you most about the Roma?

Participants' answers to this bold[18] and somewhat leading[19] question are quite revealing. They demonstrate that on condition of anonymity, non-Roma from these two towns in Slovenia are quite willing to express prejudice. For example, a participant from Novo mesto was bothered that Roma

> [b]eg from house to house despite social benefits and government child support; that they steal; that they engage in illegitimate business (drugs, weapons). That they don't work; they are not clean; that they don't educate themselves. And the state gives them a lot without them having to do much in return.

Another, also from Novo mesto, took issue with

> [b]egging, dumpster diving and leaving trash lying all around; laziness/unwillingness to work, because he [a Roma person] expects the state to support them financially, pay their bills and take care of their dwellings; irresponsible use of the financial aid obtained; violence, engagement in crime; improper maintenance and filth (both bodily and of their houses and the surroundings).

A third, from Murska Sobota, wrote

> they know about rights, of which they take advantage, but are not aware of responsibilities.

[18] While asking such a blunt question may be inappropriate in some contexts, Slovenes are typically not bothered by directness. None of the participants complained about the question and most were quite comfortable providing blunt answers. Participants were free to skip any question they did not wish to answer; only 35 participants (about 26 percent of the sample) opted to skip this one.

[19] While this question may be leading, it also sounds quite absurd to a person who is not prejudiced. In fact, the obvious answer such a person might give is "nothing bothers me about the Roma"; for good measure, they might also complain about the question. While I did not receive any complaints about the question, a high number of participants (25) answered "nothing," and 4 more gave specific answers as to why nothing bothered them. Overall, "nothing" was one of the two most common answers given; the other one was that Roma "refuse to work."

A fourth, also from Murska Sobota, was bothered by Roma women:

> [t]hat they knock on doors begging, while their clothes and make-up are impeccable (nice), with small children.

Categorizing the answers into 21 categories reveals substantial overlap between the two towns on some issues, and substantial divergence on others (see Figures 5.10 and 5.11 for an illustration).[20] Non-Roma from Novo mesto and Murska Sobota both wrote that Roma refuse to work, that they lie and beg; that they are cunning and violent; that they have no interest in education, and that they behave inappropriately in public. Consider the following matching statements. A participant from Murska Sobota wrote "they don't like to work and they lie," while a participant from Novo mesto was bothered by "crime, thefts, dishonesty, refusal to work." In Murska Sobota, someone simply wrote "cunning," while someone in Novo mesto explained further: "they are cunning, you can't trust everything they say." A participant in Murska Sobota was bothered by Roma "ringing the bell, [at] home, intruding into private space without an invitation," while one from Novo mesto felt similarly about Roma "encroaching onto the property of others." While there is remarkable overlap on a subset of mentioned issues, non-Roma from the two towns did not agree on everything.

The statements from the two towns diverge in two ways. First, participants from Murska Sobota were less critical. They were more likely to skip this question; of the 35 who did not answer the question, 26 were from Murska Sobota (there are a total of 136 non-Roma participants). Participants from Murska Sobota were also more likely to write that "nothing" bothers them (15, compared to 10 from Novo mesto), or that "Roma are no different from non-Roma" (3, compared to one from Novo mesto). One participant from Murska Sobota perceptively wrote

> I don't know them enough to have something specific to be bothered by. A lot of Roma are disadvantaged because of a hundred years of discrimination. If the attitudes of non-Roma towards Roma changed, it would be easier for everyone.

[20] The negative categories were: steal; lie; workless; cunning; extorting rights; loud; welfare dependent; disinterest in education; disinterest in being included in society; violence; unclean; crime; begging; inappropriate behavior; dumpster diving; property intrusion; no respect for public goods and values; and distrust towards non-Roma. The neutral categories were: nothing bothers me; Roma are the same as non-Roma; and I have no experience with Roma.

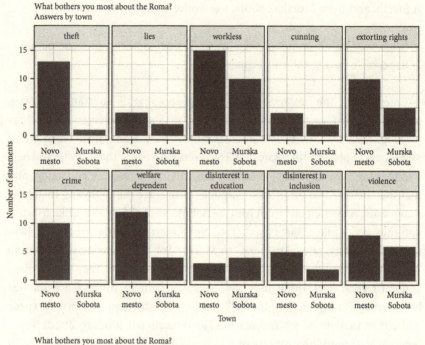

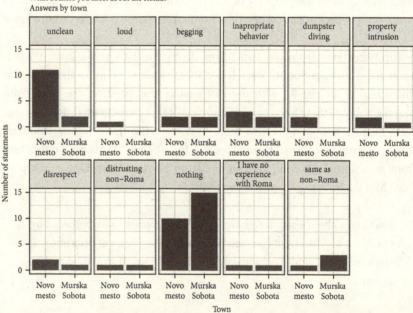

Figure 5.10 This figure shows non-Roma answers to the question "What bothers you most about the Roma?", by town. The answers are categorized into 21 categories. If a participant mentioned several issues, each issue is counted separately in the appropriate category.

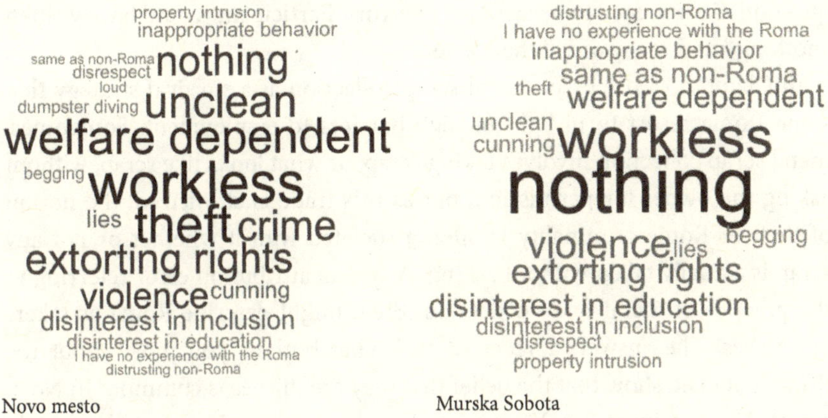

property intrusion
inappropriate behavior
same as non-Roma **nothing**
disrespect
loud
dumpster diving **unclean**
welfare dependent
begging **workless**
lies **theft** crime
extorting rights
violence cunning
disinterest in inclusion
disinterest in education
I have no experience with the Roma
distrusting non-Roma

distrusting non-Roma
I have no experience with the Roma
inappropriate behavior
theft **same as non-Roma**
welfare dependent
unclean
cunning **workless**
nothing
violence lies begging
extorting rights
disinterest in education
disinterest in inclusion
disrespect
property intrusion

Novo mesto   Murska Sobota

Figure 5.11 This figure shows non-Roma answers to the question "What bothers you most about the Roma?", by town. Novo mesto is on the left; Murska Sobota is on the right.

In contrast, none of the participants from Novo mesto acknowledged any sort of discrimination against the Roma, although one did lament "they trust me less than they could." Overall, participants from Novo mesto were far more disapproving of Roma; counting the total number of times each of the 18 negative categories was mentioned, participants from Novo mesto together mentioned something negative 108 times, while participants from Murska Sobota mentioned something negative 45 times.

Second, participants from Novo mesto were much more likely to write that Roma are thieves, that they are unclean, that they exploit their rights, that they receive excessive social assistance from the state, and that they have no interest in being included in society (a refusal to assimilate). While 10 participants from Novo mesto wrote that Roma were criminals, no participant from Murska Sobota mentioned crime. That non-Roma from Novo mesto had more than twice as many negative things to say about Roma provides additional evidence that there, mistreatment of Roma is at least partly due to animus.

The responses to "What bothers you most about the Roma?" speak to the exclusion cycle in two ways. Non-Roma answers quite clearly demonstrate the presence of anti-Roma culture and discourse in both towns, though more so in Novo mesto, and thus provide evidence for anti-minority culture. By asking participants "What bothers you most *about the Roma*?" (emphasis not in survey) the question also targets the practice of assigning survival behaviors to the very nature of Roma: committing the attribution error. Answers to this question did not need to be attribution errors. Participants could have written "nothing," and many did. Others erred.

In Chapter 3 I discussed metal scrap collection as a survival strategy that some Roma resort to in light of high barriers to employment. Sometimes, metal scrap collection involves taking scrap, or what looks like scrap, without asking the owner for permission, but as this trade is ethnicized, the notion of theft or Roma criminality is often associated with it whether or not any scrap is actually taken without asking. A typical attribution error referring to the practice of metal scrap collection, then, might describe Roma as takers or thieves. The answers I received to "What bothers you most about the Roma?" indeed show that the belief that they are thieves is common. In Novo mesto, 13 participants, or 20 percent, thought so; but in Murska Sobota, only one did. The belief that Roma are thieves, however, is not the primary way in which the attribution error related to discrimination in employment is expressed. Instead, non-Roma believe that Roma refuse to work. This was the most commonly identified "bothersome" Roma characteristic in both towns. In Novo mesto, 15 participants wrote it down, while in Murska Sobota, 10 did. Participants were remarkably precise in their language. The consistent use of a single, unusual word ("nedelo") lays the responsibility for not having a job entirely at the feet of Roma. This word carries a very specific negative, judgmental connotation and roughly translates as "workless". It is not usually used to refer to unemployment, and so tends not to be a part of common parlance in Slovenia. In fact, I have only ever heard it used in the context of the Roma. Precisely because it is not commonly used otherwise, its recurrence in my surveys suggests that the idea that Roma refuse to work is quite salient in the two towns.[21]

Low levels of education among Roma were similarly attributed to the Roma themselves, with no recognition given to discrimination in education. Two participants independently wrote that "they [Roma] do not educate themselves"; another was bothered by the fact that "they live from social assistance, without any interest in getting educated." Overall, 3 participants from Novo mesto and 4 from Murska Sobota were bothered by Roma "disinterest in" education.

Roma reliance on social assistance, a survival strategy that is a clear consequence of barriers to education and employment, was another characteristic commonly attributed to the Roma themselves and not their circumstances.

---

[21] If they did not wish to assign judgment, participants might have said "nezaposlenost," which is commonly used and means unemployment.

In Novo mesto, 12 participants were bothered by their excessive reliance on social assistance; in Murska Sobota, 4 agreed. Combining several errors, one participant from Novo mesto was bothered by the fact "that they steal, that they lie, that they receive social assistance instead of putting in some effort and working honestly." Another wrote that "they do nothing themselves, they expect to be entirely supported by the state, state institutions." A third participant was bothered by "[t]heir refusal to work and abuse of social assistance by the state." There is a degree of rancor that accompanies some of the statements on excessive reliance on state assistance; the participant I just quoted called it "abuse," as did several others. Another wrote that "the rules that hold for other citizens don't hold for them and they abuse that;" while a third was bothered because they "extort rights."[22] Although reliance on social assistance is a frequent topic in the media, not a single non-Roma who brought up social assistance mentioned that non-Roma also engage in this practice. Instead, their answers suggest that this practice is exclusively ethnicized.

Answers to open-ended questions offer a glimpse into the thoughts of participants. Inviting complexity, such questions produce answers that do not easily lend themselves to a quick snapshot. While they present a diverse range of attribution errors, they do not tell us how many participants are apt to agree with any particular one. To complement the varied answers just discussed, I asked participants to answer a question designed to pin down their level of agreement with a commonly committed attribution error regarding barriers to employment. I asked them—after they answered a more general question—to what extent they agreed with the following statement: "Most Roma earn a living by engaging in criminal activity, even though they have other options." This statement identifies a rather extreme survival strategy and specifies that engaging in this activity is purely a matter of choice. It attributes engagement in crime to Roma and their preferences, not their circumstances. In light of Roma exclusion from the formal labor market, this statement seems awfully unfair, and frankly, absurd.[23]

Still, in Novo mesto the modal response was "strongly agree." Overall, 62 percent of participants there either agreed or strongly agreed with the statement. In Murska Sobota, most participants who answered this question chose "neutral", and only 16 percent of them agreed or strongly agreed with

[22] This participant likely referred to the idea that Roma get too many special favors; another participant wrote that Roma "leverage their rights too well," likely speaking about excessive reliance on social assistance and alleged crimes that go unpunished.

[23] See Chapter 6 for specifics on exclusion from formal employment in Novo mesto and Murska Sobota.

it.[24] This suggests that non-Roma from both towns are apt to commit this particular attribution error, but that those from Novo mesto appear to commit it far more often.

My examination of open prejudice thus far demonstrates that while prejudice persists in both towns, there appears to be much less of it Murska Sobota, the intergroup-contact town. The attribution error is likewise committed in both towns, but to a much greater degree in Novo mesto. In the following section I examine discriminatory behavior together with open prejudice to explore the puzzling nature of people in Murska Sobota who appear prejudiced yet do not discriminate.

As if it weren't there

"The Roma cannot be trusted" is among the most common expressions about Roma that I have encountered. It derives from the stereotypes of Roma as cheaters, thieves, and takers. I used this phrase to probe participants about prejudice, asking them to indicate how much they agreed with it. The top panel of Figure 5.12 shows the answers. In Murska Sobota, 28 percent of participants either agreed or strongly agreed with this statement. The modal response was neutral, while 25 percent either disagreed or strongly disagreed. It is jarring to see 1 out of 4 participants in Murska Sobota agree with this claim, especially as it leaves no room for doubt—the claim does not state that *some* Roma *may* not be trusted, but instead quite clearly that none of them can be trusted. The answers from Novo mesto are even more unsettling. There, 62 percent, or almost 2 out of 3 participants either agreed or strongly agreed with this sweeping claim. 26 percent were neutral and the remaining 12 percent either disagreed or strongly disagreed. Answers to this question confirm what the free-form answers presented in the previous section suggested: non-Roma from both towns are openly prejudiced against the Roma, but those in Novo mesto are much more so.

How does open prejudice translate into action? In Novo mesto, very well, but in Murska Sobota, not at all. The bottom panel of Figure 5.12 reveals that in Murska Sobota, there is no relationship between a non-Roma's belief that

---

[24] While 63 participants from Novo mesto answered this question, only 48 participants from Murska Sobota did the same. This question followed a more general question of whether participants thought Roma in their town had a bad reputation. Those who answered affirmatively (almost all in the case of Novo mesto and almost three-quarters in the case of Murska Sobota) were then invited to answer this question.

Roma cannot be trusted and her average contributions to the tower.[25] Even those who strongly agreed with this prejudiced statement did not discriminate. In fact, all but one group contributed to the tower equally; the group that did not (strongly disagree), contributed more in the mixed scenario. The disconnect between open prejudice and discriminatory behavior in Murska Sobota is even more conspicuous when we consider the clear relationship between the two in Novo mesto. There, participants who agreed and strongly agreed with the prejudiced statement contributed significantly less to the tower in the mixed game. As in Murska Sobota, those who disagreed or were neutral contributed the same amount, and those who strongly disagreed contributed more in the mixed scenario. In Novo mesto, then, participants who were openly prejudiced discriminated, while those who were not openly prejudiced did not. The two contrasting findings speak to how intergroup contact might take effect: not by eliminating prejudice and stereotypes entirely, but by preventing people from acting on them.

Indeed, prejudice does not always lead to discrimination. Consider overt racism and vote choice in the US. Mendelberg (2001) writes that voters in the US tend to be much more susceptible to implicit racism than its explicit alternative. This is not necessarily because they are any less prejudiced. As racism has become socially unacceptable, people who are prejudiced wish neither to be seen as racist nor to see themselves as racist. To avoid this, they might conceal their prejudiced preferences by, say, not voting for an explicitly racist candidate. If, however, a candidate were to make implicitly racial claims—speaking about welfare or crime in the inner cities—that can be interpreted as orthogonal to race, voters who are prejudiced might vote for him, especially if they believe that their preferences on crime and welfare have nothing to do with race.

Following a similar logic, non-Roma from Murska Sobota may curb their disparate treatment of Roma because discrimination seems less socially acceptable there. With increasing rates of voluntary positive intergroup contact ensured by the NGO, such contact was more commonly observed and norms about group interactions, or people's perceptions of such norms, might have changed. As the norm of positive intergroup contact became more salient, discrimination might have become a less socially desirable alternative. A person can follow new norms of intergroup interaction even if she is prejudiced, and over time, her prejudice may even abate (Olson and

<hr />

[25] The correlation between the two is very low (-0.07) and not statistically significant ($p=.60$). In Novo mesto, the correlation between the two is moderate ($-.50$) and statistically significant ($p<0.001$).

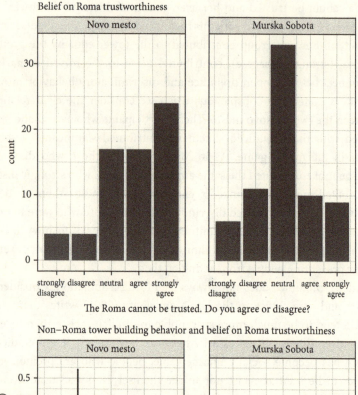

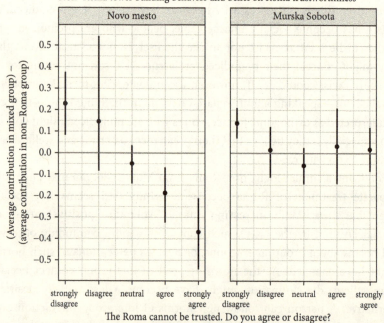

Figure 5.12 The top panel of this figure shows non-Roma agreement with the statement "the Roma cannot be trusted," by town. The bottom panel plots agreement with this statement along with the mean difference in average participant contributions to the tower in the mixed and coethnic games.

Stone 2005). In fact, research in social psychology suggests that attitude change often follows behavioral change, and not the other way around (Olson and Stone 2005). Linking this to intergroup contact, Tropp and Pettigrew (2011) write that "optimally structured intergroup contact offers a means of behavior modification, with new behavior leading to changed attitudes" (90).

Having observed and captured open prejudice and discriminatory behaviors in the two towns, I can conclude that discrimination against the Roma in Novo mesto is not merely a case of ingroup favoritism. Anti-Roma sentiment I recorded in both towns, but in Novo mesto especially, demonstrates open derogation of Roma. While this evidence by no means proves that voluntary positive intergroup contact in Murska Sobota eliminated discrimination, it does suggest that it might have helped. As positive cross-group interactions became more normatively salient there, non-Roma were perhaps encouraged to avoid acting on their prejudice and, eventually, to express less of it.

But what if ... ?

What if I found greater discrimination in Novo mesto because non-Roma there are more intolerant in general—that is, of all outgroups and not just of the Roma—and not because the town lacks a contact promoting NGO? This is one of two concerns that pose a serious challenge to the findings; both are addressed in this section, starting with this one. The information I presented in the matching section suggests that non-Roma in the two towns do not appear to differ substantially in their general level of intolerance. To further test for this possibility, I explored how participants in both towns felt about a completely different outgroup. If the findings were indeed picking up general anti-outgroup sentiment and not merely anti-Roma sentiment, then participants' attitudes towards a different outgroup should match up with their discriminatory behavior against the Roma; that is, a generally intolerant participant should also discriminate against the Roma. If however, discrimination against the Roma is related to Roma-specific intolerance, there should be no relationship between how participants feel about a different outgroup and how they treat Roma.

To establish how the participants felt about a different outgroup, I asked them to indicate the extent to which they were bothered by "Slovenia potentially receiving several hundred African migrants."[26] Besides Roma, African

---

[26] This number is based on widely publicized EU refugee quotas.

migrants were at the time of data collection the most visible outgroup in the otherwise fairly homogenous Slovenia. I chose this particular question because Slovenia is not a destination country[27] and sentiment about someone who is passing through might be different from sentiment about someone who is posed to stay. I chose to use the word "migrants" and not "refugees" because I wanted to avoid underscoring that the people arriving were victims, chiefly because Roma are generally not seen as such. This should result in a cleaner comparison. Figure 5.13 presents how participants from both towns reacted to this statement (top panel) and how those reactions stack up against their behavior in the tower game (bottom panel).

The top panel of Figure 5.13 shows that participants from the two towns felt quite similarly about the migrants who might stay. The modal responses in both towns were "not at all bothered," while the second most likely answers in both were bothered "some." Quite a few participants were "very bothered" or bothered "a fair amount"—18 percent in Novo mesto and 25 percent in Murska Sobota. The similar overall response to this question suggests that non-Roma from Novo mesto were not substantially more prejudiced when it came to a different outgroup (for their anti-Roma sentiment, take another look at Figures 5.10 and 5.11).

Further, the bottom panel of Figure 5.13 shows that in *both* towns participants who were "very bothered" about migrants contributed equivalent average amounts to the tower. In Murska Sobota, participants contributed equivalent average amounts regardless of how they felt about migrants. And, notably, participants from Novo mesto who were "not at all bothered" about migrants still discriminated against the Roma. These findings therefore not only suggest that participants from Novo mesto are not generally more intolerant than those from Murska Sobota, but also show that in both towns, prejudice against the migrant outgroup is unrelated to discrimination against the Roma.[28] This again suggests that in Novo mesto, the differential treatment of Roma is not merely due to coethnic favoritism among the non-Roma—which would more likely result in generalized intolerance towards all outgroups—but is instead a result of Roma-specific animus.

The second challenging question is this: what if I found greater discrimination in Novo mesto because non-Roma there have had worse personal experiences with Roma? This is a tough question. Given that non-Roma

---

[27] Refugees traveling north along the Balkan route typically travelled to Germany and beyond.
[28] The correlation between the reactions to migrants and the average difference in contributions to the mixed and coethnic games was 0.02 (p=0.91) in Novo mesto and 0.03 (p=0.84) in Murska Sobota.

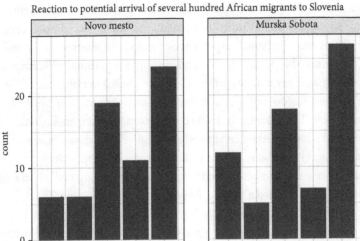

Reaction to potential arrival of several hundred African migrants to Slovenia

On a scale from 1 to 5, where 1 is very bothered at all and 5 is not at all bothered, how bothered are you with Slovenia potentially receiving several hundred African migrants?

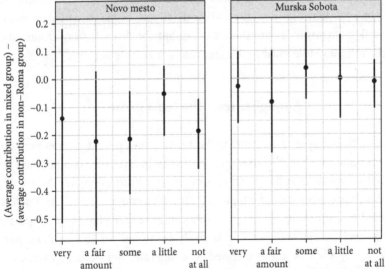

Non–Roma tower building behavior and reaction to potential arrival of several hundred African migrants to Slovenia

On a scale from 1 to 5, where 1 is very bothered at all and 5 is not at all bothered, how bothered are you with Slovenia potentially receiving several hundred African migrants?

Figure 5.13 The top panel of this figure shows non-Roma reactions to the potential arrival of migrants, by town. The bottom panel plots these reactions along with the mean difference in average participant contributions to the tower in the mixed and coethnic games.

in Novo mesto discriminate against the Roma and that mistreatment spurs survival strategies, Roma/non-Roma relations there are almost certainly worse. Unpleasant personal experiences related to intergroup interaction might therefore be unavoidable, and in light of those, discrimination motivated by bad personal experiences seems almost certain. Yet while that might be true, we do not know if bad personal experiences are linked to discrimination. To explore this, I asked non-Roma participants whether they had ever had a bad experience with Roma. Figure 5.14 shows how many did (top panel), and how that is related to their tower contributions.

In Novo mesto, 44 percent of participants report having had a bad experience with Roma; in Murska Sobota, 24 percent report the same. The difference is not surprising. More unexpected, perhaps, is the finding that having a bad experience does not appear to matter. In Novo mesto, participants who reported having had a bad experience contributed significantly less in the mixed game, but so did those who had no bad experiences. Both discriminated, and to a very similar degree. In Murska Sobota, there was no difference either, as both types of participants contributed essentially equivalent amounts in both games.[29] These findings, then, suggest that discrimination observed in Novo mesto was in fact unrelated to bad personal experiences with Roma.[30] What sorts of unpleasant experiences did non-Roma report? Most described theft, some vandalism, and some childhood bullying. Some were preposterous. One participant wrote "I gave them a dress, but she threw it away around the next corner; they stole mushrooms from my car and ate our dog."

A tougher test: The trust game

Earlier in this chapter I wrote that the tower game provides an easier test of discrimination than the trust game. This is because the combination of repeated interactions and indirect reciprocity (rewarding) nudges the participant towards cooperation; first, participants who cooperate early and defect late stand to gain more—as long as they can get other players to cooperate as well—and second, cooperating is likely rewarded. In this context, participants may then be more inclined to cooperate, not because they don't want to discriminate, but rather because they want to get the most out of

---

[29] The 24 percent of participants with a history of bad experiences in Murska Sobota did contribute more to the coethnic group, on average, but the difference was not statistically significant at the 5 percent level.

[30] In Novo mesto, the correlation was -0.08 (p=0.53); in Murska Sobota it was -0.16 (p=0.2).

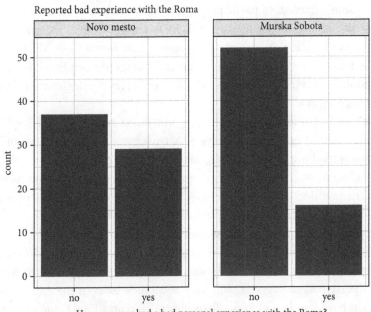

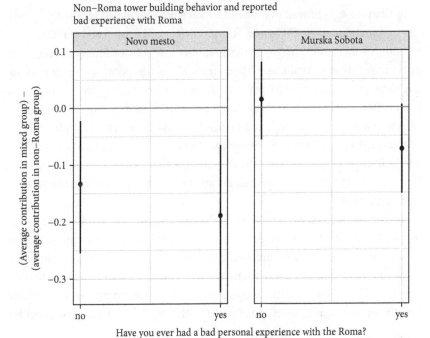

Figure 5.14 The top panel of this figure shows non-Roma reports of bad personal experience with Roma, by town. The bottom panel plots reports of bad experience along with the mean difference in average participant contributions to the tower in the mixed and coethnic games.

the game. Granted, as participants from both towns played the tower game, any difference between the two is likely to emerge despite the game encouraging cooperation. Nonetheless, to subject non-Roma from Murska Sobota to a tougher test—one that does not encourage cooperation—I asked 101 randomly sampled participants in each town to play the single interaction trust game (Berg et al. 1995).[31]

Crudely, I wanted to see whether non-Roma senders would send less to Roma than to non-Roma receivers. A trust game sender is better off if she sends something to the receiver, but only if she is paired with a receiver who is willing to send enough back. If, however, she does not trust her receiver to return anything, or enough, she should keep her 6-euro endowment and send nothing. When deciding how much of the endowment to send, the senders had very limited information about their partners, but they knew that they were either Roma or non-Roma. A widespread stereotype about the Roma is that they are cheaters and thieves. If non-Roma senders expected Roma to behave as the stereotype suggests, and keep too much or even the entire pot, they might have sent less to Roma than they sent to non-Roma. Such a difference in behavior would suggest discrimination.

In Chapter 4, I showed that non-Roma from Novo mesto sent significantly less to Roma than they did to non-Roma receivers. The top panel of Figure 5.15 reproduces this result. It also shows that non-Roma from Murska Sobota did not behave this way. Again, non-Roma from Murska Sobota did not treat Roma any differently. They sent 57 percent of their endowment to their non-Roma partners and 58 percent to their Roma partners. This difference is negligible. Effectively, they sent no more and no less to Roma, a result that stands in sharp contrast to the result from Novo mesto, where non-Roma clearly favored their coethnic trust game partners. When paired with coethnics, non-Roma from Novo mesto sent 78 percent of their endowment; when paired with Roma, they sent 58 percent.

Regression results, presented in Table 4.1 in Chapter 4, confirm this finding and provide further insight. The logit regression analysis controlled for education, gender, income bracket, risk preference, and people's willingness to donate money to an anonymous family in need; it also included interaction terms between the control covariates and the treatment variable (ethnic identity of the receiver, labeled as Roma).[32] The conditional marginal effect for

[31] See Chapter 4 for game rules.
[32] As each town was treated as a block, each treated observation (sender partnered with a Roma receiver) was weighted by the inverse of the proportion of subjects in its block (town) who were assigned to the treatment condition, and each control subject was weighted by the inverse of the proportion of subjects in its block who were assigned to the control condition (Gerber and Green 2012).

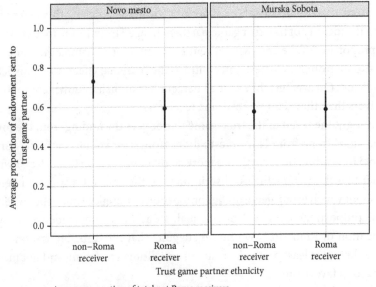

Average proportion of endowment non–Roma senders sent to receivers in the trust game, by receiver ethnicity

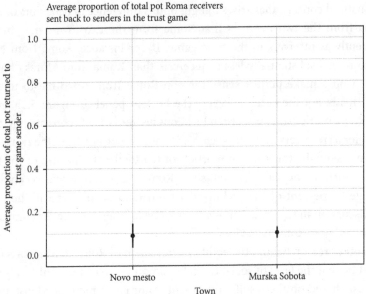

Average proportion of total pot Roma receivers sent back to senders in the trust game

Figure 5.15 The top panel presents the average proportion of the trust game endowment that non-Roma participants sent to their non-Roma and Roma receivers, respectively. The plot also shows 95 percent confidence intervals. For Novo mesto, the difference between the two means is statistically significant the 5 percent level ($p < 0.05$). For Murska Sobota, the difference between the means is not statistically significant and is negligible. The bottom panel shows the average proportion of the total pot that Roma receivers returned to their non-Roma senders in the trust game (all senders were non-Roma). The difference between the two is not statistically significant.

non-Roma from Murska Sobota is not statistically significant. This means that when the identity of the trust game partner changed from Roma to non-Roma, the proportion of the endowment sent to the partner remained the same. For non-Roma from Novo mesto, in contrast, the marginal effect was statistically significant. On average, they sent 33 percent less of their endowment to Roma receivers than they did to non-Roma receivers.

Fittingly, the result of the trust game reproduces the finding from the tower game: non-Roma from Novo mesto differ from their counterparts in Murska Sobota by sending their coethnics more, and not by sending Roma less. I wrote earlier that this is nonetheless discrimination; the relevant distinction here is not about which group gets a higher proportion of the endowment but whether those proportions are equal or unequal. In addition, my evidence of open derogation of Roma in Novo mesto suggests that the disparate treatment of Roma there is at least partly the result of anti-Roma sentiment, and not merely of ingroup favoritism.

A natural concern that arises in light of this difference in behaviors of non-Roma from the two towns is that Roma from the two towns may behave differently as receivers in the trust game. If, for instance, Roma from Novo mesto return substantially less as receivers than Roma from Murska Sobota do, it would make perfect sense for non-Roma from Novo mesto to send less. This is not the case, however. The bottom panel of Figure 5.15 shows that Roma participants from both locations are remarkably consistent in their behavior as receivers in the trust game. On average, Roma from the two towns return essentially the same proportion of the total pot. The size of the total pot, in turn, is the same as well, since Roma from both towns received on average 58 percent of the endowment from their senders (recall, however, the discussion in Chapter 4 on why this game is inappropriate for comparing Roma and non-Roma behaviors).

Another reason behind the equitable treatment of Roma in Murska Sobota might be that the level of social capital is simply higher there. This is also not the case. Based on the results from the dictator game mentioned just above, in which the senders were asked to divide 6 euros between themselves and a local family in need, altruism levels are actually higher in Novo mesto. Senders in Novo mesto sent on average 83 percent of their endowment to the family in need, while those from Murska Sobota sent on average 70 percent. The difference between these amounts is statistically significant ($p < 0.05$). The same people who systematically sent less to Roma partners in the trust game, were therefore *more* generous, not less, when it came to the family in need. This finding does not support the idea that social capital is higher in Murska

Sobota; if anything, it suggests the opposite. Thus, non-Roma from Murska Sobota appear to treat Roma no differently than they treat non-Roma, despite the fact that overall levels of social capital there do not appear higher and despite the fact that Roma there behave the same way as receivers as Roma in Novo mesto.

This finding is notable because it ocurred in the context of a one-shot game played confidentially with an anonymous partner. Completely ruling out a need to exhibit high trust on account of future interactions, the game captures a sender's gut-level reaction to the information that her partner is either Roma or not. Non-Roma from Murska Sobota who played this game indicated that they trusted Roma just as much as they trusted non-Roma. Whether or not they believed the stereotype that Roma are cheaters and thieves, their decisions reflect a profound disregard for it.

Conclusion

Using the example of Novo mesto, this chapter demonstrates how non-Roma contribute to the exclusion cycle. Non-Roma in this town discriminate against the Roma in the context of both repeated and single interactions. When presented with an option to update their behavior in response to Roma avatars who are just as cooperative as non-Roma avatars, non-Roma from Novo mesto keep discriminating. They also discriminate when rewarding Roma and non-Roma for past behaviors, where good behavior by Roma is rewarded less often than identical good behavior by non-Roma, while bad behavior by Roma is punished more than identical bad behavior by non-Roma. Not everyone in this town discriminates, but non-Roma who do also express prejudice against the Roma. Anti-migrant sentiment, while present, is not related to discrimination against the Roma, which suggests that discrimination against the Roma is linked to anti-Roma culture specifically and not to intolerance expressed toward outgroups in general. Having had a bad personal experience with a Roma person is also unrelated to discrimination. Non-Roma in Novo mesto commit a wide array of attribution errors with a relatively high frequency.

The case of Murska Sobota, which matches Novo mesto well on all relevant covariates but one, suggests that Roma-led intergroup contact promotion might help break the exclusion cycle. Non-Roma there consistently do not discriminate against the Roma; those who are familiar with the contact-promoting NGO or attend its events in fact contribute more to the tower in the mixed game. While they express prejudice against the Roma, non-Roma from Murska Sobota express less of it than non-Roma from Novo mesto. Importantly, they do not act on it in the context of the tower game. Similarly, non-Roma from Murska Sobota commit attribution errors, but to a lesser extent. As the contact-promoting Roma NGO was not randomly assigned to one of these two towns, I cannot conclude that lower levels of discrimination in Murska Sobota are due to NGO action. The findings are nevertheless promising, even if only suggestive.

6

From the Other Side

Chances are that a Roma child born today will be born into exclusion. For many, this is how their personal exclusion cycle begins. A Roma child born in Novo mesto, for example, experiences disparate treatment hours into life, years before she might become aware of it, when she is placed next to her mother in the segregated "Roma room" of the maternity ward. Living with anti-minority culture and facing more discrimination as she grows up, the young woman might eventually resort to survival strategies. Each time she does so, her strategy is likely to be perceived by non-Roma as something inherent, not as something she is compelled to do because she has few other options. The cycle of prejudice, mistreatment, survival strategies, and attribution errors could easily then repeat, over and over again.

Chapter 5 focused on the non-Roma part of this cycle. I presented evidence of anti-Roma culture, of discrimination against the Roma, and of the attribution errors that non-Roma commit when judging Roma behaviors. Here, I turn to Roma and ask the remaining crucial questions. Do Roma use survival strategies? If yes, under what circumstances?

I begin this chapter with a brief overview of survival strategies, informed by interviews with Roma participants. Examining Roma answers to an extensive survey, I next discuss why some Roma might want or need to use survival strategies. First, I present information on deprivation that likely results from persistent exclusion. Second, I discuss the extent to which Roma perceive discrimination that's directed at them and the forms that it takes. Third, I examine Roma perceptions of stereotype intractability. I find that Roma in my sample experience material deprivation, that a vast majority reports having experienced discrimination, and that many see their reputation strongly tied to that of their ethnic group. Each of these factors alone points to a propensity to use survival strategies. Together, they suggest their inevitability.

The chapter then takes up Roma behaviors, examining the extent to which Roma use survival strategies in the context of the tower-building videogame. I find that Roma uses of survival strategies are not overwhelmingly high, but that some Roma nevertheless resort to them. Deprivation and survival strategies do

Breaking the Exclusion Cycle: How to Promote Cooperation between Majority and Minority Ethnic Groups.
Ana Bracic, Oxford University Press (2020). © Oxford University Press. DOI: 10.1093/oso/9780190050672.001.0001

not appear to be linked, and Roma who believe that stereotyping against them is deeply entrenched are no more likely to engage in them than Roma who do not believe the same. Roma who have personally experienced discrimination, however, are more likely to engage in survival strategies.

In demonstrating how Roma behaviors fit into an exclusion cycle, the findings in this chapter provide the final block of evidence in support of my argument. The relationship between discrimination and survival strategies I uncover here is particularly significant, as it bolsters several findings discussed in Chapters 4 and 5 where I also explored the significance of discrimination, but through a direct focus on non-Roma behaviors. The findings here provide a counterpart to those results, together showing not only how some non-Roma discriminate against the Roma, but also how some Roma perceive that discrimination and react to it.

Examining Roma and non-Roma behaviors at once demonstrates the challenge of sustaining cross-group cooperation. Non-Roma participants in Novo mesto consistently discriminate against the Roma by contributing less to the tower when Roma avatars are in play. Roma participants expect this and accordingly contribute even less to the tower. Anticipating that, non-Roma in turn contribute even less, and so on. Behaviors of the two groups fall into a negative feedback loop in which cross-group cooperation cannot be sustained. By contrast, Roma and non-Roma in Murska Sobota are able to sustain cross-group cooperation, as members of both groups on average contribute to the tower at equal levels.

Survival strategies

People develop survival strategies in order to persevere and thrive in difficult circumstances. For members of marginalized minorities, survival strategies often become a necessity because the discrimination they experience significantly curtails their options. Thus, Roma who experience high barriers to formal employment engage in scrap metal collection or seasonal agricultural work; forage and sell mushrooms, blueberries, and wood (most Slovene forests are by convention open to anyone to forage); rely on social assistance; sell goods door to door; take up minimum-wage work, if they can get it; and more.

While I primarily discuss these strategies in the context of Roma, they are not quintessentially ethnic activities; non-Roma engage in them too, sometimes to a greater extent than Roma. There are more non-Roma than Roma among Slovenes who rely on social assistance to make ends meet. Slovene

Roma and non-Roma alike forage mushrooms, and while many wander the woods for recreation, plenty from both groups pick mushrooms for a living. Similarly, scrap metal collection is not a Roma trade in Slovenia, and neither is selling goods door-to-door.

Many survival strategies are nevertheless ethnicized. Non-Roma tend to see metal scrap collection as something Roma engage in; the same holds for relying on social assistance (Messing and Molnár 2011). When my enumerators and I recruited study participants door to door, we were on occasion rudely turned away; once, a participant apologized to a pair of enumerators for having been rude, explaining that she thought they were Roma. She'd made that assumption because my research teams carried experiment and survey materials in large shoulder bags, reminiscent of those Roma women often carry when they sell goods door to door.

The occupations I listed above typically pay little, while requiring strenuous work. As picking mushrooms is a popular activity in Slovenia, hobby mushroom pickers likely have a strong misconception of what foraging looks like when done for subsistence. A Roma mushroom forager explained that they typically wake up at 3 or 4 in the morning in order to be deep into the forest by daybreak; the terrain varies from meadows to steep forested hills, depending on the time of year and the type of mushroom.[1] She explained that foragers often pick what grows and might switch from wild blueberries to mushrooms as summer turns to fall. Wild blueberries, she said, are particularly challenging to pick since the fruit is very small and the plant close to the ground; on the steep hills in the forests where she and her teammates forage, it takes well over an hour to fill up a glass that might sell for 6 euros at the farmer's market or a roadside stand.

Survival strategies are usually other-benefitting; they informally provide goods and services that are in demand, but not provided by the formal market. And yet, survival strategies are often disliked, particularly when Roma engage in them; when this happens, their typical other-benefitting nature is muddied by uncharitable non-Roma interpretations or instances of sporadic bad behaviors by individual Roma. An uncharitable non-Roma interpretation of relying on social assistance thus concludes that Roma who employ this strategy are "extorting the state"; the same is seldom said of their non-Roma counterparts.

Sporadic bad behavior by individuals, such as taking what looks like scrap metal without permission (which, again, is something Roma and non-Roma

---

[1] In-person interview, notes. July 2017.

may do), often leads non-Roma to conclude that Roma in general engage in metal theft. Roma who collect scrap find different ways to navigate the resulting hostility. A participant explained that she and her husband collect scrap together because it is safer to go in pairs—non-Roma are sometimes hesitant to accuse when women collect scrap alongside men.[2] Regardless, she noted that they have been accused of stealing plenty of times. She also said that some non-Roma have been very nice and respectful, offiering them water on a hot day.

On a different occasion, a Roma entrepreneur who trades in scrap metal that others collect explained that when he started collecting many years ago, he would travel further and further out from the region, eventually to cover Slovenia in its entirety; business was better where non-Roma did not know that he was Roma.[3] Another participant said that she and other Roma follow a similar logic and find seasonal agricultural work, like picking apples during the harvest, in neighboring Austria. The Austrians for whom they work either don't know they are Roma or don't care, for all that matters is how well the work gets done. Slovene farmers, she said, are often less welcoming.[4]

While many survival strategies are other-benefitting, some are not. Tapping electricity lines where there is no infrastructure for safe provision of electricity is such a practice (moreover, it's illegal). As it often results in cables strewn over roofs, fences, and trees, this strategy is dangerous and can lead to severe injuries and death. Commenting on this, a participant from Novo mesto pointed out of the back of her house across her backyard, a ditch, and tall bushes, saying "this is where my electricity comes from. I do not like it this way, I would prefer to have it directly, from the municipality."[5] When people engage in this strategy they often do so out of need, turning to it because the only other alternative is living in darkness.

Why might Roma use survival strategies?

Roma might engage in such ethnicized survival strategies because of deprivation, because of personal experience of discrimination and ostracism, and because of intractable stereotypes that depict their engagement in them. What follows is an explanation of the possibilities I have just outlined that relies

[2] In-person interview, notes. July 2018. See Chapter 3 for more on scrap collection.
[3] In-person interview, notes. July 2018.
[4] In-person conversation, December 2015.
[5] In person interview, notes. July 2018.

heavily on Roma answers to an extensive survey. These three factors are not the only ones that potentially influence engagement in survival strategies, but they are especially salient because of their direct link to exclusion. Examining other factors must fall to future scholarship.

Deprivation

Exclusion can lead to material deprivation. Personal experience of deprivation can in turn lead individuals to behave differently from those who are not deprived. For instance, people who experience deprivation are more likely to incur debt (Lea et al. 1993) and save less for the future (Shapiro and Wu 2011). They are more likely to have children sooner (Imamura et al. 2007), to smoke, and to suffer from obesity (Adams and White 2009). They are more likely to express pessimism about their future (Robb et al. 2009), and less likely to invest in education (Blanden and Gregg 2004). Scholarship in evolutionary behavioral science shows that such behaviors are contextually appropriate responses to economic hardship (Pepper and Nettle 2007).

Behaviors associated with deprivation at least partly develop when individuals who experience economic hardship have, or perceive themselves as having, limited control over their futures (Lundberg et al. 2007). A lesser sense of personal control leads to trade-offs between present and future rewards that differ from those typically made by individuals who are not deprived; people who experience deprivation are comparatively more likely to value present rewards than future rewards, even if the rewards in the present are smaller (Pepper and Nettle 2017). In the context of material deprivation, for example, a person might discount the future if she lacks the ability to afford solutions to problems like environmentally hazardous or otherwise unsafe housing, whether it is by moving away or by repairing the home (Pepper and Nettle 2007). Similarly, an individual might be less worried about accruing debt if the likelihood she will have to pay it is limited (Pepper and Nettle 2017), and less concerned still about damaging future effects of an activity that is rewarding in the short term if she might not be alive when the negative consequences take their toll (Daly and Wilson 2005). Therefore, if survival strategies privilege the present over the future, an individual's propensity to engage in them may be informed by her experience of deprivation.

Typically, deprivation is measured through the lens of socio-economic status, focusing on factors such as income, occupation, or wealth; factors such as a person's perception of her or her group's political power also matter, as do neighborhood-level factors, like average house price or general level of disrepair (Pepper and Nettle 2017). The following touches on a few of these factors, as reported by Roma participants from the two towns. The comparison of disparities shows some progress in Murska Sobota, but also reflects the anchoring nature of systemic exclusion. Though Roma in Murska Sobota on occasion appear ahead of those in Novo mesto, overall their levels of deprivation are quite close.

I first asked Roma trust game participants about their income, a question which resulted in remarkably low variation. The first income category was 0 to 600 euros per month; 91 percent of Roma trust game participants indicated this as their income category. Some circled "0" to indicate that they had no income at all. The same year, in 2011, the Slovene Statistical Office reported that the monthly income threshold for people who were considered at risk for poverty was 600 euros. With almost all Roma participants below that line, and many quite far below, this finding leaves little room for doubt. As a group, the Roma in the two towns are financially disadvantaged.[6]

Seeking more variation, I asked Roma tower game participants about their living conditions. Among them, 90 from Novo mesto and 86 percent from Murska Sobota had heating at home. This does not deviate dramatically from the national estimate: in 2015, 93 percent of Slovene households had adequate heat. Roma participants' access to sewerage was considerably lower, at 57 and 63 percent in Novo mesto and Murska Sobota, respectively. For Slovenia, these numbers are striking. Outside of a Roma settlement, I have never heard of a Slovene house without access to sewerage. I am unable to compare these figures to the national estimate; the Slovene Statistical Office does not list access to sewerage in its data on residence conditions.[7] Likely, access to sewerage is assumed and so not included in the yearly household survey. As every third Roma participant in my second study does not have access to sewerage, this omission, while not surprising, is perhaps premature.

According to Burchardt et al. (2002), people who are unemployed, self-employed, retired early, in education or training, disabled, or looking after family at home are excluded from participation in production. Among the

---

[6] The median income category for non-Roma participants in the trust game was 600-1,200 euros per month.

[7] See the tables available through the data portal of the Republic of Slovenia Statistical Office. Here, I refer to "Stanovanjske razmere, glede na tip gospodinjstva, Slovenija, letno" for year 2015 and "Posedovanje izbranih dobrin po: dohodek gospodinjstva - kvintil, leto, dobrina, meritve", also for 2015. See https://pxweb.stat.si.

Roma tower game participants, 90 percent in Novo mesto and 72 percent in Murska Sobota qualify as excluded. Most are unemployed; a few are retired. With Slovene unemployment at 9 percent in 2015, the rates of unemployment among Roma are egregious.[8] I probed further. I asked Roma participants whether they had applied for a job in the past 12 months. In Novo mesto, 38 percent had; of those, 9 percent were employed. In Murska Sobota, 43 percent applied; of those, 22 percent were working. I also asked Roma participants if they ever looked for a job via the Employment Service of Slovenia;[9] in Novo mesto, 73 percent did, and in Murska Sobota, 76 percent did. Of those, 10 percent from Novo mesto and 25 percent from Murska Sobota had a job. While Roma seek formal employment, they predominantly do not possess it. I asked them to what extent they agreed with the statement: "people from my settlement usually do not get the job after they interview for one." In Novo mesto, 55 percent either agreed or strongly agreed; in Murska Sobota, 52 percent did the same.

To establish their level of political engagement, I asked all study participants whether they voted in the latest election. Among non-Roma participants, 75 percent said they did; among Roma, 57 percent said the same (53 percent in Novo mesto and 60 percent in Murska Sobota).[10] I then asked Roma participants whether they agreed or disagreed with the view that "it's irrelevant who the Roma vote for as no political party would fight for their well-being." In Novo mesto, 85 percent either strongly agreed, agreed, or somewhat agreed; in Murska Sobota 80 percent answered the same way. Thus, while Roma rates of political participation are lower than those of non-Roma, they do not appear to be excluded from political participation. However, they do not tend to trust their elected officials to represent them or protect their interests.

It is important to note that spatial segregation plays a role in sustaining the disparities just listed. For example, Roma families would likely find it easier to get connected to the sewage system if they were dispersed among non-Roma in the main part of the city. As they are isolated, those who perhaps could otherwise get connected find it more challenging because securing the

---

[8] See the tables available through the data portal of the Republic of Slovenia Statistical Office. The table I refer to here is "Aktivno in neaktivno prebivalstvo po: meritve, četrtletje." See https://pxweb.stat.si.

[9] The Employment Service of Slovenia is an independent legal entity with a public institute status. It operates throughout the state and offers job-brokering services, employment and career advice, unemployment benefits and unemployment insurance, etc. Typically, people who are looking for jobs and entities looking to hire register with this service.

[10] I could not ask participants how they voted because vote choice is typically seen as a very private matter in Slovenia.

necessary infrastructure is quite costly.[11] Further, in a town with poor public transportation, spatial isolation makes it costlier for Roma from a far removed settlement to go to work or school; along the same lines, social interactions between Roma and non-Roma in contexts other than work or school are costlier and less likely when members of both groups are spatially isolated. Moreover, as Roma settlements are out of sight, they may also be out of mind. While deprivation observed every day may instill a sense of urgency in some public servants, unseen deprivation can be more easily ignored. Indeed, Roma from Novo mesto recounted a visit from the Slovene Human Rights Ombudsperson, who appeared genuinely horrified at the conditions in the settlement, not having expected them to be so bad. But politicians, Roma said, visit only before it's time to vote.

Consequently, Roma participants are deprived on a number of dimensions. They have substantially lower incomes than their non-Roma counterparts and less access to basic amenities that are considered essential for everyday life in Slovenia, like sewerage. They are grievously under-employed, with about 80 percent not having a job. Most do not trust elected officials to represent them or protect their interests.

Discrimination

In demonstrating that discrimination exists, we naturally aim to capture the behaviors of those who discriminate. Another approach might be to ask their targets whether they have experienced discrimination. While it sounds sensible, relying on victim accounts is not common. Indeed, Williams and Mohammed (2009) write that "perceived discrimination is a historically neglected race-related aspect of life" (34). As a measure of discrimination, perceived discrimination has a clear weakness. It does not comprehensively capture one's experience of discrimination; instead, it is merely one of its components. Before I discuss why perceived discrimination must nonetheless be considered, the section that follows describes, in more detail, what measures of perceived discrimination may or may not capture.

---

[11] This is not confined to Romani settlements; in conversation with a Bosnian activist and NGO leader, I learned of a Bosnian municipality that stopped laying new water pipes intended for the entire town once they reached the border of where the displaced Serbian population lived. We need not go that far to see beyond the case of the Roma; people who live in Flint, Michigan, including about 10,000 children, were exposed to lead in water, which causes irreversible brain damage (Hanna-Attisha 2017). Most of the population affected is Black and poor (The New York Times Editorial Board 2016).

In life, we observe what is happening, while failing to observe what is not. The alternative scenario—that which did not happen—is called a counterfactual. Our inability to observe counterfactuals can blind us to the realities of disparate treatment. Consider this example, simplified, but based on a field experiment conducted by Pager et al. (2009). Joe, who is Black, fills out an application for a retail job. He is told that his references will have to be checked before he can interview. Simon, who is White but otherwise identically qualified and of similar attractiveness, also applies, and is interviewed on the spot, without a reference check. Simon is offered the job two days later. Unless Joe and Simon talk to each other (or are part of an experiment, as they were) neither is going to know how the other was treated. Because Joe does not observe the counterfactual of how he would likely be treated were he not Black, he might not think that the employer mistreated him. But she did.

Paradies (2006) writes that individuals frequently do not perceive racism because of "its pervasive nature in contemporary societies" (888). Even worse are cases where victims of discrimination have "internalized oppression," (Krieger 1999, p.324) believing that their status and the accompanying mistreatment are deserved. In such an instance, discrimination might not be perceived at all, and if it were, it would not be recognized as mistreatment at all.

We usually have more trouble recognizing mistreatment when it affects us personally. If, instead, a friend or a family member is affected, or if we observe how others are variously mistreated over time, recognizing discrimination tends to be easier (Krieger 1999). As a result, people typically report greater levels of discrimination directed toward their group, and not toward themselves. This discrepancy may be due to our relative inability to recognize patterns based on our own experience (Krieger 1999). It may also be due to self-protection mechanisms that benefit from denying the experience of mistreatment, in favor of optimism or even illusions of invulnerability (Krieger 1999).

In misperceiving discrimination, people can even interpret it as something positive, rather than negative. Krieger (1999) notes that where some women see sexual harassment, others may see a compliment on their looks. There is also a chance that people might see discrimination where there is none, possibly due to paranoia, a misinterpretation of rude behavior (Gee et al. 2009), or as a way to avoid blaming themselves when they fail (Krieger 1999).

Of course, people may perceive mistreatment exactly for what it is, but may nonetheless choose not to report it. Reasons behind choosing silence vary. Sometimes, people who experience discrimination wish to present themselves in a socially favorable way and, often correctly, see reporting discrimination as undesirable (Gee et al. 2009; Krieger 1999). Sometimes victims of mistreatment wish to avoid "losing face" (Gee et al. 2009, p.145) or shaming themselves or their families. Sometimes, speaking about discrimination is distressing and unhelpful (Krieger 1999), particularly if victims who speak out are then challenged to prove that discrimination indeed exists (Gee et al. 2009).

And sometimes, underreporting stems from a fear of repercussions and a deep distrust of a system that ought to protect the victims, but at best does very little and at worst actually protects perpetrators. For example, in response to formal reports of workplace sexual harassment, workplaces may erect barriers that prevent the victims from asserting their rights to protection from harassment (Marshall 2014; also see Bracic et al. 2019). Rape and sexual assault more generally tend to be massively underreported, whether in the US (Kruttschnitt et al. 2014), across EU member states (FRA 2014b), or in South Africa (Jewkes et al. 2012). Alongside grievous consequences for the victims, this practice results in data that cannot be trusted. As rates of underreporting likely change in response to a variety of factors, ranging from policies that aim to reduce underreporting to outcomes of trials that exonerate perpetrators, generating estimates of actual assaults is quite challenging. That is, if we cannot accurately estimate what the rate of underreporting is, and how it changes over time, we cannot know how many people are assaulted.[12] This logic can easily be extended to other cases of mistreatment, ranging from police brutality—like that against the Roma in a number of states[13]—to schoolyard discrimination. What results is a number that we know is wrong, but we can only guess how wrong.

People, then, might not notice that they are targets of discrimination; they might misperceive it; or they may choose not to report it. That doesn't mean we shouldn't ask them about it. Without asking people about their experiences, we are at risk of failing to understand how those experiences shape their daily lives. If, when passing a young Roma man on the street at night, a woman switches her purse to the side that's opposite of the man, she may blithely continue on her way home, without thinking twice about what she did. The man, however, may take this encounter home with him, adding it to a number

---

[12] For an exposition of how challenging it is to determine rates of underreporting, see Kruttschnitt et al. (2014).

[13] In the early 1990s, police often looked the other way and, in some cases, supported perpetrators or even themselves engaged in brutality against the Roma; excessive force was used routinely and a number of Roma "inexplicably died" (Barany 2002, p.315) in police custody. The damage was aggravated by courts that often engaged in discriminatory treatment, sometimes blaming the Roma for the violence (Romania) and other times refusing to recognize that attacks against the Roma could be motivated by racism (Czech Republic and Slovakia). For more, see Barany (2002).

of other indignities he has experienced. Over time, these indignities may come to inform his behavior. He may decide to cross the street every time he sees a woman walking towards him on the sidewalk in the evening. He may decide to stubbornly keep his hands in his pockets when he's taking a bus. He may consider shoplifting, as those people see him as a thief anyway.

One could argue that people's behaviors are likely to change in response to discrimination that they have perceived, and not to that which they have not (although it is, of course, also possible that our behaviors change in response to stimuli of which we are unaware). Certainly, research in psychology demonstrates that even short bursts of social exclusion and ostracism can lead to devastating consequences, including temporary feelings of abject misery, anger, sadness, and increased stress (Williams 2007); lower levels of empathy and trust (Twenge et al. 2007); higher aggression towards innocent bystanders (Catanese and Tice 2005); and less engagement in other-benefitting behaviors like altruism and cooperation (Twenge et al. 2007). Taking heed of this research, I explore the relationship between personal experience of discrimination and uses of survival strategies among marginalized Roma.

Measuring perceived discrimination requires some caution. Consider the following pitfall. Suppose that a local human rights NGO is raising awareness of mistreatment and as a result the word discrimination is heard quite often and assigned particular meanings. Suppose next that the neighboring town has no such NGO and the concept of discrimination tends not to be brought up in everyday conversation there. If a researcher wants to collect data on perceived discrimination in these towns, she should not ask people directly if they have experienced it, for two reasons. First, the people from the first town have likely become more familiar with discrimination and what it entails, and may therefore be more likely to recognize it and report it. Second, the meaning of the word "discrimination" likely varies not only across the two towns but also from one individual to another. What I consider discrimination, someone else may see as a fact of life. A researcher asking about discrimination directly, then, might fall into the trap of having it overestimated in the town that is more aware of it and underestimated in the town that is less aware. Further, she is likely to capture a range of behaviors and experiences that different people recognize as discrimination, but not have the knowledge of which experiences, exactly, she captured. To avoid this, even if just as a precaution, it is better to ask about specific experiences of mistreatment.

I therefore asked the Roma from Novo mesto and Murska Sobota a battery of questions on how they were treated at different points in their lives. In Murska Sobota, 23 percent report having been treated badly in school; in Novo mesto, 30 percent report the same. When I asked them to describe how, several answered that they were verbally abused; one participant wrote "they said I stank and heckled me, called me gypsy". Others wrote that they were held to a higher standard, having to "always know more for the same grade," while "not being worth as much as a non-Roma." One participant wrote "they yelled at me and beat me," and another, "they were mean and didn't want me to come to school." Almost half of those who reported having been treated badly in school wrote that it was the teachers who mistreated them.

I next asked Roma participants about how they were treated when they last saw a doctor. On a five-point scale, from very badly to very well, the modal response from both towns was very well; in Novo mesto, 54 percent answered that way and in Murska Sobota, 53 percent did. In this general question, the distribution of answers was nearly identical. In my next health-related question, not so. I asked the women whether they had given birth within the past 5 years, and if yes, who shared their hospital room with them.[14] This question may be unusual, but I asked it because I had heard reports that the hospital in Novo mesto has "Roma rooms," where Roma patients are told they'd be "more comfortable." The probability that several Roma women but no non-Roma women would be giving birth at the same time is quite low, as the proportion of Roma inhabitants in Novo mesto is low (at most 2.8 percent). Since we can reasonably expect more non-Roma women giving birth at the same time, sharing rooms with just Roma by pure chance would be unlikely. In accordance with this expectation, none of the participants from Murska Sobota had shared a maternity room just with other Roma; half reported they were in a mixed room and half were in a room with just non-Roma. None reported that they were treated badly. Among participants from Novo mesto, however, 68 percent shared their maternity room with just other Roma. Eleven percent reported that they were badly treated; all who did stayed in a "Roma room."

The answers to my questions about school and health-related mistreatment happen to be quite clear as to the source of mistreatment. Describing how they were treated in school, a number of participants wrote that they were verbally abused with the common slur. In the context of disparate treatment in the maternity ward in Novo mesto, the "Roma rooms" are also quite clear— Roma women giving birth are placed in those rooms because they are Roma. In perceived mistreatment (and likely also in mistreatment generally) the source of discrimination might be unclear, especially when directed at people with multiple minority status. A Roma woman may be mistreated because she is

---

[14] All Roma participants who gave birth within the past 5 years gave birth in their local hospital.

Roma, because she is a woman, or because she is a Roma woman. I do not engage with this compelling question here; I do, however, try to establish the extent to which Roma interpret the discrimination they perceive as directed towards their ethnic identity. I therefore posed my remaining questions on personal perceived discrimination in two parts: I first asked if the participant had experienced a particular type of disparate treatment, and if yes, whether they thought that had happened because they were Roma. I asked 10 such questions. They are modeled after those in Andriessen et al. (2014) and listed in Table 6.1.

These direct questions aim to capture disparate treatment of different types and in different contexts. The first composite question, for example, asks whether, when the participant rides the bus, people switch their bags to the side facing away from from the participant or visibly secure their hold on their bags. If the participant answers "yes," the question then asks whether the participant thinks this happens because she or he is Roma. I only consider a survey answer

Table 6.1 Perceived discrimination questions

1	When you ride the bus, do people sometimes switch their bags to the side facing away from you or visibly secure their hold on their bags? [yes/no] If yes, do you think this is because you're Roma? [yes/no]
2	When you sit down next to other people in a waiting room (doctor's office, bus stop, municipal office, PTA meeting), do people sometimes get up or move somewhere else? [yes/no] If yes, do you think this is because you're Roma? [yes/no]
3	Has a shop clerk or a waiter ever ignored you to help another customer even though you arrived in the store/restaurant first? [yes/no] If yes, do you think this is because you're Roma? [yes/no]
4	Have you been refused entrance to a restaurant, bar, or cinema? [yes/no] If yes, do you think this is because you're Roma? [yes/no]
5	Do you feel like non-Roma seem wary when you interact? [yes/no] If yes, do you think this is because you're Roma? [yes/no]
6	Do you feel like non-Roma think that you can't handle a job or do certain things? [yes/no] If yes, do you think this is because you're Roma? [yes/no]
7	Do you feel like non-Roma behave as if you were lazy? [yes/no] If yes, do you think this is because you're Roma? [yes/no]
8	Do non-Roma make you feel excluded? [yes/no] If yes, do you think this is because you're Roma? [yes/no]
9	Do you feel like non-Roma blame you when something untoward has happened? [yes/no] If yes, do you think this is because you're Roma? [yes/no]
10	Do you feel like non-Roma don't trust you? [yes/no] If yes, do you think this is because you're Roma? [yes/no]

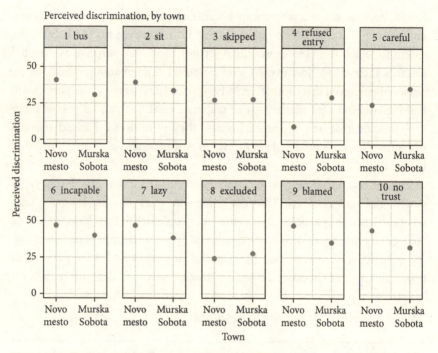

Figure 6.1 Perceived discrimination, by town. The subplots are numbered to match the questions listed in Table 6.1. Each plot shows the percent of Roma who answered both questions affirmatively—first, that they experienced discrimination and second, that they thought they experienced it because they were Roma.

as reporting discrimination if the participant answers "yes" to both parts of the composite question. In Novo mesto, 41 percent of participants answered yes to both of these questions; in Murska Sobota, 31 percent did the same. Figure 6.1 presents the answers to each of the 10 composite questions; each plot shows the percent of Roma in both towns who answered both questions affirmatively— that is, that they experienced mistreatment, and that they thought it happened because they were Roma.

The advantage of these direct questions is twofold. First, they avoid the trap of capturing a range of experiences under the common term "discrimination" by asking participants to think about specific instances of mistreatment. Second, as different people experience mistreatment under a variety of circumstances, the direct and specific questions also provide insight into which forms of mistreatment are most commonly perceived. They also allow me to see the extent to which the same individuals perceive discrimination across different circumstances, and the extent to which participants are likely to experience one type of mistreatment but not others. Overall, 73 percent of Roma participants report experiencing at least one type of mistreatment—that is, they answered affirmatively to both questions of at least one of the 10 composite questions. Perceived discrimination is not balanced across the two towns (see Figure 6.2). In Novo mesto, 82 percent of Roma participants report experiencing at least one type of mistreatment. In Murska Sobota, 63 percent report the same.

Who reports discrimination? Roma women are not more likely to report discrimination than are Roma men; there is no systematic variation across levels of employment, and none based on education.[15] There is some variation across age, however. Among older age groups, there is no statistically significant difference between the two towns. Importantly, instead of asking whether participants experienced discrimination over the past 5 years, the questions do not specify a time frame. Older generations are therefore more likely to report having experienced discrimination; in Murska Sobota, they may have experienced it in earlier in their lives, and not once the effects of NGO action manifested. The overlap in the number of older participants from both towns reporting discrimination thus speaks to the quality of the match of the two towns. It suggests that Murska Sobota did not always have better Roma/non-Roma relations than Novo mesto, but that instead, the difference manifested fairly recently.[16]

Indeed, participants in the youngest age group, those who are between 18 and 25 years old, are significantly less likely to report having experienced discrimination in Murska Sobota than in Novo mesto (see Figure 6.2). This discrepancy among younger Roma, combined with no difference in reporting by older generations, likely reflects the findings I presented in Chapter 5. If NGO efforts to promote intergroup contact with the aim of reducing discrimination worked, we would most likely see that reflected in what the youngest generation reports. Since this is precisely what Roma survey answers suggest, they provide an independent corroboration of the findings I presented using the trust and tower building games in the previous chapter: today, non-Roma from Novo mesto discriminate against the Roma to a substantially higher degree than non-Roma from Murska Sobota.

To summarize, individual reports of perceived discrimination in Novo mesto and Murska Sobota are high. The difference in reports between the two

---

[15] While Roma who are more educated are less likely to report having experienced discrimination, the number of observations in my sample is too low for the difference to be statistically significant.

[16] As levels of intolerance increased after the post-socialist states in Central/Eastern Europe began democratizing, the difference in reports of discrimination in the two towns manifests as a substantial increase in reports in Novo mesto and a much less substantial increase in Murska Sobota.

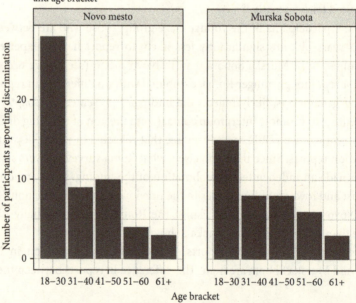

Figure 6.2 The top panel shows the number of Roma who answered yes to at least one of the composite questions on discrimination (reported) and Roma who answered no to all of them (not reported), by town. The bottom panel shows the same, but broken down by town and age bracket. See Table 6.1 for the composite questions.

towns reflects the difference in discriminatory behavior I presented in Chapter 5—the reports are higher in Novo mesto, particularly among the younger generation of Roma—and the raw numbers are sobering. In Murska Sobota, 6 out of 10 Roma report experiencing discrimination. In Novo mesto, 8 out of 10 do. If engagement in survival strategies is indeed linked to the experience of discrimination or ostracism (Twenge et al. 2007), we can expect to find it in both towns.

Perceived stereotype intractability

Scholarship on stereotype threat suggests that people who are stereotyped to behave a particular way are indeed more likely to behave in that manner—when the stereotype is activated (Steele and Aronson 1995). Scholars further suggest that individuals who are stereotyped might embrace the stereotype to protect their self-esteem (Burkley and Blanton 2008). Research on stereotype threat is predominantly conducted in educational contexts and laboratory settings; it explores, for example, whether Asian women perform poorly on a math test after being reminded that as women, they are stereotyped as inferior in math (Shih et al. 1999). They indeed perform worse, but they also perform much better when reminded that as Asians, they are stereotyped as superior in math (Shih et al. 1999).

Often, the everyday experience of stereotype threat differs somewhat from those induced in a laboratory setting. Recall the example of boys of color from Oakland, which I discussed in Chapter 2 (Rios 2011). Many boys from Rios's study contend with the system of punitive control on a daily basis as salespeople follow them in shops expecting them to steal; as teachers and parents tell them they will amount to nothing; and as police officers stop them for frequent searches because they match descriptions of gang members (Rios 2011). When stereotype threat is inescapable, people are likely to respond to it; not only unawares, as we might when taking a math test, but also deliberately, by considering how widespread the threat is and what decisions and actions it might preclude. Having been persistently stopped by police and asked where he was keeping drugs, Tyrell, one of the young men in Rios's study, indeed eventually turned to the survival strategy of selling marijuana, partly because he internalized the assumption that he was inherently criminal, partly because of financial struggles and lack of access to formal employment, and partly because intractable stereotyping left him with little control over his reputation (Rios 2011). That is, since he was already paying the social and psychological costs of being treated as a criminal, he might as well have fed his family. While this example uses a rather extreme survival strategy, the logic can apply to activities like scrap metal collection, collecting wood, and relying on social assistance. To what extent might beliefs regarding stereotype intractability inform Roma behaviors?

I began exploring this possibility by asking Roma participants three questions that might offer insight into their perception of stereotype threat as well as their agency in countering it. With the first question, I aimed to capture their perception of how deeply entrenched stereotyping was. I asked Roma from both towns to what extent they agreed with the following statement: "As long as non-Roma think that one Roma is a criminal, they won't trust any Roma at all." Seventy-three percent of Roma from Novo mesto either agreed or strongly agreed with this statement; the modal response was "strongly agree," with 57 percent of participants answering this way (see Figure 6.3). In Murska Sobota, agreement was less pronounced but nonetheless substantial; 48 percent of participants either agreed or strongly agreed. The statement provided was purposefully weak—it refers to a single individual and avoids stating whether that individual is actually responsible for a crime. That so many Roma agreed with this statement suggests that in their view, questionable behavior of a *single* individual could be sufficient to motivate non-Roma mistrust, and that the mere *presumption* of guilt, and not actual responsibility, also suffices.

This is a grievous finding regardless of context. Except in the most utopian of societies, it is reasonable to expect that someone will engage in crime. In a community where 8 out of 10 people cannot get a job and most families subsist on the basis of social benefits, the chance that someone will resort to crime out of need is appreciable, even if low. In the eyes of many Roma, then, widespread stereotyping is all but certain.

My second question thus aimed to uncover the extent to which Roma participants still thought that they had control over their own reputations. I asked them whether they agreed or disagreed with the following statement: "For non-Roma I am not an individual with personal interests; they only see me as a member of the Roma community." In Novo mesto, "strongly agree" was the modal response, with 37 percent of participants answering this way (see Figure 6.3). Fifty-three percent either agreed or strongly agreed. In Murska Sobota, participants were most likely to say they neither agreed nor disagreed with this statement; still, 36 percent either agreed or strongly agreed. In Novo mesto, half of Roma believe that they are not seen as individuals, only as Roma; in Murska Sobota, one third believe the same. This finding signifies that not

Trust repercussions of Roma being accused of crime, by town

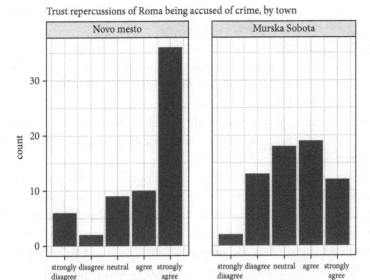

As long as non–Roma think that one Roma is a criminal, they won't trust any Roma at all. Do you agree or disagree?

Being seen as an individual by non–Roma, by town

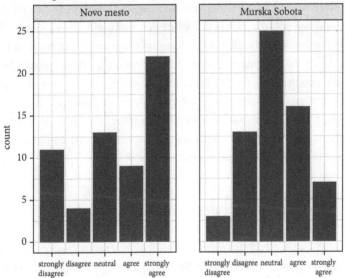

For non–Roma I am not an individual with personal interests, they only see me as a member of the Roma community. Do you agree or disagree?

Figure 6.3 The number of Roma who agree with two statements on stereotyping. Both statements aim to capture perceptions of stereotype intractability.

only is there a damaging group reputation, but also that a substantial number of Roma feel that they cannot escape it.

As the stigma sticks, some may internalize it. To see to what extent this might be the case, I asked Roma whether they agreed or disagreed with the following statement: "Some Roma from my town generally cannot be trusted." In Novo mesto, the modal response was "strongly agree," and 54 percent of participants either agreed or strongly agreed. In Murska Sobota, the modal response was "neither agree nor disagree," but 23 percent nonetheless agreed or strongly agreed.

Consistently, Roma from Novo mesto exhibited stronger agreement with the statements on stereotyping. This makes sense. When I surveyed non-Roma on their attitudes towards the Roma, I asked them to list what bothered them most about the Roma. Together, non-Roma participants from Novo mesto listed something negative and prejudiced 108 times; non-Roma participants from Murska Sobota listed something negative and prejudiced 45 times.[17] Non-Roma from Novo mesto are substantially more prejudiced and Roma know it. Roma perceptions of prejudice matter because they might more likely react to stereotyping they perceive and not to stereotyping which they do not. Thus, if stereotype threat is a mechanism through which mistreatment by non-Roma could drive Roma to survival strategies, we might expect Roma who find stereotyping particularly intractable to more often engage in such strategies.

Here, I showed that many Roma see their own reputations strongly tied to that of the group. Who they are, as individuals, is rendered invisible in favor of a single, damaging label. Many, especially from Novo mesto, believe the stereotype to be inescapable and some even internalize it. I now turn to the tower game, and will revisit deprivation, discrimination, and perceptions of stereotype intractability in the pages that follow.

Survival strategies and the tower game

In the tower game, which involves repeated interactions, early decisions influence later success (see Chapter 4 for a full description). If players had the opportunity to build the tower only once, free-riding (not contributing their brick to the tower), would be the optimal strategy.[18] Since players have the

---

[17] For more, see Chapter 5.
[18] Recall that the tower game is played in a group of 8 players that includes the participant and 7 avatars.

opportunity to build the tower together over several interactions, however, the optimal strategy changes. In order to achieve the best outcome, the group must consistently cooperate. Contributing bricks to the tower, or cooperating, benefits the players twofold: first, all players earn points from the tower as the tower grows, and second, individual players have the option of earning points through the rewarding mechanism, provided that other players in their group reward them for cooperating. A participant can thus achieve the best outcome by contributing her brick early and then continuing to contribute, but this strategy only works if other players contribute as well. While persistent cooperation leads to good outcomes for all players, defecting—not contributing a brick—when all other players cooperate results in the highest payoff for the defector (at the expense of the players who cooperated). Once this happens, sustaining cooperation in subsequent interactions is challenging; since someone already defected, chances are higher that other players will cut their losses and also defect, which makes defection the best option for any and all players. Group cooperation thus easily breaks down. And if players keep their bricks early on, group cooperation might not develop at all because it makes little sense to contribute when others free ride. Success at the end is therefore tied to cooperation throughout.

A player's decision to contribute (or not) to the tower typically rests on their assessment of the likelihood that other players will cooperate. This assessment need not be logical or rational; a player might in fact not be strategic at all, playing entirely without intent. Their decisions are nevertheless meaningful, as they might reflect mental shortcuts, "instincts, habits, or imitation" (Axelrod 1984, p.18). Chapter 5 thus reveals that game decisions of many non-Roma from Novo mesto reflect their beliefs on whether "Roma cannot be trusted," with non-Roma who think that this is so contributing significantly less to the tower when Roma avatars are in play.

For marginalized Roma, the tower game reproduces real-life interactions because it recreates constraints that sometimes govern daily decision-making. Like many such constrains in real life, these come from non-Roma. If Roma expect non-Roma players to discriminate (that is, cooperate less when Roma avatars are in play), it makes sense to defect. Roma players are thus left with a constrained set of options; they might wish to contribute to the tower, but contributing is likely to leave them worse off. Not contributing to the tower is thus equivalent to a survival strategy: it is an action that might not be preferred, but one which is under the limiting circumstances the best remaining alternative. Typical real-life survival strategies are often precisely that—not preferred, but the best available options given the circumstances.

Numerous Roma in my sample who persistently seek formal employment (which is their preferred option for subsistence) but cannot secure it (often due to discrimination by non-Roma) so turn to the best available alternatives, like selling goods door to door, foraging and selling mushrooms, collecting scrap metal, and relying on social assistance.

While the tower game primarily provides a reflection of reality because it allows for constraints imposed by non-Roma, it also reflects some characteristics typical of survival strategies. First, according to the rules of the game, not contributing bricks to the tower is a perfectly acceptable strategy. In real life, relying on social assistance to make ends meet is also perfectly acceptable, as is collecting scrap metal and foraging for mushrooms and blueberries in the forest. Second, not contributing to the tower is nevertheless disliked. The real-life survival strategies I mentioned are also disliked, especially when Roma engage in them; recall the rancor with which some non-Roma talked about what Roma do in Chapter 5 or the way the press wrote about the circumstances surrounding the murder-suicide in Novo mesto in Chapter 3. Third, not contributing bricks to the tower is ethnicized. Although the game rules named it a valid strategy and enumerators took great pains to communicate very clearly that defecting was allowed and was not cheating, non-Roma interpreted defection as cheating and attributed the action to the Roma as such. Notably, a participant from Murska Sobota reacted to game instructions by exclaiming "The Gypsies!" when the enumerator described that a player can keep the brick instead of contributing it to the tower; at the time, the participant did not know that ethnicity was a part of the study.[19] Real-life survival strategies are similarly ethnicized. A journalist need only mention individuals who "trade in . . . colorful metals" or "certain recipients of social assistance" (Radio Krka 2011) to effectively communicate to his audience that he is referring to Roma. Although non-Roma also collect scrap metal, forage in forests, and rely on social assistance, these activities are all associated with Roma (Messing and Molnár 2011).

While the survival strategy in the tower game reflects most real-life survival strategies in being perfectly acceptable but nonetheless disliked and ethnicized, it falls short in one crucial aspect: not contributing a brick to the tower is not other-benefitting. This is *not* representative of survival strategies. Some survival strategies are indeed not other-benefitting; tapping the electricity line is an example of such a strategy. However, many survival strategies are

---

[19] Before they played the tower game participants were only told that the study explored interpersonal relations between people in their town.

other-benefitting; scrap metal collection is perhaps the clearest example, since it both provides a service to individuals who need it and protects the environment. A hasty interpretation of the tower game might *incorrectly* conclude that survival strategies in general are not other-benefitting. I urge readers to think carefully before drawing that conclusion.

In Chapter 4, I presented findings from this game that show that Roma do not behave as stereotyped and that their uses of survival strategies vary from one individual to another. I also showed that Roma levels of cooperation do not decrease when they play with non-Roma avatars. Here, I build on these findings.

As in Chapters 4 and 5, the three main games of interest are those in which the decisions made by all avatars are identical, but in which the avatars have different ethnic identifiers. The first game is the baseline, which assigns no ethnic identifiers; the second is coethnic; and the third mixed. The figures I present here partly reproduce the figures from Chapter 4; I again show the behaviors of Roma from Novo mesto, but compare them to behaviors of Roma from Murska Sobota (see Figures 6.4 and 6.5).[20] As discussed in Chapter 4, Roma from Novo mesto behave quite consistently. Between the baseline, the coethnic, and the mixed game their behaviors change very little. The same holds for Roma participants from Murska Sobota: they, too, behave consistently and do not appear to contribute more to the tower when they play with just other Roma. While Roma in Murska Sobota contribute more to the tower than do Roma from Novo mesto, this difference is not statistically significant. Roma from both towns invariably contribute to the tower about half the time, a remarkable finding.

Numerous studies have shown that people tend to favor members of their ingroups and that they sometimes derogate members of outgroups (Balliet et al. 2014; Pettigrew and Greenwald 2014; Riek et al. 2006; Tajfel and Turner 1979). As this happens when group divisions are haphazard, and even random (Billing and Tajfel 1973), it seems natural to expect it when divisions are not at all arbitrary. When group membership is repeatedly reinforced by discrimination and ingroup members find themselves treated as members of the group first and as individuals second, if at all, sharp lines between the ingroup and the outgroup that discriminates are unavoidable. Members of the marginalized ingroup may unsurprisingly favor ingroup members over

[20] Figure 6.5 presents predicted probabilities of Roma from Novo mesto and Murska Sobota contributing to the tower. They are based on a logit model with individual clustered standard errors that included covariates for gender, age, employment, and education. The model also controlled for the order in which each participant played the randomized games.

Roma tower building behavior in identical baseline, mixed, and coethnic scenarios (Novo mesto)

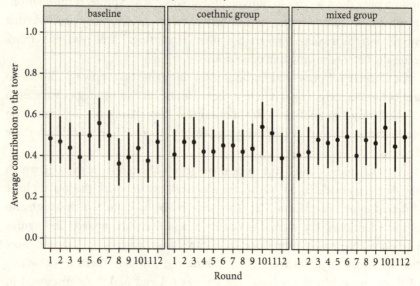

Roma tower building behavior in identical baseline, mixed, and coethnic scenarios (Murska Sobota)

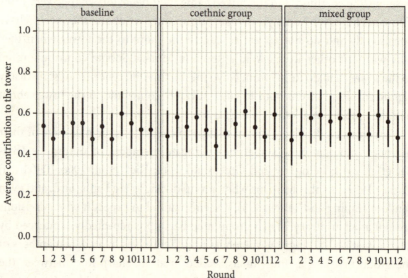

Figure 6.4 This figure presents the average contribution to the tower, along with the 95 percent confidence intervals, that participants made in each round of the three games.

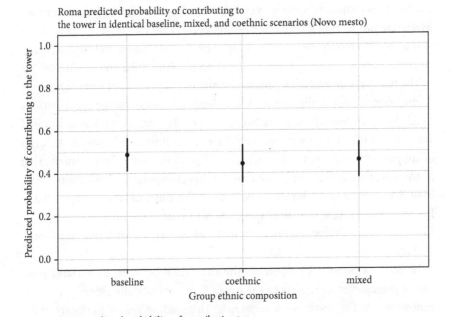

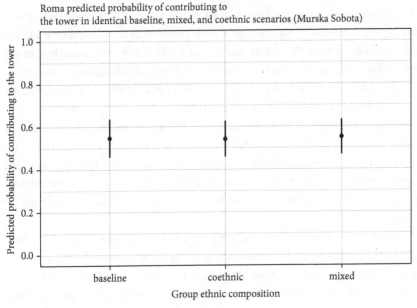

Figure 6.5 This figure presents the predicted probability of contributing to the tower in the first three games, for Roma from Novo mesto on the top and for Roma from Murska Sobota on the bottom. The predicted probabilities with their 95 percent confidence intervals are based on logit models with individual clustered standard errors that included covariates for gender, age, employment, and education. The model also controlled for the order in which each participant played the randomized games. There are no statistically significant differences between any of these predicted probabilities.

outsiders. Yet Roma who have been mistreated by non-Roma for generations cooperate just as much when non-Roma avatars are included in interactions as they do when only Roma avatars are in play. This finding is unexpected and demands further inquiry. I return to its implications at the end of Chapter 7.

The tower game enables a proper, if limited comparison of Roma and non-Roma cooperation in the two towns.[21] Figure 6.6 plots average contributions to the tower in the mixed game, where half of the players are Roma and half are not.[22] While not enormous, the difference in Roma and non-Roma levels of cooperation in Novo mesto is clearly visible. Non-Roma there, contributing to the tower on average 63 percent of the time, cooperated significantly more than Roma, who contributed 47 percent of the time, on average (p < 0.05). Recall, however, that non-Roma from Novo mesto discriminated against the Roma and contributed significantly more when playing with just non-Roma avatars.

In Murska Sobota, by contrast, the difference between Roma and non-Roma average contributions to the tower is not statistically significant—*they contributed to the tower at the same rate*. This finding gets at the heart of the difference between the two towns. In Novo mesto, members of the two groups on average cannot sustain cross-group cooperation as non-Roma consistently discriminate against the Roma and Roma consistently contribute less to the tower than non-Roma. The two behaviors fall into a feedback loop. Since non-Roma discriminate and contribute less to the tower, it makes sense for Roma to contribute less as well; when Roma contribute less, it makes sense for non-Roma to lower their contributions even further, and so on. By contrast, Murska Sobota sees sustainable cross-group cooperation as members of both groups are equally as likely (or unlikely) to defect. Since non-Roma don't discriminate, Roma have no unequal treatment to which to react; and as the survival strategy of low cooperation doesn't manifest itself, non-Roma likewise have no basis for disparate treatment.

Equal levels of cooperation among Roma and non-Roma in Murska Sobota are further meaningful. If the absence of discrimination is the first step toward good intergroup relations, matching levels of cooperation are the second. One could imagine a situation where non-Roma do not discriminate but Roma

---

[21] As Roma and non-Roma might arrive at their tower game behaviors through different processes, analyzing the behaviors of both groups together is problematic (Israel-Trummel 2015). Nevertheless, it is useful to plot average contributions to the tower together solely for the purpose of illustrating the gaps between average contributions.

[22] For Roma participants, 3 avatars are Roma and 4 are non-Roma; for non-Roma participants, 3 avatars are non-Roma and 4 are Roma.

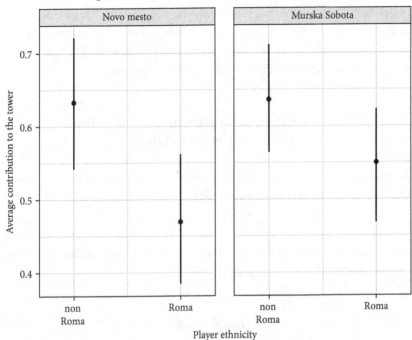

Tower building behavior in the mixed game, by player ethnicity

Figure 6.6 This figure presents the average contributions to the tower in the mixed game, first by towns and then by non-Roma and Roma participants.

continue to contribute less to the tower, perhaps because their levels of trust in non-Roma cooperation remain low due to recent experience of discrimination. Such a situation is likely to develop because neither discrimination nor survival strategies disappear overnight. Experiencing discrimination can be traumatic. The expectation that upon observing lower levels of discrimination Roma who have previously experienced discrimination would immediately adjust their behaviors is both deeply unrealistic and deeply problematic. Yet non-Roma who (newly) do not discriminate might expect precisely such an adjustment and might, upon not observing such a change, regress back into discriminatory behaviors. The findings from Murska Sobota suggest that Roma/non-Roma relations there are not in this fragile state where discrimination has decreased but the usage of survival strategies has not yet caught up; instead, Roma and non-Roma there can sustainably cooperate with one another.

It is important to note here that a breakdown of cooperation is not in fact observed in the tower game. This is so because participants play identical scenarios, which are determined beforehand. In those scenarios, the avatars cooperate with the same probability and do not react to the decisions that the participant is making (except in rewarding, where cooperation is always rewarded and defection never). In real life such reactions are likely in at least some cases, and might lead to a breakdown of cooperation.

Deprivation, discrimination, and perceptions of stereotype intractability

The findings from the tower game deal a serious blow to commonplace stereotyping of Roma as cheaters, thieves, and takers. In the paragraphs that follow, I explore variation in Roma uses of survival strategies in the tower game. In particular, I examine the relationship between Roma contributions to the tower and three factors: deprivation, personal experience of discrimination, and perceptions of stereotype intractability.[23]

Deprivation

I first turn briefly to deprivation. Scholars have found that people who have been deprived often behave differently from people who have not (Ramos et al. 2013). Experiences associated with economic hardship can reduce a person's actual or perceived ability to control her future; as a result, she might value present rewards more highly than future rewards, even if present rewards are smaller (Pepper and Nettle 2017). Deprived individuals thus sometimes invest less in education (Blanden and Gregg 2004) and smoke more (Adams and White 2009).

Since the tower game is played in several rounds, we can explore whether deprivation is linked to different levels of cooperation in the game. A participant who discounts the future to a substantial degree would be more likely to defect in the context of the tower game. The logic is as follows. Sustained cooperation among all 8 players over time leads to higher payoffs for everyone—this is the tower game version of a higher reward in the future. Such an outcome, however, is only possible if everyone cooperates. If a participant cannot trust the other players to cooperate (and keep cooperating), it is better for her to defect and keep her brick. This is the tower game version of a small

---

[23] As Roma contribute to the tower consistently regardless of the ethnic identities of the avatars, all my plots in this section are based on average contributions to the tower in the mixed game (half Roma and half-non-Roma players).

reward in the present. A participant who has experienced deprivation and who, as a result, may feel that she has less control over her future—particularly when it depends on the behavior of other players—might thus prefer to keep her bricks instead of contributing them to the tower. Although the tower game has several rounds, we might expect participants who discount the future to begin defecting right away; when the game starts, the only decision that happens in the present is the one that happens first.

I have not been able to capture much variation in socioeconomic status among Roma participants (recall that most fall into the lowest income bracket), but access to sewerage nevertheless offers an opportunity to see whether gradations in deprivation are linked to survival strategies. The top panel in Figure 6.7 plots access to sewerage against average contributions to the tower in the first round of the baseline game, which was the very first decision participants made in the tower game. The results suggest that in both towns, Roma who do not have access to sewerage contributed no more and no less to the tower than Roma who have sewerage. While a difference in cooperation that stems from discounting the future is likely to appear in the first round, an overall higher tendency to defect might also lead to lower average contributions in all rounds of the game, especially as early defection makes later cooperation unlikely. The bottom panel of Figure 6.7 thus examines average Roma contributions to the tower in the mixed game, across all rounds. Here, too, tower contributions did not vary significantly based on access to sewerage. Gradations of deprivation, as captured by access to sewerage, thus do not appear to be linked to Roma uses of survival strategies in the game.

While I have not established a link between deprivation and survival strategies here, that does not mean that the two are unrelated. Access to sewerage is a limited indicator because it does not capture the full array of factors that contribute to deprivation. Perhaps this measure fails to capture the full extent of deprivation and with it variation that is, in fact, linked to uses of survival strategies. Alternatively, relative (and not absolute) deprivation could shape behaviors, such that people who feel more deprived compared to others might engage in more risk-seeking behaviors (Mo 2017). As my data are limited, I cannot explore these questions here. However, studying this relationship further would be a worthwhile endeavor.

Discrimination

Here, I examine the relationship between survival strategies and reported personal experience of discrimination. Personal experience of ostracism can

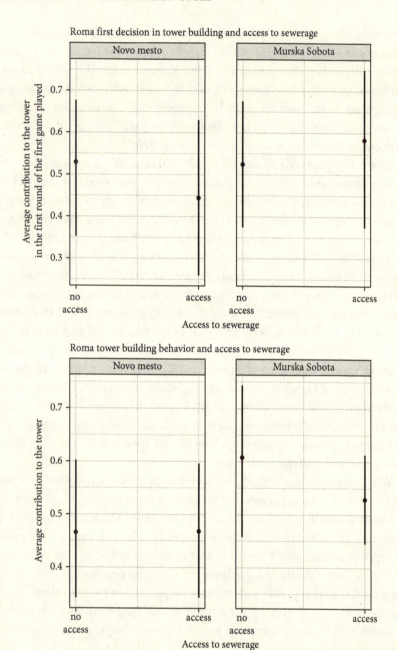

Figure 6.7 This figure presents the average Roma contributions to the tower in the mixed game, first by towns and then by access to sewerage.

have profoundly damaging effects, ranging from abject misery and aggression to low levels of altruism and cooperation (Twenge 2007; Williams 2007). Earlier in this chapter, I introduced ten composite questions that I used to capture perceived discrimination among Roma. The plots I present here all rely on a dichotomous variable, coded 1 if the participant reports that she has experienced *at least one* type of discrimination, which she believes happened because she is Roma, and coded 0 if the participant does not report having experienced discrimination.[24] Based on this variable, about 7 out of 10 Roma report having experienced discrimination. In Novo mesto, 82 percent report it and in Murska Sobota, 63 percent do the same.

As the number of Roma who did not report any experience of discrimination is quite low—12 in Novo mesto and 24 in Murska Sobota—I combine the data from the two towns.[25] The top panel of Figure 6.8 plots the predicted probabilities of contributing to the tower by reported experience of discrimination—first for participants who did not report having experienced discrimination and then for participants who did.[26] Participants who reported personal experience of discrimination contributed significantly less to the tower than participants who did not report the same. Those who reported having experienced discrimination contributed about 46 percent of the time, while those who did not contributed about 60 percent of the time. This is a meaningful divide. Personal experience of discrimination divides Roma participants into those who kept their bricks more often than they parted with them and those who were more likely to contribute than not.

Challenging questions emerge from these findings. Do Roma with personal experiences of discrimination use more survival strategies? Or do Roma who use survival strategies face more discrimination? Since I did not experimentally manipulate exposure to discrimination, my findings cannot speak to the

[24] The composite questions are listed in Table 6.1. I only consider a survey answer as reporting discrimination if the participant answers "yes" to both parts of the composite question—that is, that she has experienced discrimination and that she believes it happened because she is Roma. If she answers "no" to at least one part of the composite question, I do not count that report as perceived discrimination.

[25] Examining contributions to the tower by town reveals that in both Novo mesto and Murska Sobota, Roma who reported experiencing at least one type of mistreatment contributed less than Roma who did not. The differences, however, were not statistically significant, possibly because the number of Roma who did not report experiencing discrimination is quite low.

[26] The predicted probabilities are based on a logit model with individual clustered standard errors that included the dichotomous reported discrimination variable, a dichotomous perception of stereotype intractability variable as well as covariates for gender, age, employment, education, and game order.

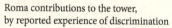

Roma contributions to the tower,
by reported experience of discrimination

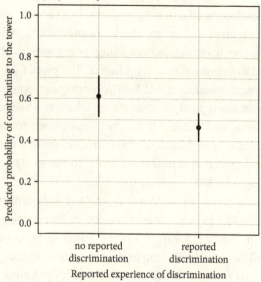

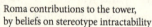

Roma contributions to the tower,
by beliefs on stereotype intractability

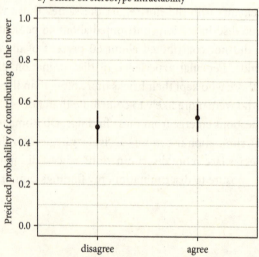

Figure 6.8 The top panel presents the predicted probability of contributing to the tower in the mixed game, by town and reported experience of discrimination. The bottom presents the same, by town and perceived stereotype intractability. The predicted probabilities and the 95 percent confidence intervals are based on a logit model with individual clustered standard errors that included the dichotomous reported discrimination variable, the dichotomous perceived stereotype intractability variable, as well as covariates for gender, age, employment, education, and game order.

directionality of the relationship.[27] Short-term manipulations of exposure to ostracism demonstrate that even a few minutes of such exposure can lead to damaging consequences, including low levels of cooperation (Twenge 2007). But it is also easy to imagine that someone who engages in behaviors that are not other-benefitting might be treated poorly as a result—after all, criminals are ostracized, people who try cutting in line at the DMV receive dirty looks and more, and rowdy guests are often not invited to the next barbecue gathering. Ostracism leads to low cooperation, but individuals who do not cooperate are also shunned.

The cyclical nature of the relationship between discrimination and survival strategies renders the question of what came first difficult to answer. This is especially true in the context of systemic discrimination against the Roma that has lasted for generations, both at the level of the individual as well as the state and beyond. If we must look for a beginning, we might focus on anti-minority culture, which is in place before a child is born to a marginalized community. As I mentioned in the introduction to this chapter, a Roma child born today in the Novo mesto hospital is likely placed in a "Roma room" in the maternity ward, experiencing discrimination before she can even be aware of it. Her introduction to discrimination occurs before she develops the capacity to engage in a survival strategy, which she might grasp by the time she turns three and develops selectivity in how she treats others (Olson and Spelke 2008). While most Roma who experience exclusion probably encounter anti-minority culture and discrimination first, perhaps some don't. Exclusion cycles can likely develop regardless. There are many questions to ask regarding the emergence of exclusion cycles. As they extend beyond the scope of this book, I do not approach them here. Instead, I turn to the third factor that might influence Roma decision making in the tower game.

Perceptions of stereotype intractability

Perceptions of stereotype intractability may shape Roma engagement in ethnicized survival strategies. Scholarship on stereotype threat shows that a mere mention of a stereotype might lead a member of the stereotyped group to behave as the stereotype dictates (Steele and Aronson 1995). While people can

---

[27] While experimental manipulations of short-term exposure to ostracism exist (i.e. playing Cyberball for 15 minutes; see Gonsalkorale and Williams 2007), approximating anything more extensive would be ethically unacceptable.

respond to contextually relevant stereotypes without intent and perhaps even without awareness, some responses can be deliberate, going as far as embracing the stigma and collectively reconstructing it (Ashforth and Kreiner 1999). Thus, if an individual believes that stereotyping is intractable, she might be more likely to engage in a stereotyped, ethnicized survival strategy—deliberately or not.

Earlier in this chapter, I discussed Roma answers to questions on stereotyping. In Novo mesto, almost 3 out of 4 Roma find stereotyping deeply entrenched; they believe that as long as non-Roma think that one Roma is a criminal, non-Roma won't trust any Roma at all. In Murska Sobota, half of Roma believe the same. Further, half of Roma in Novo mesto believe they are seen only as Roma and not as an individuals; the same is true for a third of Roma in Murska Sobota. Lastly, half of Roma in Novo mesto agree that some Roma in their town generally cannot be trusted; in Murska Sobota, 1 in 4 agree. Here, I explore whether these beliefs are linked to cooperative behaviors in the tower game.

In the context of the game, the potential link between perceptions of stereotype intractability and Roma uses of survival strategies is quite straightforward. Perceptions of stereotype intractability could be viewed as prior beliefs: the more a Roma participant finds stereotypes intractable, the more she might believe that non-Roma would expect any Roma to defect in the tower game. This, in turn, would then influence her own behavior in the game—the stronger her belief that non-Roma would expect Roma to defect, the stronger her expectation that non-Roma, upon seeing a Roma co-player, will then also defect. As she expects non-Roma to defect, she should then also defect herself as cooperating while others defect results in a loss.

Are Roma who perceive stereotypes as particularly intractable less likely to contribute to the tower? The top panel of Figure 6.9 suggests that they might be. This panel plots the average Roma contribution to the tower in the mixed game along with their agreement with the following statement: "as long as non-Roma think that one Roma is a criminal, they won't trust any Roma at all."[28] Roma who agreed with this statement contributed significantly less to the tower than did Roma who did not agree ($p < 0.05$).[29]

---

[28] On the survey, the question asked for agreement on a 5-point scale. I re-scaled the answers for the graph into "yes" and "no". "Yes" stands for "agree" and "strongly agree." No stands for "disagree," "strongly disagree," and "neutral".

[29] This difference is only statistically significant when Roma from both towns are examined together; when looking at the two towns separately, the difference remains, but loses significance.

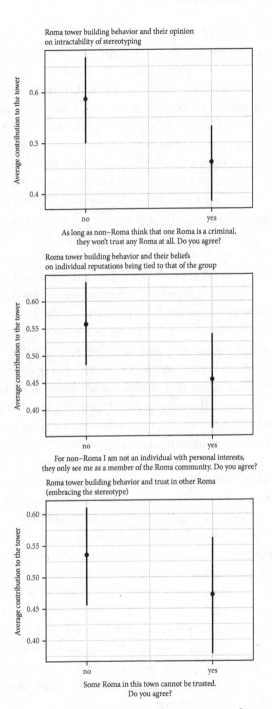

Figure 6.9 Roma tower building behavior and perceptions of stereotype intractability.

The other two plots of Figure 6.9 provide little support to this finding, however. The bottom two panels of this figure show the average contribution to the tower in the mixed game and agreement with two statements, "for non-Roma I am not an individual with personal interests; they only see me as a member of the Roma community" and "some Roma from my town generally cannot be trusted." In both, the direction of the relationship is as anticipated—Roma who agree with the statements contribute less—but neither is statistically significant.[30] Whether or not a participant believes that she is only seen as a Roma and not as an individual thus has no bearing on how she played the tower game. Likewise, Roma attitudes on whether some Roma from their town can be trusted are not linked to their game decision making. Thus far, the findings therefore present only limited support for the link between beliefs on stereotype intractability and tower contributions.

As reports of personal experience of discrimination and perceptions of stereotype intractability are correlated, I next examine them and Roma tower contributions together. Figure 6.8 presents the results of a regression that included both of these factors in addition to the usual population controls (this analysis uses the measure of stereotype intractability that was predictive of tower contributions before—agreement with "as long as non-Roma think that one Roma is a criminal, they won't trust any Roma at all"). As discussed in the previous section, the top panel of Figure 6.8 shows that even when controlling for beliefs on stereotype intractability, reported personal experience of discrimination remains predictive of tower contributions. The bottom panel of Figure 6.8 instead shows that when the model accounts for personal experience of discrimination, beliefs on stereotype intractability lose statistical significance. In short, the findings suggest that personal experience of discrimination matters in determining Roma uses of survival strategies, while beliefs on stereotype intractability don't. Although many Roma participants believe that stereotyping is deeply entrenched and difficult to escape, those beliefs do not appear to shape their behaviors in the tower game.

Altogether, my findings suggest that in the context of the tower game, reported experience of discrimination affects Roma uses of a survival strategy, while deprivation and perceptions regarding stereotype intractability do not. What does this tell us about the NGOs in Murska Sobota and Novo mesto? The conclusion regarding deprivation and perceptions of stereotype intractability is uncomplicated as the results were consistently insignificant in the models that considered the towns separately.

---

[30] The same holds when Roma behaviors and beliefs are examined separately, by town.

By contrast, personal experience of discrimination demands some caution in interpretation. When I combined the observations from both towns, comparing Roma who either reported experiencing discrimination or didn't, the experience of discrimination was consistently significant. Once I split the results by town, however, experience of discrimination lost statistical significance. This may be due to the low number of Roma who reported that they have not experienced discrimination. It's important to note that two thirds of Roma who reported no such experience were from Murska Sobota. Nevertheless, I cannot conclude that not experiencing discrimination in Murska Sobota or in Novo mesto *specifically* mattered for Roma behaviors in the tower game, but only that overall, participants who did not experience discrimination contributed significantly more to the tower.

A test of persistence

My conclusion that personal experience of discrimination shapes Roma contributions to the tower is consistent with research on the consequences of exclusion of ostracism, which shows that even short periods of exclusion result in lower levels of cooperation (Twenge et al. 2007). While some participants may have acted intuitively or without a plan, a logic for those who may have acted strategically can be imagined rather easily. A participant who has experienced discrimination before may be more likely to expect discrimination in the context of the game; if that is the case, defecting makes sense. She might then reckon that other Roma players, or some of them, may have also experienced discrimination and are likely making the same calculation. As the game requires only one participant to defect in order for cooperation to dissolve, and both Roma and non-Roma are likely to defect following this logic, the optimal choice is indeed not to contribute any bricks to the tower.

My next and final test examines what happens when this reasonable expectation is wrong. If all other players cooperate, can a participant who has experienced discrimination increase her own cooperation? Answering this question speaks to the persistence of discrimination's dampening effect on cooperation as well as to the role that Roma who have not experienced discrimination play in sustaining cross-group cooperation.

In the final game, Roma participants see only cooperators. I achieve this through the reward phase: where in the other scenarios participants would see a selection of Roma and non-Roma cooperators and defectors, in this game they see only cooperators. The game is otherwise identical to the regular mixed

218   BREAKING THE EXCLUSION CYCLE

game. The avatars are making the same decisions, and the reward phase shows both Roma and non-Roma, except only those who are cooperators.[31] This difference is established quickly. In the regular mixed game, a participant sees a cooperator in the reward phase of the first round, and then two defectors— once in the rewarding phase of the second round and then again in the third. In the "cooperators-only-shown" game, the participant sees three cooperators in the first 3 rounds of the game; this continues for all rounds. This game thus presents the participant with a promising scenario. If she, too, contributes to the tower, she can help sustain a high level of cooperation among all players, ensuring that everyone is better off as the game proceeds through the rounds. If, unlike everyone else, she does not contribute to the tower, she becomes the single defector, jeopardizing the cooperative success of the group.

The results reveal an unmistakable gap between Roma who reported personal experience of discrimination and Roma who did not. Figure 6.10 plots this gap. Roma who reported personal experience of discrimination contributed to the tower 47 percent of the time, on average. They were entirely unswayed by the apparently constant cooperation of other avatars. They contributed to the tower at essentially the same level as in the mixed game, which was otherwise identical but in which half the avatars presented in the reward phase were defectors.[32] Roma who did not report personal experience of discrimination, in contrast, adjusted their behaviors and raised their levels of cooperation. They were significantly more likely to contribute to the tower in this apparently highly cooperative game, which they did on average 70 percent of the time. Crucially, this adjustment in behaviors had to have happened quite quickly because the "cooperators-only-shown" game only lasted for a total of 12 rounds.

The findings suggest that even under the most auspicious circumstances, personal experience of discrimination presents a barrier to raising levels of cooperation. The consequences of trauma are deeply-rooted and enduring, and they require interventions that extend beyond a momentary change in circumstances, like that in the tower game, as well as tempered expectations regarding quick behavioral change. To be sure, the findings do not suggest that Roma who have experienced discrimination would never have adjusted their game decision-making; they merely show that a 12-round game is too short for that to happen. The 12 rounds were sufficient, however, for Roma who did

---

[31] See the Online Appendix for game details.

[32] In that game, Roma who reported experiencing discrimination contributed 48 percent of the time, on average.

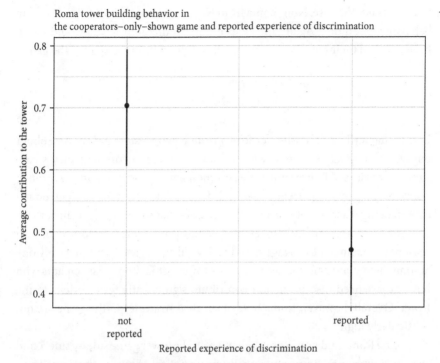

Roma tower building behavior in
the cooperators–only–shown game and reported experience of discrimination

Figure 6.10 The average contribution to the tower in the highly cooperative game (where all avatars shown are cooperators), by reported experience of discrimination.

not report experiencing discrimination to adjust their behaviors. This shows exceptional promise for future efforts to eliminate discrimination against the Roma and promote Roma/non-Roma cooperation. If efforts to reduce discrimination work, Roma treated fairly may engage in high levels of intergroup cooperation very quickly. In light of recent widespread discrimination, this is noteworthy.

Two additional points are worth mentioning. First, Roma behaviors are not uniform. I have already demonstrated this several times, but in light of persistent and pervasive stereotyping it bears repeating. Second, Roma behaviors in the highly cooperative game demonstrate that the tower game design allows participants to observe the behaviors of others and adjust their own, if they so desire. Recall that non-Roma from Novo mesto consistently contributed less to the tower when Roma avatars were in play, even though Roma and non-Roma avatars behaved identically. Observing that game, one might have questioned whether this happened because the game design somehow discouraged changes in behavior; here, Roma participants demonstrate that this is not the case. Non-Roma from Novo mesto could have adjusted their behaviors, but didn't. Again, this does not mean that non-Roma would never have adjusted their behaviors, just that they didn't within the span of the game.

Conclusion

In this chapter I explore whether Roma from Novo mesto and Murska Sobota engage in survival strategies, with a focus on three factors that may shape Roma behaviors. All three are quite common among the Roma in my sample; many participants experience material deprivation; many report personally experiencing discrimination; and many believe that stereotyping against them is intractable and difficult to escape. While these three factors could all reasonably be linked to engagement in survival strategies, I find that only one among them matters in the context of the tower game. Roma participants who have experienced discrimination contribute significantly fewer bricks to the tower. Overall, however, Roma uses of survival strategies in the game are not particularly high.

Placing Roma and non-Roma behaviors in the tower game side by side, I find that, in Novo mesto, Roma and non-Roma do not contribute to the tower at the same rate, while in Murska Sobota they do. Participants from Murska Sobota are thus able to establish sustainable cross-group cooperation in the context of the game, which is not possible for participants in Novo mesto. Although I do not have conclusive evidence that Roma who don't report experiencing discrimination drive the finding in Murska Sobota, results from the mixed and the highly cooperative mixed games suggest that this might be the case. Certainly, personal experience of discrimination affects Roma uses of survival strategies, which suggests that any efforts to curb discrimination might, over time, lead to fewer survival strategies.

7

Full Circle

I have now constructed an empirical example of an exclusion cycle and presented evidence in support of one mechanism that can help break it. This chapter offers a brief summary of the findings and a short discussion on animus and statistical discrimination. I then address the question of generalization and continue with open questions, of which there are many. I conclude with the main takeaways.

Summary

There is no doubt that anti-Roma culture exists in Slovenia; it is written into the dictionary of Slovene itself. This general environment creates space for anti-Roma sentiment, which I find in both towns I examine. In Novo mesto, far more non-Roma express it. Those who express it also discriminate against the Roma in the tower game. Roma participants from this town in turn engage in a survival strategy in the game and contribute even fewer bricks to the tower (but do not discriminate). These behaviors lead to a breakdown of cooperation between Roma and non-Roma, where contributing less and less (or, in fact, nothing) is the optimal action for all. As Roma engage in survival strategies, non-Roma dislike these strategies and ethnicize them, even though non-Roma resort to them as well. These attribution errors affirm stereotypes, feed anti-minority culture, and start the exclusion cycle over again.

While non-Roma in Murska Sobota do voice anti-Roma sentiment, they express less of it. They also do not act on it in the tower game; instead, they treat everyone the same. Roma participants do, too. More importantly, Roma and non-Roma contribute to the tower at the same rate, which leads to sustained cooperation between members of the two groups. Non-Roma still commit attribution errors, but make fewer of these mistakes than their counterparts in Novo mesto. In the context of the tower game, the feedback loop of discrimination and survival strategies does not manifest itself. That doesn't mean that there are no exclusion cycles in everyday life in Murska

Sobota, but it does mean that there might be fewer in this town than in Novo mesto.

Discrimination is at the core of the cyclical dynamic in the tower game. When non-Roma discriminate, Roma engage in survival strategies; the opposite is also true. Notably, not all Roma engage in survival strategies in the tower game; only those who have personally experienced discrimination in real life do. My findings thus suggest that in order to break the cycle, interventions should be aimed at discrimination.

As the two towns match on a host of relevant factors but differ in the type of Roma-led NGO action, the difference in discriminatory non-Roma behaviors may be at least partly due to contact-promotion activities of the NGO in Murska Sobota. Non-Roma who are familiar with the NGO indeed contribute significantly more to the tower in the mixed game than non-Roma who are unfamiliar with the organization. However, as I neither randomly assigned 25 years of contact-promoting NGO action to one of these towns nor selected the inhabitants of the treated town to participate in said contact, interpreting the link between contact promotion and no discrimination requires caution. It is nevertheless exciting, even if just suggestive.

Animus or statistical discrimination?

When Adida et al. (2016) describe an interactive dynamic between the rooted French and Muslim immigrants in France, they call it "a discriminatory equilibrium":

> By "discriminatory equilibrium" we mean a vicious circle in which both [rooted French] and Muslims in France are acting negatively toward one another in ways that are mutually reinforcing. We describe this equilibrium as follows: (1) Muslim immigrants display behaviors that feed into French statistical discrimination against them in the labor market...; (2) rooted French exhibit unprovoked taste-based discrimination against Muslims...; and (3) Muslims, perceiving more hostility in France, separate more from the host society than do their Christian counterparts.   (Adida et al. 2016, p.108)

Adida et al. (2016) distinguish between two types of discrimination traditionally singled out in scholarship that aims to explain why discrimination happens. The first is statistical discrimination. This concept, coined by Phelps (1972) and Arrow (1973), denotes discrimination based on rational optimizing behavior and limited information. As we generally cannot tell how strangers with whom we interact will behave, but want to have some sense of it, we form expectations based on their group characteristics (Arrow 1973; Phelps 1972). Suppose a Black woman is looking to buy a car. The salesman, who harbors no animus but believes that Black women are willing to pay more for a car because they have an aversion to bargaining, quotes her a higher price than he would quote to a White man (Ayres and Siegelman 1995).[1] This is statistical discrimination. Suppose instead that the salesman quotes a higher price because he harbors anti-Black sentiment. This is an example of animus, or discrimination based on hatred (Becker 1957). The two concepts are typically contrasted, and numerous scholars have grappled with isolating one from the other (Guryan and Charles 2013; Riach and Rich 2002).

The complicated relationship between Roma and non-Roma fits exactly into this space. It makes perfect sense that non-Roma from Novo mesto would contribute less to the tower when Roma avatars are in play if Roma from this town in fact defect more often than non-Roma. This looks like a textbook case of statistical discrimination. Yet non-Roma from Novo mesto not only express alarming levels of anti-Roma sentiment, but they also behave consistently with it and contribute less to the tower if prejudiced. Moreover, when given the opportunity to learn and adjust their behaviors upon interacting with Roma and non-Roma avatars that behave identically—which a pure statistical discriminator might do—non-Roma from Novo mesto keep discriminating. Of course, that does not mean that they would never adjust, only that they didn't within the span of the game (unlike the Roma participants I discussed a few pages ago). I thus appear to have evidence of both animus and statistical discrimination in Novo mesto.

I do not try to separate animus from statistical discrimination in Novo mesto, for two reasons. First, the two likely feed into one another. As Ayres and Siegelman write, "it may be that simple theories of discrimination fail to capture the mutually reinforcing nature of multiple causes. In the end, it may prove impossible to parse out the various elements of animus and rational inferences from irrational stereotypes" (Siegelman 1995, p.319). Second, in

---

[1] In an audit study of bargaining for a new car, Ayres and Siegelman (1995) found that Black and female testers received significantly higher price quotes than White male testers, even though all testers used identical bargaining strategies and all other relevant factors (socioeconomic class, etc.) were controlled for. Offers to Black male testers, for example, were on average $935 higher than offers to White male testers. While they find no direct evidence suggesting that women or minorities have more aversion to bargaining, they do find that sellers force non-White-male customers to overcome additional hurdles, like putting down a deposit. They associate that treatment with bargaining aversion. For more, see Ayres and Siegelman (1995).

the case of groups that have been marginalized for generations, statistical discrimination may stem, at least partly, from animus. To demonstrate, I return briefly to the hypothetical example of the Black woman buying a car. Suppose that the salesman who quoted his customer a higher price in fact felt no animus towards her. Suppose also that the hypothetical customer, in turn, did not experience animus while buying the car. Years before, however, her mother might have, and years before that, her grandmother might have as well. While bargaining for a car might be bereft of animus today, it was not always, and therefore what the salesman sees as statistical discrimination now may in fact be a legacy of past animus. The reason for his belief that Black women are averse to bargaining now may very well stem from behaviors learned generations ago, when animus was acute, making bargaining unbearable for some. Taking a snapshot of the interaction in the car dealership without fully considering the past might, in the absence of evidence of animus, lead one to chalk up the difference in treatment to statistical discrimination. But life is not a snapshot, and while this conclusion might be correct in the moment, it misses the bigger picture. And as the snapshot allows the salesman to engage in disparate treatment without owning up to his contribution to systemic inequality—in fact, he might not be aware of it at all—instances of such statistical discrimination, even if individually small, maintain and widen disparities along the intersections of race, class, gender, and more. Animus casts a long shadow. If today's statistical discrimination is caught in that shadow, it is not truly free of animus.

Generalization challenges

The findings I have presented in this book are based on two studies that involve experiments, an extensive survey, semi-structured interviews of experts and regular citizens, field observations I have made, and countless conversations I have had with Roma and non-Roma over the past 8 years. Yet rich as they are, the data are limited to the behaviors and attitudes of people from two towns in a small country in the middle of Europe. I would therefore caution *against* generalizing the results of my analyses to other contexts. The findings should not serve as an indication that such exclusion cycles exist elsewhere, but rather as an impetus to explore whether they actually do.

That said, there are a number of reasons for why we *might* find exclusion cycles in other contexts, should we choose to look for them. Consider first the case of Roma and non-Roma in other places. In Chapter 3, I discussed a number of ways in which Roma communities differ from one another. These include variations in dialect, religion, customs, and traditional occupations, as well as distinct present and past political and economic circumstances.

Despite this diversity, a number of commonalities—not only across communities but also across states—suggest that variations of what I observed in Slovenia might be observed elsewhere. First, the nature of Roma exclusion itself provides an unexpected constancy across different Roma communities. Roma exclusion has withstood decades, even centuries, of challenges. Even though Roma differed from one another, and even though the local circumstances they encountered wherever they travelled or settled surely varied, their *Otherness* and, often though not always, their exclusion was common.

Table 7.1 presents a range of socioeconomic and quality of life indicators for a set of 12 European countries with Roma populations and for the Slovene

Table 7.1 Socioeconomic and quality of life indicators of Slovene Roma participants, based on my survey, and Roma populations in 12 other European states, based on the 2012 UNDP/World Bank/EC Regional Roma Survey

country	sanitation[a]	washing machine[c]	household size[d]	rooms per person[e]	education[f]	employment[g]
Slovenia	76 (59)[b]	80	4.3	0.93	65	20
Albania	50	34	5	0.44	63	42
Bosnia and Herzegovina	30	36	6	0.62	70	19
Bulgaria	62	54	5	0.94	86	34
Czech Rep.	1	82	5	0.55	99	31
Hungary	30	83	5	0.68	99	23
Croatia	48	66	7	0.48	89	14
Moldova	79	32	6	1.08	67	21
Montengro	35	55	5	0.65	63	27
Macedonia	34	4	6	0.66	83	23
Romania	78	33	6	0.67	83	30
Serbia	44	55	6	0.63	86	26
Slovakia	38	76	6	0.54	98	15

[a]The questions on the UNDP survey asked about a toilet or shower inside, but not about access to sewerage; I asked about having a bathroom (not specifying toilet or shower) and whether they had access to sewerage.; [b]For Slovene Roma participants, 76 indicates the percent of Roma who said they had a bathroom and 59 indicates the percent of Roma who said they had access to sewerage; [c]Ownership of a washing machine; [d]Average number of persons in a given household; [e]Average number of rooms per household member; [f]Young Roma population with at least primary education. In the case of Slovene Roma participants, the age group included in this number are Roma who are between 18 and 24 years old. In the case of the UNDP survey, the age group included are Roma who are 14 to 20 years old; [g]Employment rates. Any type of paying job included.

Roma communities in Novo mesto and Murska Sobota.[2] On measures ranging from indoor plumbing to education, housing, and employment, the two localities in my study are well within the norm. This suggests that at least as a first cut, the Roma communities from which I recruited my participants may be relatively typical.

Further, the nature of stereotyping and anti-Roma speech across a number of states suggests the presence of a similar anti-Roma culture. The Bulgarian press uses racist language when reporting on crime allegedly perpetrated by Roma, ascribing criminal acts to a "specific ethnic nature" (Scicluna 2007, p.49). As discussed in Chapter 3, the Slovene press does the same, often referring to the "Roma question or the Roma problem" (Erjavec et al. 2000, p.15), as does the press in Croatia (Kanižaj 2004), Hungary (Bogdan 2015), and almost all Western European Union states,[3] where the stereotype of criminality is consistently associated with Roma and is, along with stereotyping of Muslims, "the most pernicious and the most negative" of all stereotypes (ter Wal 2002, p.48). Such reporting contributes not only to general anti-Roma culture but also commonly commits attribution errors.

Anti-Roma speech by public officials, also contributing to anti-Roma culture, is present across a number of European states. A Slovene independent presidential candidate stated that "It is known that [Roma] steal, that they have social problems..." (Erjavec et al. 2002, p.27), while the Prefect of Rome in Italy reported having visited a Roma settlement to find that "... [Roma] women were not around because they [were] at the metro stealing purses" (Egenberger and Colacicchi 2007, p.2). In response to a crime in which one of the assailants was Roma, a founding member of the Hungarian political party Fidesz, Zsolt Bayer, wrote "... [t]hese Roma are animals, and they behave like animals" (Guy 2017, p.159). When a Czech mayor forcibly evicted Roma families from the town center of Vsetin, he called his actions "the removal of an ulcer" (Guy 2017, p.157). In Slovakia, Marián Kotleba was elected governor of Banská Bystrica on a manifesto promising to fight "unfair favoritism of Gypsy parasites" (Nosko 2013). And after fielding questions from a journalist, the President of Romania remarked:"[h]ow aggressive that stinky gypsy was" (Scicluna 2007, p.47). Across a number of Central and Eastern European states, including

---

[2] The 12 countries are: Albania, Bosnia and Herzegovina, Bulgaria, Croatia, Czech Republic, Hungary, Macedonia, Moldova, Montenegro, Romania, Serbia, and Slovakia. These are the countries that were included in the 2012 UNDP/World Bank/EC Regional Roma Survey, which collected data on the socioeconomic and quality of life measures presented in Table 7.1 (with the exception of Slovenia). See O'Higgins (2012), Perić (2012), Brüggemann (2012), Ivanov et al. (2012), and Mihailov (2012).

[3] Some Finnish and Greek media offer welcome exceptions. For more, see ter Wal (2002).

Slovenia, hate speech does not merely appear in private communications or on the street, but also on the national stage.

Finally, across these states Roma face substantial discrimination in employment (Hyde 2006; O'Higgins 2012); a higher probability of being disabled or having a chronic illness (Mihailov 2012); a higher likelihood of being unable to afford medicine (Mihailov 2012); and a near certainty that their children and their peers won't learn Romani or Roma history in school (Brüggemann 2012).

In broad strokes, stereotyping, anti-Roma hate speech, and discrimination against the Roma in Slovenia are similar to the same in a number of other Central and Eastern European states. In socioeconomic status, Slovene Roma participants do not deviate much from Roma in the 12 European countries that were included in the UNDP household survey. While they are sometimes better off and sometimes worse off, on average, than the majority of Roma from these countries, they never stray far from the group. Of course, this does not mean that exclusion cycles necessarily exist in any of these other states; it merely means that on some indicators, Roma participants in my study are fairly representative of Roma elsewhere in Europe and therefore looking for exclusion cycles there might be fruitful.

If Roma diversity poses a challenge to generalization beyond Novo mesto and Murska Sobota, altogether different groups might pose an even bigger challenge. Still, there are some parallels to be drawn between my case, other marginalized communities, and the communities that exclude them. Let me start with an anecdote. A few years ago, at a conference reception, I had a conversation with an educator from one of the post-Yugoslav states. She was an expert on primary education, working on a program that would better integrate Serbian, Croatian, and Bosnian children, some of whom were children of refugees displaced during the Yugoslav wars in the 1990s. Excited about her program, I asked enthusiastically whether local Roma children also attended. "Of course not," she scoffed, "they're animals."

This conversation calls to mind the discussion from Chapter 2 on Batwa and boys of color in Oakland. While he was conducting his fieldwork in Uganda, Kidd (2008) was cautioned against driving his motorcycle through the forest, as "that was where the animals belonged" (Kidd 2008, p.118). Such speech appears in the general US context as well; in December 2016, Pamela Taylor, a non-profit director, celebrated the imminent arrival of Melania Trump to the White house by writing on Facebook "[i]t will be so refreshing to have a classy, beautiful, dignified First Lady back in the White House. I'm tired of seeing a Ape in heels" (Phillips 2016). Rios's study participants in Oakland, too, reported that teachers "treat us like if we were animals" (Rios 2011, p.144).

There are still more parallels. Both Black Americans and Roma are stereo-typed as criminal (Alexander 2010, McGarry 2017), and all three groups are sterotyped as lazy or unwilling to work (Alexander 2010; McGarry 2017; Kidd 2008). In the case of Black Americans, the lazy stereotype is gendered and classed, and applied predominantly to women in the trope of a "welfare queen," describing a "lazy, greedy, black ghetto mother" (Alexander 2010, p.49). Roma women are similarly accused of having a multitude of children in order to extract child benefits from the government. More generally, Black Americans and Roma are often seen as receiving too many special favors, typically in the form of social benefits, which they purportedly do not deserve (Green et al. 2006; McGarry 2017). Further, just like Black men have been hypersexualized and portrayed as a danger to White womanhood (hooks 1981, 2004), so too have Roma men (Bardi 2006). Batwa, too, are generally seen as sexually immodest (Kidd 2008). And for all three groups, stereotyping is tied to location: the forest for Batwa, the settlement for Roma, and inner cities for Black Americans. Though marginalized Batwa, marginalized Roma, and marginalized Black Americans lead different lives thousands of miles apart, they are stereotyped in remarkably similar ways.

Rooted in these stereotypes, discrimination against one group often resem-bles that directed at another. In Chapter 2, I wrote about the tradition in Uganda of breaking the cups from which Batwa drank, or of dropping food into their cupped hands from a height, in order to avoid contact. This degrading practice may seem of another world, but not long ago, Black and White Americans drank from separate water fountains (Alexander 2010). While Jim Crow laws are consigned to the past, there are still restaurants that bar entry to Roma and Travellers (BBC 2008); in fact, a number of Roma participants in the tower game study reported being turned away at a restaurant, bar, or cinema because they were Roma. Marginalized children of all three groups often receive inferior education (Brown 2015; Brüggemann 2012; Fenning and Rose 2007; Kidd 2008), experience discrimination on the job market as adults (Hyde 2006; Kidd 2008; Pager et al. 2009), and face disparities in access to healthcare (Hoffman et al. 2016; Kidd 2008; Mihailov 2012) and housing (Kidd 2008; Pager and Shepherd 2008; Perić 2012).

Of course, these similarities do not mean that we would get the same results if we were to conduct this study in the context of marginalized Batwa, Black Americans, or other Roma communities and their respective majority populations. They do suggest, however, that Roma in Novo mesto might not be the only ones trapped in an exclusion cycle, and that therefore, further exploration is warranted.

Open questions

In this section I consider a number of questions that I have not answered in the preceding chapters. The first part looks inward and names a few points that the exclusion cycle I wrote about does not take into account; these points complicate the simple cycle and present an array of compelling questions to pursue in the future. I also discuss what empirical steps would be prudent to take next. The second part looks outward and considers a few outside factors that might affect exclusion cycles.

Inward

The logic of the exclusion cycle I have presented here is quite simple. This simple version, however, is not the only cycle that exists. Other cycles may be more complex, and others still completely different. For example, the direction in which different parts of the cycle succeed one another in this version goes one way, from anti-minority culture to discrimination to survival strategies, and so on. It could be, however, that sometimes directionality is not as strictly determined, with prejudice leading to discrimination and discrimination then affirming or even reinforcing prejudice, thus adding additional complexity to the simple cycle. Or perhaps members of the majority might sometimes react to a survival strategy they dislike with outright animus, not needing to attribute the action to the nature of the group, dispensing with the attribution error altogether.

My description of this simple cycle also does not mention other, competing ways in which exclusion may be worsened further. In some situations those surely exist. For example, are there factors other than discrimination that might compel an individual to pursue a survival strategy? Consider the possibility of an elite within the marginalized minority that benefits, for one reason or another, from the minority engaging in one particular survival strategy. Suppose further that the favored survival strategy is among those most intensely disliked by the majority. If the elite has the power sufficient to make its preferences respected, that influence enters the logic of the cycle alongside discrimination. The case of Jewish metal peddlers in 16th and 17th century Europe is one such example (Israel 1989, cited in Laitin (1995)). Rich metal-dealing merchants living in Prague, Hamburg, and Frankfurt had a material interest in socially and geographically isolating the thousands of poor peddlers who collected scrap and old coins in the villages of Central

Europe; this kept the labor force cheap and ensured that metal was collected from rural, isolated villages. It also contributed to keeping indigent Eastern European Jewish peddlers excluded. The same case also presents an example of an opposing elite interest in Court Jews, who were instead "interested in normalizing Jews in the pale"[4] (Laitin 1995, p.50). Whether elite preferences are in favor of assimilation or a survival strategy that furthers exclusion, if those preferences manifest as action, they contribute to the cycle.

Elite interests are not the only such determinant; community norms of non-assimilation emerging from regular members of the marginalized group might play the same function (Laitin 1995). Exploring these two possibilities in a number of conversations with Roma from Novo mesto and Murska Sobota, I found no evidence of powerful elite interests either incentivizing or coercing Roma into one survival strategy over another. They did, however, confirm the existence of a powerful non-assimilationist norm in the past; if one left the settlement to live outside with non-Roma, one was often not welcome back. Typically, Roma who left were educated and had secured good jobs; Šiftar (1994) mentions them, too, when he writes about educated Roma leaving settlements, not returning, and forgetting where they came from. Roma I have talked to explained that this is no longer the case today and has not been for many decades. Some now routinely leave to work abroad, and then return; activists, too, often live or work in bigger cities, and neither are shamed for having left. Still, while these factors appear not to be in effect in Novo mesto and Murska Sobota, they might matter in other contexts.

Examining a full repertoire of possible survival strategies, future work might also ask who chooses what strategy and why. As one survival strategy is typically insufficient for subsistence—recall that social assistance provides the bare minimum—strategies are often complementary and the choice of just one is unlikely. Whether one might supplement social assistance with foraging in the forest or collecting scrap metal, however, poses an interesting question. Elite interests, as mentioned above, might inform that choice; having a particular skillset likely matters as well, as do personal networks and resources, like owning a truck or having space where scrap metal can be stored.

Expanding in a different direction, we might explore strategies that are not primarily aimed at material survival, but still affect exclusion and likely feed into the cycle, like resistance (Scott 1985). Recall Rios's (2011) example of a boy from Oakland pointedly stealing a bag of chips that he had intended to pay for

---

[4] The pale was a demarcation of the Western part of the Russian Empire in which Jews were allowed to permanently settle (from 1791 to 1917).

before the store manager treated him as a potential thief. This was a strategy of resistance integral to the preservation of dignity and is, in my view, closely linked to survival. I have probed for elements of resistance in my conversations with Roma and have repeatedly been unable to obtain information in support of them, either as a part of survival strategies or unrelated to them. Roma participants speak of survival and not of resistance. That does not necessarily mean that there is no resistance—there is a chance that as an outsider and a non-Roma, I have been unable to uncover evidence of it. The issue of resistance, or of resistance as survival, does not only matter in the context of a potential exclusion cycle at the level of the individual but may also have implications at the community level or for a group as a whole, uncovering an entirely new set of questions. What happens to exclusion cycles when the marginalized group resists exclusion? If there is little resistance, does exclusion become more deeply entrenched over time? And does the type of resistance matter? An endeavor that aims to explain how exclusion cycles emerge and how they end might consider these questions, among others.

In this book, I provide an empirical illustration of an exclusion cycle. This illustration is not a test. While I do present suggestive evidence of the links between the different parts of the cycle—in Novo mesto, non-Roma who are prejudiced discriminate against the Roma, and overall, Roma who have experienced discrimination in real life resort to survival strategies in the tower game—this evidence is far from conclusive. Systematically testing the links between each part of the cycle would therefore be a logical next step, allowing for a deeper dive and speaking to numerous situations in which exclusion cycles do not appear or do not persist. For example, one could explore under what conditions engagement in survival strategies leads to the attribution error, and how that error differs based on the strategy used. Further, one could test the extent to which reacting to disliked survival strategies might lead directly to prejudice instead of first leading to attribution error. Or one might explore the persistence of cycles, examining how long it takes a population that appears to be trapped in a cycle to adjust and, possibly, exit. I already show some variation in adjusting; on the one hand, non-Roma from Novo mesto failed to raise their cooperation levels in the mixed game even though Roma avatars in that game contributed just as much as non-Roma avatars in the coethnic game. On the other hand, in a highly cooperative scenario, Roma who did not experience discrimination quickly adjusted to overall increases in cooperation and contributed more. What would it take for non-Roma to adjust in the mixed game? Is it a question of time or of information? Would communication help? And would interventions that might help non-Roma adjust be equally successful in helping Roma who experienced discrimination do the same in a highly cooperative scenario? Perhaps not. But we should know.

Outward

My argument in this book only concerns individuals. I limit my focus in order to grapple with a puzzle that is manageable, even if quite substantial nevertheless. In paring off a small slice of a large problem, I leave out much that matters in real life, on the ground; individual acts of discrimination and of survival don't happen in a vacuum, but in a world where lives are shaped by institutions, economic conditions, violence, migration, and more. As Novo mesto and Murska Sobota match quite well with respect to these and other factors (by which they are likely shaped), focusing on just individual behaviors was possible. Expanding the view, however, would require reckoning with numerous sources of variation, which may themselves affect potential exclusion cycles by influencing, constraining, or enabling different individual behaviors and attitudes.

Consider, for example, the vast difference in how Roma students are treated in Rokycany, Slovakia and in La Paz, Spain. There is no mainstream primary school in Rokycany; the nearest school is 3 km away in a neighboring village. Roma children from Rokycany used to go there, but many have transferred once a new special school opened in Rokycany (ERRC 2017). Special schools teach a curriculum adjusted for children with mild mental disabilities. For decades, pedagogical experts in Slovakia have been using culturally inappropriate tests to asses school preparedness of young Roma children (recall that many children speak primarily or only Romani before they start school) and have grossly over-diagnosed Roma children as having such disabilities (ERRC 2017). Like in many special schools across Slovakia, all the students in the Rokycany school are Roma. Among them are students who had been tested by a state diagnostic center and found to have no disabilities, attended a mainstream school, were then re-tested by a private institution, and transferred to the special school closer to home (ERRC 2017). While the report cards of students in this school reflect the requisite subjects, including the Slovak language, parents and children report that "the children are often instructed to draw and paint during the Slovak language classes" (ERRC 2017, p.39). Once children turn 16 or have completed 10 years of education, they are discouraged from continuing; as state funding drops by 90 percent when that happens, the school has no incentives to keep teaching. Legislation in Slovakia has addressed some of these issues—the mental disability tests are no longer recognized as legitimate, for example—but implementation lags. The Ministry of Education in fact decided to close down the school in Rokycany, but the school has since been renovated and has received state funding for teaching assistants (ERRC 2017).

La Milagrosa in Albacete provides a stark contrast. It is one of the poorest neighborhoods in Spain; in 2006, its unemployment rate was nearly 100 percent (Sordé Martí and Macías 2017). It is a predominantly Roma neighborhood. The school that has since been renamed La Paz used to be plagued by mutual distrust between teachers and Roma families and was eventually closed by the government. Drastic reforms to the school were agreed upon and implemented by experts from the international research community and locals, mostly Roma families from the neighborhood. Early implementation was challenging due to reluctance of all parties to trust and engage with one another, but as everyone persisted and helped re-build the dilapidated school, the hostility disappeared. The reforms include classrooms of small heterogeneous groups; family participation in which family members help younger children learn; increases in learning time that include students and supporting volunteers helping one another; and active participation of teachers, families, and community members in school decision-making processes (Sordé Martí and Macías 2017). The last development is particularly important for parental ability to hold the school accountable for its educational results— and the school delivers. In the first year, the rate of school enrollment increased from 45 to 114 students and educational performance "improved enormously" (Sordé Martí and Macías 2017, p.195); almost every student who finishes primary school enrolls in secondary school and graduates. The success of the school inspired changes in the neighborhood, improving housing, employment, health outcomes, and raising political participation.

In both examples, individual behaviors clearly matter. The teachers in Rokycany who refuse to teach Roma children the Slovak language immediately and directly contribute to their exclusion, while the teachers in La Milagrosa who work with Roma families in the classroom fight against it. The institutional sources of disparity, however, are at the core of the difference between these two examples. In Slovakia, the government still tacitly supports the illegitimate testing of mental disability and invests in the special school. This environment enables the teachers not to teach and to discourage Roma students from seeking more education, drastically affecting their futures. In Spain, the government instead closed the dysfunctional school and relocated the teachers from the old program. Supporting the rather unconventional approach of egalitarian decision-making, the government then issued a call for new teachers who were willing to work very closely with the children's families. As a result of the school's success, children might find it easier to exit out of employment-related survival strategies by finding formal employment; parents who had the opportunity to receive vocational training in the school and secured regular employment did so within a short time span. In both cases, the institutional factors are connected to individual behaviors and attitudes—of both Roma and non-Roma—and can greatly affect whether and to what extent exclusion cycles form and persist.

The UK Scrap Metal Dealers Act of 2013 is another example of a structural factor that affects exclusion cycles (Le Bas 2013). Ostensibly intended to reduce scrap metal thefts across the UK, the law in fact disproportionately affects Roma and other Travellers—not only because scrap metal collection represents a substantially larger share of trades in which they engage, but also because the law makes scrap collection substantially costlier for those who travel to collect scrap (Le Bas 2013). I mentioned in Chapter 6 that Roma who are not itinerant regularly travel to collect scrap both to increase their yield and to work where they are less likely to be recognized as Roma; in the UK, the 2013 law requires a separate license, along with a fee set by the local authorities, for every area in which collectors operate (Le Bas 2013). This raises the cost of a commonly practiced, other-benefitting survival strategy and curtails the repertoire of strategies that are available. If, as a result, some collectors switch to strategies that are not other-benefitting and therefore more disliked, exclusion cycles could become more deeply entrenched.

In Chapter 3, I discussed how survival strategies employed by many Roma do not have an intrinsic ethnic character but are instead activities to which people who are poor resort. In localities where poor Roma and non-Roma compete for the same jobs, structural factors that affect people with low socioeconomic status might impact exclusion cycles within that subgroup of individuals. In Hungary, for example, mayors can exercise discretion over the allocation of jobs in the anti-poverty or workfare programs, which provide a monthly income in exchange for performing public work in the interest of the community (Mares and Young 2019).[5] In a small locality close to the Hungarian border with Slovakia in which poverty levels are high and substantial numbers of Roma and non-Roma are excluded from the labor market, competition for workfare is reflected in anti-Roma sentiment, as many

---

[5] In Slovenia, mayors do not have this discretion.

non-Roma claim that "Roma abuse the workfare program, while failing to perform the required work" (Mares and Young 2019, p.3). The implications for potential exclusion cycles occur on at least two dimensions. First, workfare job allocation is vulnerable to mayor prejudice. Second, in places of high competition, the programming might exacerbate anti-Roma sentiment among poor non-Roma whether or not Roma receive workfare. If Roma receive workfare, non-Roma might resent losing jobs to Roma; if Roma do not receive it, they might instead turn to other survival strategies. Either way, further anti-Roma sentiment may result.

Finally, structural factors are not only linked to individual behaviors and attitudes that make up the components of exclusion cycles, but also affect interventions that aim to break them. Consider this example from Slovenia. In 2017, the Slovene government unveiled a 1.7 million euro plan to help finance 11 Roma centers across Slovene municipalities that have significant Roma populations. As Slovene Roma-led NGOs have been successful in serving their target populations (recall that every single Roma in my sample knew the local NGO and many expressed praise), one might expect the government call to target such NGOs or Roma communities in general. Instead, requirements attached to the call are too financially and administratively challenging for Roma communities to take on, seemingly designed for NGOs, private entities, or municipal departments with more organizational capacity and larger coffers, which are also likely to have predominantly or exclusively non-Roma staff (Kramberger 2017). Roma communities are not locked out completely, as they could partner with a non-Roma entity, but whether they could participate as full and equal partners is unclear. Writing about the successes and shortcomings of Roma or pro-Roma NGOs, (predominantly) Romani scholars and activists note that organizations are most successful when they are not financially dependent on external donors; when grassroots activism can escape NGO-ization and donor-driven agendas (Acton and Ryder 2015); and when Roma participate in efforts not as token representatives, but instead as decision-makers in leading positions, which is rare (Nasture 2015; Rostaş et al. 2015). As the government design precludes such independence from the very beginning, it risks developing interventions that members of the minority might not find helpful. Indeed, an informal conversation with a municipal employee from Novo mesto revealed that the city plans on building a Roma center like those envisioned by the government and that it plans to place it inside the Roma settlement. This is precisely what the example of Roma NGO action from Murska Sobota might advise against—they purposefully organize activities in the main part of the city—and what many Roma from Novo mesto don't want, as it would reinforce segregation, which they wish to eliminate. A Roma center located in the settlement probably would contribute to further exclusion, as non-Roma would be unlikely to attend events there; any parallel alternative effort aimed at building something in the city proper would receive less support on account of being redundant.

Having considered a few of the many remaining open questions, I now turn to the main takeaways from this book, which include a puzzle, a game, a cycle, and a few thoughts on NGO-promoted contact.

In conclusion

A puzzle

Of the findings I presented in this book, the uniformity of Roma behaviors across coethnic and mixed groups in the tower building videogame is among the most remarkable. I first started to question whether Roma might favor their own during data collection in Novo mesto. While we were waiting for a participant to finish the videogame, my research team and I chatted with some Roma from the settlement. We were talking about gardening. Reflecting on the work required to cultivate a field, a Roma man remarked "people around here are not in the habit of working together. Elsewhere, people will help their neighbors build their house. Not here. They'd sooner be jealous of your good fortune."[6] Looking over the grassy patch of land, we could see a few Roma children playing. A couple of kids, also Roma, from across the field ran to join them. In a gesture that seemed uncanny at the time, two kids from the first group echoed what the man had said. They traced a line with their shoes along an imagined border in the grass and told the newcomers they had better stay on the other side of it.

Interpreting the absence of ingroup favoritism among Roma, we might conclude that their behavior is exemplary, as they do not appear to discriminate against members of the group that has mistreated them for generations and continues to do so today. This behavior is indeed admirable. Consider, however, its implications for the Roma community. The tower game is a public goods game; the decision of whether to contribute to the tower simulates a decision to contribute to a public good that benefits all—like participating in a

---

[6] He was talking about the Slovene practice of having neighbors help build one another's house; as someone always had work to be done, neighbors would work together on one house or the other.

"clean the park" community drive. The statement by the man I quoted above, that people from the settlement "are not in the habit of working together," paints an ominous picture, especially as municipalities tend to neglect settlements and the people who live there often rely on their own ingenuity. What does the reluctance to favor a Roma-only group in the context of the game imply about Roma engagement in community building or ground-up political and civil mobilization?

While Roma have long been politically active, and many now have increasingly effective political representation, they still face numerous challenges to mobilization (Mark 2017; Vermeersch 2017). Roma candidates run for office and are sometimes elected, but in many communities the political base among Roma is weak (Mark 2017), while mainstream political parties co-opt Roma organizations to gain Roma votes or engage in outright vote buying (Vermeersch 2017, but see Mares et al. 2017).[7] Could the lack of ingroup favoritism be linked to challenges in mobilization? Might variation in ingroup favoritism—here, I capture none, but that may vary across locations—help explain why mainstream political parties have been successful at co-opting some Roma organizations, or why vote buying might be successful in some communities but not in others? Further, what could this tell us about the relationship between strength of community building and political and civil mobilization elsewhere?

A game

The tower game offers a significant departure from the way public goods games are typically played for the purpose of political science research. I developed this game in response to three fairly common constraints. First, as relations can be contentious, it was untenable to put Roma and non-Roma participants in a room together to play in a group, face to face, which is how the game tends to be delivered in other contexts. Second, as significant subset of Roma cannot read, especially women and the elderly, a simple substitute that presented the decision choices in writing was unacceptable. Third, as a

---

[7] There are a number of other challenges to Romani political participation, ranging from an ironic lack of accountability and electoral competition inherent in the policies that aim to secure Romani representation (Mark 2017) to the fact that running for office as a Roma can be profoundly challenging, especially in light of a recent rise in anti-Roma sentiment that rightwing parties have harnessed to court intolerant voters (Vermeersch 2017). Often, the disconnect between Romani politicians, who cannot always be held accountable, and the Romani constituencies they are meant to serve is substantial. For more, see Mark (2017) and Vermeersch (2017).

substantial proportion of Roma and non-Roma don't own a computer or have access to the internet, a simultaneous multi-player variant of the game was not an option.

The tower game of course does not mirror real-life interactions and thus sacrifices valuable realism. But it allowed members of the two groups to participate in an environment that was safe and confidential, without the threat of contention. It also enabled the participation of Roma who cannot read, who are thus particularly vulnerable, and who are sometimes excluded from study participation on this basis. Finally, the tower game gave me more analytical leverage than the traditional game, as the game experience was the same for every participant (aside from order randomization). The traditional public goods game delivery results in variation in how participants experience the game, not only between different groups but also within their own group. With the tower game, I instead capture how each participant behaves across different scenarios as well as how different participants behave in the same scenario. Since numerous other research contexts face constraints similar to mine, the videogame approach might offer a way to negotiate them in those contexts as well.

A cycle

In order to fully understand how individuals contribute to social exclusion, we must consider the behaviors of those who exclude and their targets together. The logic of the simple cycle I present and illustrate in this book begins to bring light into the complexity and the intransigence of exclusion, but these are early steps. The simple cycle does not account for multiple causes of discrimination; it does not consider when prejudice might lead to discrimination and when not; and does not say when members of the marginalized group might engage in survival strategies that are disliked and when they might instead choose strategies of which the majority approves. The simple cycle further does not connect individual behaviors with larger, structural factors that both influence those behaviors and are in turn influenced by them. Considered as one whole and not a sum of parts, exclusion is a multi-dimensional complex phenomenon in which micro and macro factors intersect, combine, and reinforce one another. Reckoning with this vastly more intractable whole is a task of lifetimes. In this work, I hope to have made a convincing case for the interactive and cyclical nature of minority and majority behaviors in the context of exclusion, and to have contributed to an effort of building towards interventions that would make such cycles obsolete.

Roma NGOs, contact, and dialogue

The nature of contact and dialogue promotion I examine in this book dif substantially from contact interventions typically used in experimental stud ies. Externally imposed interventions are far more controlled, often appear quite suddenly, and tend to be more intense on a day-to-day basis, but they are overall shorter in duration. The Roma NGO, in contrast, slowly grew out of the Romani community, presenting opportunities for positive intergroup contact as well as promoting dialogue in a relaxed manner, without imposing contact on any one individual,[8] and yet exposing a high number of them to it over the period of 25 years.[9] Their intervention was far more subtle, but also far more sustained. Where relations between groups can be contentious, the slower-but-sustained approach offers some advantages over sudden interventions of fairly intense contact, which carry a higher risk of triggering a negative interaction. To experimental work that randomly assigns intense contact in shorter time spans, this work therefore adds another dimension, examining the effects of low-key, positive, and disarming ways of promoting contact that developed organically, on the ground, under Romani leadership and execution.

Given the success of the organization in Murska Sobota, where are the other NGOs that promote contact between Roma and non-Roma? To be sure, we do observe a few—but only a few. Vzájemné Soužití supports the "Coexistence Village," an artificially integrated Roma/non-Roma community in Ostrava, Czech Republic. In Ferentari, Romania, the Policy Center for Roma and Minorities promotes contact among Roma and non-Roma children through alternative education and soccer. In addition to these two organizations, I was able to track down the beginnings of a third, in Prague in 2013, which was fighting to secure initial funding, but failed (Anonymous 2013).

The experience of this last organization suggests that limited funding may be why we see so few groups with a contact-promoting focus. In an environment where many Roma NGOs compete for limited funding, a contact-promoting NGO has a natural disadvantage. Most Roma organizations focus on service provision; most that do not, engage in Roma rights advocacy. Since marginalized Roma communities are in need of both, NGOs that provide them can make powerful appeals that lead to success in obtaining funds (Anonymous 2013). Perhaps service provision and rights advocacy are indeed

---

[8] Pettigrew and Tropp (2011) write that the benefits of positive intergroup contact are greater when contact is voluntary.

[9] Recall that almost every other non-Roma in Murska Sobota can name the NGO, while only 2 percent of non-Roma in Novo mesto are able to do the same.

foci that deserve precedence—ignoring the lack of electricity, heat, and access of sewerage would be inhuman, while not mobilizing for the enforcement of adopted anti-discrimination legislation would be a lost opportunity. And as needs of Roma communities are often acute, efforts to allay immediate concerns are favored among funding agencies. In contrast to providing much needed services or rights advocacy, positive intergroup contact does not carry urgency. Some might also argue that it would impose an additional burden upon the Romani community at a time when such burdens are unwelcome; there is certainly truth to this argument, as contact can induce stress and expose members of the minority to more discrimination. But my findings suggest that focusing on services and advocacy to the effective exclusion of contact-promoting organizations is short-sighted.

Does that mean that Roma-led NGOs should as a rule aim to involve non-Roma? Not at all. The NGO in Novo mesto, run by Roma for the Roma, is not only helpful to the Roma community there—according to community testimonies, it is necessary. Roma organizers know best what their communities need, and under numerous circumstances they might be better able to serve them by turning inward. However, with full inclusion as the ultimate goal, this approach, while necessary, is insufficient. The exclusion cycle is pernicious and self-sustaining; if discrimination continues at the level of the individual, marginalized communities may never be fully included, even if services are provided and national laws are passed (Nasture 2015). For that to happen, non-Roma must change. Just as the exclusion cycle involves both Roma and non-Roma, so too should solutions that aim to break it.

Bibliography

Acton, Thomas, and Andrew Ryder. 2015. "The Gypsy Council—Approaching 50 Years of Struggle". *Roma Rights: Quarterly Journal of the European Roma Rights Centre* 18 (2): 11–16.

Adams, Jean, and Martin White. 2009. "Time Perspective in Socioeconomic Inequalities in Smoking and Body Mass Index". *Health Psychology* 28 (1): 83–90.

Adida, Claire L., David D. Laitin, and Marie-Anne Valfort. 2010. "Identifying Barriers to Muslim Integration in France". *PNAS* 107 (52): 22384–90.

Adida, Claire L., David D. Laitin, and Marie-Anne Valfort. 2016. *Why Muslim Integration Fails in Christian-Heritage Societies*. Cambridge, MA: Harvard University Press.

African International Christian Ministry. 2005. The Batwa of Uganda: *A Denial of Basic Human Rights*. Kabale: African International Christian Ministry.

Ajdič, Karmen. 2008. *Diplomsko delo: Romska Naseljakot Primer Prostorske Segregacije v Sloveniji*. Ljubljana: Univerza v Ljubljani, Fakulteta za družbene vede.

Albert, Gwendolyn. 2011. "Three Roma Families Repeatedly Attacked in Slovakia Over Easter", http://www.romea.cz/en/news/world/three-romafamilies-repeatedly-attacked-in-slovakia-over-easter.

Alexander, Marcus, and Fotini Christia. 2011."Context Modularity of Human Altruism". *Science* 334 (6061): 1392–94.

Alexander, Michelle. 2010. *The New Jim Crow: Mass Incarceration in the Age of Colorblindness*. New York, NY: The New Press.

Allport, Gordon Willard. 1954. *The Nature of Prejudice*. Cambridge, MA: Addison-Wesley.

Allport, Gordon, and Leo Postman. 1947. *The Psychology of Rumor*. New York, NY: Henry Holt/Company.

Amnesty International. 2016. *Brazil: Police Killings, Impunity and Attacks on Defenders: Amnesty International Submission for the UN Universal Periodic Review-27th Session of the UPR Working Group, May 2017*. London, UK: Amnesty International Ltd.

Amsel, Rhonda, and Catherine Fichten. 1988. "Effects of Contact on Thoughts About Interaction With Students Who Have a Physical Disability". *Journal of Rehabilitation* 54 (1): 61–5.

Anderson, Benedict. 1983. *Imagined Communities: Reflections on the Origin and Spread of Nationalism*. New York, NY: Verso.

Andreoni, James, William Harbaugh, and Lise Vesterlund. 2003. "The Carrot or the Stick: Rewards, Punishments, and Cooperation". *The American Economic Review* 93 (3): 893–902.

Andriessen, Iris, Henk Fernee, and Karin Wittebrood. 2014. *Perceived Discrimination in the Netherlands*. The Hague: The Netherlands Institute for Social Research.

Anonymous. 2013. Anonymous Official from the Office of the Government of the Czech Republic. Interview by Author. Notes. Prague.

Arrow, Kenneth J. 1973. "The Theory of Discrimination". In *Discrimination in Labor Markets*, edited by Orley Ashenfelter and Albert Rees, 3–33. Princeton University Press.

Ashforth, Blake, and Glen Kreiner. 1999. "How Can You Do It? Dirty Work and the Challenge of Constructing a Positive Identity". *Academy of Management Review* 24 (3): 413–34.

Axelrod, Robert. 1984. *The Evolution of Cooperation*. New York, NY: Basic Books.

Ayres, Ian, and Peter Siegelman. 1995. "Race and Gender Discrimination in Bargaining for a New Car". *The American Economic Review* 85 (3): 304–21.

Baggett, Travis P., et al. 2013. "Mortality Among Homeless Adults in Boston: Shifts in Causes of Death Over a 15-year Period". *JAMA Internal Medicine* 173 (3): 189–95.

Bajec, Anton et al. 2008. *Slovar slovenskega knjižnega jezika*. Edited by Slovenska akademija znanosti in umetnosti in Znanstvenoraziskovalni center Slovenske akademije znanosti in umetnosti, Inštitut za slovenski jezik Frana Ramovša ZRC SAZU. Ljubljana: Založba ZRC.

Balažek, Dušica. 2012. Interview by Author. Voice Recording. Novo mesto.

Balliet, Daniel, Junhui Wu, and Carsten K. W. De Dreu. 2014. "Ingroup Favoritism in Cooperation: A Meta-Analysis". *Psychological Bulletin* 140 (6): 1556–81.

Baluh, Stane. 2012. Interview by Author. Voice Recording. Ljubljana.

Barany, Zoltan. 2002. *The East European Gypsies: Regime Change, Marginality, and Ethnopolitics*. Cambridge: Cambridge University Press.

Barclay, Pat. 2004. "Trustworthiness and Competitive Altruism can also Solve the "Tragedy of the Commons". *Evolution and Human Behavior* 25 (4): 209–20.

Bardi, Abby. 2006. "The Gypsy as Trope in Victorian and Modern British Literature". *Romani Studies* 16 (1): 31–42.

Barič, Tamara. 2011. "Zalog: Romi želeli podjetnika okrasti?" *Žurnal* 24(). http://www.zurnal24.si/slovenija/crna-kronika/zalog-romi-zeleli-podjetnika-okrasti112479.

Barlow, Fiona, et al. 2012. "The Contact Caveat: Negative Contact Predicts Increased Prejudice More Than Positive Contact Predicts Reduced Prejudice". *Personality and Social Psychology Bulletin* 38 (12): 1629–43.

Barr, Abigail. 2004. "Kinship, familiarity, and Trust: An Experimental Investigation". In *Foundations of Human Sociality: Economic Experiments and Ethnographic Evidence from Fifteen Small-Scale Societies*, edited by Joseph Henrich et al. Oxford, UK: Oxford University Press.

Barrie, Janet. 1999. "Hiding Gypsies Behind a Wall", http://news.bbc.co.uk/2/hi/europe/286704.stm.

Barry, Brian. 2002. "Social Exclusion, Social Isolation and the Distribution of Income". In *Understanding Social Exclusion*, edited by John Hills, Julian Le Grand, and David Piachaud, 13–29. Oxford, UK: Oxford University Press.

Batson, C. Daniel. 2010. "Empathy-Induced Altruistic Motivation". In *Prosocial Motives, Emotions, and Behavior: The Better Angels of Our Nature*, 15–34. Washington, DC: American Psychological Association.

Bauman, Zygmunt. 1988. "Entry Tickets and Exit Visas: Paradoxes of Jewish Identity". Telos 77: 45–77.

Baumeister, Roy F., and C. Nathan De Wall. 2005. "The Inner Dimension of Social Exclusion: Intelligent Thought and Self-Regulation among Rejected Persons". In *The Social Outcast: Ostracism, Social Exclusion, Rejection, and Bullying*, edited by Kipling D. Williams, Joseph D. Forgas, and Willim von Hippel, 53–73. Psychology Press.

Bayat, Asef. 1997. *Street Politics: Poor People's Movements in Iran*. New York, NY: Columbia University Press.

BBC. 2008. "Pub Anti-Traveller Sign Removed". May 28, 2008, *BBC NEWS*.

Beaudoin, Julianna. 2015. "Exploring the Contemporary Relevance of "Gypsy' Steretypes in the Buffyverse". *The Journal of Popular Culture* 48 (2): 313–27.

Becker, Gary S. 1957. *The Economics of Discrimination*. Chicago, IL: The University of Chicago Press.

Berg, Joyce, John Dickhaut, and Kevin McCabe. 1995. "Trust, Reciprocity, and Social History". *Games and Economic Behavior* 10: 122–42.

Bilefsky, Dan. 2010. "Walls, Real and Imagined, Surround the Roma". April 2, 2010, *The New York Times*.

Bitenc, Maja. 2013. "Slovene, Between Purism and Plurilingualism". In *Survival and Development of Language Communities: Prospects and Challenges*, edited by F. Xavier Vila. Bristol, UK: Multilingual Matters.

Blanden, Jo, and Paul Gregg. 2004. "Family Income and Educational Attainment: A Review of Approaches and Evidence for Britain". *Oxford Review of Economic Policy* 20 (2): 245–63.

Blascovich, Jim, et al. 2001. "Perceiver Threat in Social Interactions With Stigmatized Others". *Journal of Personality and Social Psychology* 80 (2): 253–67.

Blinder, Scott, Robert Ford, and Elisabeth Ivarsflaten. 2013. "The Better Angels of Our Nature: How the Antiprejudice Norm Affects Policy and Party Preferences in Great Britain and Germany." *American Journal of Political Science* 57 (4): 841–57.

Bochet, Olivier, Talbot Page, and Louis Putterman. 2006. "Communication and Punishment in Voluntary Contribution Experiments". *Journal of Economic Behavior & Organization* 60 (1): 11–26.

Bogdan, Maria. 2015. "Challenging Perspectives—The Role of Media Representation in Knowledge Production about Roma". *Roma Rights: Quarterly Journal of the European Roma Rights Centre* 18 (2): 71–74.

Boulding, Carew E. 2010. "NGOs and Political Participation in Weak Democracies: Subnational Evidence on Protest and Voter Turnout from Bolivia". *The Journal of Politics* 72 (2): 456–68.

Bracic, Ana. 2015."European Union Accession and Roma Rights Practices in Five Eastern Enlargement States". Paper presented at the International Studies Association Annual Convention. New Orleans, LA, February 2015.

Bracic, Ana. 2018. "For Better Science: The Benefits of Community Engagement in Research". *PS: Political Science & Politics* 51 (3): 550–53.

Bracic, Ana. 2016. "Reaching the Individual: EU Accession, NGOs, and Human Rights". *American Political Science Review* 110 (3): 530–46.

Bracic, Ana, et al. 2019. "Experiences of Sexual Harassment, Support for the Me Too Movement, and the 2018 Elections".

Brazzabeni, Micol, Manuela Ivone Cunha, and Martin Fotta. 2015. "Introduction: Gypsy Economy". In *Gypsy Economy*, edited by Micol Brazzabeni, Manuela Ivone Cunha, and Martin Fotta, 1–30. New York, NY: Berghahn Books.

Brewer, Marilynn B. 1991. "The Social Self: On Being the Same and Different at the Same Time". *Personality and Social Psychology Bulletin* 17 (5): 475–82.

Brown, Emma. 2015. "In 23 States, Richer School Districts Get More Local Funding Than Poorer Districts". March 12, 2015, *The Washington Post*.

Bruggemann, Christian. 2012. *Roma Education in Comparative Perspective. Analysis of the UNDP/World Bank/EC Regional Roma Survey 2011*. Roma Inclusion Working Papers. Bratislava: United Nations Development Programme.

Burchardt, Tania, Julian Le Grand, and David Piachaud. 2002. "Introduction". In *Understanding Social Exclusion*, edited by John Hills, Julian Le Grand, and David Piachaud, 1–12. Oxford, UK: Oxford University Press.

Burkley, Melissa, and Hart Blanton. 2008. "Endorsing a Negative In-Group Stereotype as a Self-Protective Strategy: Sacrificing the Group to Save the Self". *Journal of Experimental Social Psychology* 44 (1): 37–49.

Byrne, David. 2005. *Social Exclusion*. Berkshire, UK: Open University Press.

Cahn, Claude. 2003."Privileging the Document". *Roma Rights: Quarterly Journal of the European Roma Rights Centre* 3 (3).

Cahn, Claude. 2007. "The Unseen Powers: Perception, Stigma and Roma Rights". *Roma Rights: Quarterly Journal of the European Roma Rights Centre* 10 (3): 3–8.

Camerer, Colin. 2003. *Behavioral Game Theory: Experiments in Strategic Interaction*. Princeton, NJ: Princeton University Press.

Campbell, Donald T. 1958. "Common fate, Similarity, and Other Indices of the Status of Aggregates of Persons as Social Entities". *Behavioral Science* 3 (1): 14–25.

Casella, Ronnie. 2003. "Punishing Dangerousness Through Preventive Detention: Illustrating the Institutional Link Between School and Prison". In *Deconstructing the School-to-Prison Pipeline: New Directions for Youth Development*, edited by Johanna Wald and Daniel J. Losen, 55–70. San Francisco, CA: Jossey-Bass.

Caspi, Avshalom. 1984. "Contact Hypothesis and Inter-Age Attitudes: A Field Study of Cross-Age Contact". *Social Psychology Quarterly* 47 (1): 74–80.

Catanese, Kathleen R, and Dianne M. Tice. 2005. "The Effect of Rejection on Anti-Social Behaviors: Social Exclusion Produces Aggressive Behaviors". In *The Social Outcast: Ostracism, Social Exclusion, Rejection, and Bullying*, edited by Kipling D. Williams, Joseph D. Forgas, and Willim von Hippel, 297–306. Psychology Press.

Cesarini, David, et al. 2008. "Heritability of Cooperative Behavior in the Trust Game". *PNAS* 105 (10): 3721–26.

Chandra, Kanchan. 2012. "Attributes and Categories: A New Conceptual Vocabulary for Thinking about Ethnic Identity". In *Constructivist Theories of Ethnic Politics*, edited by Kanchan Chandra, 97–131. New York, NY: Oxford University Press.

Chaudhuri, Ananish, Sara Graziano, and Pushkar Maitra. 2006. "Social Learning and Norms in a Public Goods Experiment With Inter-Generational Advice". *Review of Economic Studies* 73 (2): 357–80.

Chavez, Leo R. 2008. *The Latino Threat: Constructing Immigrants, Citizens, and the Nation*. Redwood City, CA: Stanford University Press.

Christ, Oliver, etal. 2014. "Contextual Effect of Positive Inter Group Contact On Out Group Prejudice". *PNAS* 111 (11): 3996–4000.

Cinyabuguma, Matthias, Talbot Page, and Louis Putterman. 2006. "Can Second-Order Punishment Deter Perverse Punishment?" *Experimental Economics* 9 (3): 265–79.

Cofan, Soria-Maria. 2016. "An Analysis Regarding the Roma Community from Romania". In *Corruption, Fraud, Organized Crime, and the Shadow Economy*, edited by Maximilian Edelbacher, Peter C. Kratcoski, and Bojan Dobovšek, 147–58. CRC Press.

Cohen, Jacob. 1988. *Statistical Power Analysis for Behavioral Sciences*. Hillsdale, NJ: Lawrence Erlbaum Associates.

Coleman, Martin. 2013. "Emotion and the Ultimate Attribution Error". *Current Psychology* 32 (1): 71–81.

Collins, Patricia Hill. 1990. *Black Feminist Thought: Knowledge, Consciousness, and the Politics of Empowerment*. New York, NY: Routledge.

Commonwealth v. Jimmy Warren. 2016. *SJC11956, Massachusetts Supreme Judicial Court*.

Cook, Stuart W. 1984. "Cooperative Interaction in Multiethnic Contexts". In *Groups in Contact: The Psychology of Desegregation*, edited by Norman Miller and Marylin B. Brewer, 155–85. Orlando, FL: Academic Press.

Cook, Stuart W. 1971. *The Effect of Unintended Interracial Contact Upon Racial Interaction and Attitude Change. Final Report*. Washington, DC: Office of Education (DHEW), Bureau of Research.

Csata, Zsombor, Roman Hlatky, and Amy H. Liu. 2019. "Congruence of Self-Identification and Other-Identification Strategies: A Research Note on the Implications for Ethnic Minorities".

Čupkovic, Gordana. 2015. "Diachronic Variations of Slurs and Levels of Derogation: On Some Regional, Ethnic and Racial Slurs in Croatian". *Language Sciences* 52: 215–30.

Daly, Martin, and Margo Wilson. 2005. "Carpe Diem: Adaptation and Devaluing the Future". *The Quarterly Review of Biology* 80 (1): 55–60.

Daniel, Stanko. 2010. Interview by Author. Notes. Budapest.

Darwin, Charles. 1859. *On the Origin of Species by Means of Natural Selection.* London: John Murray.

De Las Nueces, Denise. 2016. "Stigma and Prejudice Against Individuals Experiencing Homelessness". In *Stigma and Prejudice*, edited by Ranna Parekh and Ed W. Childs, 85–101. Switzerland: Springer.

Dedić, Jasminka. 2003a. "Disckriminacija v postopkih pridobivanja slovenskaga državljanstva". In *Izbrisani: Organizirana nedolžnost in politike izključevanja*, edited by Jasminka Dedić, Vlasta Jalušič, and Jelka Zorn, 2–84. Ljubljana: Mirovni inštitut.

Dedić, Jasminka. 2003b. "The Erasure: Administrative Ethnic Cleansing in Slovenia". *Roma Rights: Quarterly Journal of the European Roma Rights Centre* 6(3).

Desforges, Donna, et al. 1991. "Effects of Structured Cooperative Contact on Changing Negative Attitudes Toward Stigmatized Social Groups". *Journal of Personality and Social Psychology* 60 (4): 531–44.

Deutsch, Morton, and Mary Collins. 1951. *Interracial Housing: A Psychological Evaluation of a Social Experiment.* Minneapolis, MN: University of Minnesota Press.

Ditlmann, Ruth K., and Cyrus D. Samii. 2016. "Can Intergroup Contact Affect Ingroup Dynamics? Insights From a Field Study with Jewish and Arab-Palestinian Youth in Israel". *Peace and Conflict: Journal of Peace Psychology* 22 (4): 380–92.

Dobreva, Nikolina. 2007. "Constructing the 'Celluloid Gypsy': Tony Gatlif and Emir Kustorica's 'Gypsy films' in the context of New Europe". *Romani Studies* 17 (2): 141–54.

Dovidio, John F., et al. 2004. "Contemporary Racial Bias: When Good People do Bad Things". In The *Social Psychology of Good and Evil*, edited by Arthur G. Miller, 141–67. New York, NY: Guilford Press.

Dovidio, John F., et al. 1995. "Group Representations and Intergroup Bias: Positive Affect, Similarity, and Group Size". *Personality and Social Psychology Bulletin* 21 (8): 856–65.

Dumitru, Diana, and Carter Johnson. 2011. "Constructing Interethnic Conflict and Cooperation: Why Some People Harmed Jews and Others Helped Them during the Holocaust in Romania". *World Politics* 63 (1): 1–42.

Duncan, Birt. 1976. "Differential Social Perception and Attribution of Intergroup Violence: Testing the Lower Limits of Stereotyping of Blacks". *Journal of Personality and Social Psychology* 34 (4): 590–98.

Dunfield, Kristen A. 2014. "A Construct Divided: Prosocial Behavior as Helping, Sharing, and Comforting Subtypes". *Frontiers in Psychology* 5: 1–13.

Eberhardt, Jennifer, et al. 2004. "Seeing Black: Race, Crime, and Visual Processing". *Journal of Personality and Social Psychology* 87 (6): 876–93.

Egas, Martijn, and Arno Riedl. 2008. "The Economics of Altruistic Punishment and the Maintenance of Cooperation". *Proceedings of the Royal Society Biological Sciences* 275: 871–78.

Egenberger, Vera, and Piero Colacicchi. 2007. "Forced Eviction of More than 10,000 Roma Announced in Italy". *European Roma Rights Centre and osserv Azione.*

Elias, Brenda, et al. 2012. "Trauma and Suicide Behaviour Histories Among a Canadian Indigenous Population: An Empirical Exploration of the Potential Role of Canada's Residential School System". *Social Science & Medicine* 74 (10): 1560–69.

Enos, Ryan. 2014. "Causal Effect of Intergroup Contact on Exclusionary Attitudes". *Proceedings of the National Academy of Sciences* 111 (10): 3699–704.

Episcopal Medical Missions Foundation. 2007. "Episcopal Medical Missions Foundation: Making a Difference in Uganda", www.emmf.com/ugandasurvey.htm.

Erjavec, Karmen, Sandra B. Hrvatin, and Barbara Kelbl. 2000. *Mi o Romih: Diskriminatorski Diskurz v Medijih v Sloveniji*. Ljubljana, Slovenia: Open Society Institute.

Estrin, James. 2012. "Breaking Through Walls of Bias". November 5, 2012, *The New York Times*. http://lens.blogs.nytimes.com/2012/11/05/breaking-through-walls-of-bias/?_r=0.

European Commission. 2001. *2001 Regular Report on Slovenia's Progress Towards Accession*. Brussels: European Commission.

European Commission. 2002. *2002 Regular Report on Slovenia's Progress Towards Accession*. Brussels: European Commission.

European Roma Rights Centre. 2001. "British Officials Continue Policy of Stopping Roma at Czech airport; Czech Roma and ERRC sue U.K. government". http://www.errc.org/cikk.php?cikk=1289.

European Roma Rights Centre. 2013. "Slovakia: State Authorities Turn a Blind Eye to Police Abuse of Roma", http: //www. errc. org/article/slovakia-state-authoritiesturn-a-blind-eye-to-police-abuse-of-roma/4185.

European Roma Rights Centre and Amnesty International. 2017. *A Lesson in Discrimination: Segregation of Romani Children in Primary Education in Slovakia*. Budapest: European Roma Rights Centre/Amnesty International.

Eurostat. 2017. "Unemployment Statistics: Youth Unemployment Trends". http://ec.europa.eu/eurostat/statistics-explained/index.php/Unemployment_statistics

Feagin, Joe. 2000. *Racist America: Roots, Current Realities, and Future Reparations*. New York, NY: Routledge.

Fehr, Ernst, and Simon Gächter. 2002. "Altruistic Punishment in Humans". *Nature* 415 (6868): 137–40.

Fenning, Pamela, and Jennifer Rose. 2007. "Overrepresentation of African American Students in Exclusion Discipline: The Role of School Policy". *Urban Education* 42 (6): 536–59.

Flores, René D. 2015. "Taking the Law into Their Own Hands: Do Local Anti-Immigrant Ordinances Increase Gun Sales?" *Social Problems* 62 (3): 363–90.

FRA. 2014a. *Roma Survey—Data in Focus. Education: The Situation of Roma in 11 EU Member States*. Vienna: European Union Agency for Fundamental Rights.

FRA. 2014b. *Violence Against Women: An EU-Wide Survey. Results at a Glance*. Vienna: European Union Agency for Fundamental Rights.

Fujioka, Yuki. 1999. "Television Portrayals and African-American Stereotypes: Examination of Television Effects when Direct Contact is Lacking". *Journalism and Mass Communication Quarterly*.

Gaertner, Lowell, and Jonathan Iuzzini. 2005. "Rejection and Entitativity: A Synergistic Model of Mass Violence". In *The Social Outcast: Ostracism, Social Exclusion, Rejection, and Bullying*, edited by Kipling D. Williams, Joseph D. Forgas, and Willim von Hippel, 307–20. Psychology Press.

Gaertner, Samuel L., et al. 1999. "Reducing Intergroup Bias: Elements of Intergroup Cooperation". *Journal of Personality and Social Psychology* 76 (3): 388–402.

Gaertner, Samuel, et al. 2000. "The Common Ingroup Identity Model for Reducing Intergroup Bias: Progress and Challenges". In *Social Identity Processes: Trends in Theory and Research*, edited by Dora Capozza and Rupert Brown, 133–48. Los Angeles, CA: Sage.

Gaertner, Samuel, et al. 1993. "The Common Ingroup Identity Model: Re-categorization and the Reduction of Intergroup Bias". *European Review of Social Psychology* 4 (1): 1–26.

Galinsky, Adam, and Gordon Moskowitz. 2000. "Perspective-Taking: Decreasing Stereotype Expression, Stereotype Accessibility, and In-group Favoritism." *Journal of Personality and Social Psychology* 78 (4): 708–24.

Gazvoda, Tanja Jakše. 2011. "Sedaj tudi uradno: umor in samomor". *Dolenjski List* (). https://www.dolenjskilist.si/2011/02/18/38675/novice/kronika/sedaj_tudi_uradno_umor_in_samomor.

Gee, Gilbert, et al. 2009. "Racial Discrimination and Health Among Asian Americans: Evidence, Assessment, and Directions for Future Research". *Epidemiologic Reviews* 31: 130–51.

Gelman, Andrew, Jeffrey Fagan, and Alex Kiss. 2007. "An Analysis of the New York City Police Department's "Stop-and-Frisk" Policy in the Context of Claims of Racial Bias". *Journal of the American Statistical Association* 102 (479): 813–23.

Gerber, Alan S., and Donald P. Green. 2012. *Field Experiments: Design, Analysis, and Interpretation*. New York, NY: W. W. Norton & Company.

Gibson, Bryan. 1998. "Nonsmokers' Attributions for the Outcomes of Smokers: Some Potential Consequences of the Stigmatization of Smokers". *Journal of Applied Social Psychology* 28 (7): 581–94.

Gilligan, Michael J., Benjamin J. Pasquale, and Cyrus Samii. 2014. "Civil War and Social Cohesion: Lab-in-the-Field Evidence from Nepal". *American Journal of Political Science* 58 (3): 604–19.

Glucks, Nenad. 2016. "Ko dolenjski Rom v trgovino gre: Kako in kaj po trgovinah v Novem mestu kradejo Romi". August 21, 2016, *Reporter*.

Gonsalkorale, Karen, and Kipling D. Williams. 2007. "The KKK Won't Let Me Play: Ostracism Even by a Despised Outgroup Hurts". *European Journal of Social Psychology* 37: 1176–86.

Goyal, Monika K., et al. 2015. "Racial Disparities in Pain Management of Children With Appendicitis in Emergency Departments". *JAMA Pediatrics* 169 (11): 996–1002.

Green, Eva GT, Christian Staerklé, and David O. Sears. 2006. "Symbolic Racism and Whites' Attitudes Towards Punitive and Preventive Crime Policies." Law and Human Behavior 30 (4): 435–54.

Green, Donald P., and Janelle S. Wong. 2009. "Tolerance and the Contact Hypothesis: A Field Experiment". In *The Political Psychology of Democratic Citizenship*, edited by Eugene Borgida, Christopher M. Federico, and John L. Sullivan. Oxford University Press.

Greenwald, Anthony G., and Thomas F. Pettigrew. 2014. "With Malice Toward None and Charity for Some: Ingroup Favoritism Enables Discrimination". *American Psychologist* 69 (7): 669–84.

Guenther, Mathias. 1980. "From "Brutal Savages" to "Harmless People": Notes on the Changing Western Image of the Bushmen". *Paideuma* 26: 123–40.

Guryan, Jonathan, and Kerwin Kofi Charles. 2013. "Taste-Based or Statistical Discrimination: The Economics of Discrimination Returns to its Roots". *The Economic Journal* 123 (417–432).

Guy, Will. 2017. "Anti-Roma Violence, Hate Speech, and Discrimination in the New Europe: Czech Republic, Slovakia, and Hungary". In *Realizing Roma Rights*, edited by Jacqueline Bhabha, Andrzej Mirga, and Margareta Matache. Philadelphia, PA: University of Pennsylvania Press.

Hancock, Ange-Marie. 2004. *The Politics of Disgust and the Public Identity of the "Welfare Queen"*. New York, NY: New York University Press.

Hanna-Attisha, Mona. 2017. "Will We Lose the Doctor Who Would Stop the Next Flint?" February 11, 2017, *The New York Times*.

Hardin, Russell. 1982. *Collective Action*. Baltimore, MD: Resources for the Future.

Harding, Anna, et al. 2012. "Conducting Research With Tribal Communities: Sovereignty, Ethics, and Data-Sharing Issues". *Environmental Health Perspectives* 120 (1): 6–10.

Harteveld, Eelco, and Elisabeth Ivarsflaten. 2016. "Why Women Avoid the Radical Right: Internalized Norms and Party Reputations". *British Journal of Political Science* 48 (2): 369–84.

Herek, Gregory, and John Capitanio. 1996. " "Some of My Best Friends": Intergroup Contact, Concealable Stigma, and Heterosexuals' Attitudes Toward Gay Men and Lesbians". *Personality and Social Psychology Bulletin* 22 (4): 412–24.

Hewstone, Miles, Mark Rubin, and Hazel Willis. 2002. "Intergroup Bias". *Annual Review of Psychology* 53: 575–604.

Ho, Daniel E., et al. 2007a. "Matching as Nonparametric Preprocessing for Reducing Model Dependence in Parametric Causal Inference". *Political Analysis* 15 (3): 199–236.

Ho, Daniel E., et al. 2007b. "Matchit: Matching as Nonparametric Preprocessing for Parametric Causal Inference". *Journal of Statistical Software*.

Ho, Daniel E., et al. 2011. "MatchIt: Nonparametric Preprocessing for Parametric Causal Inference". *Journal of Statistical Software* 42: 1–28.

Hobbs, William, and Nazita Lajevardi. 2019. "Effects of Divisive Political Campaigns on the Day-to-Day Segregation of Arab and Muslim Americans". *American Political Science Review* 113 (1): 270–76.

Hoffman, Elizabeth, et al. 1994. "Preferences, Property Rights, and Anonymit in Bargaining Games". *Games and Economic Behavior* 7: 346–80.

Hoffman, Kelly M., et al. 2016. "Racial Bias in Pain Assessment and Treatment Recommendations, and False Beliefs About Biological Differences Between Blacks and Whites". *PNAS* 113 (16): 4296–301.

Hojsik, Marek. 2010. Interview by Author. Notes. Bratislava.

Holt, Charles A., and Susan K. Laury. 2002. "Risk Aversion and Incentive Effects". *American Economic Review* 92: 1644–55.

hooks, bell. 1981. *Ain't I A Woman: Black Women and Feminism*. Boston, MA: South End Press.

hooks, bell. 2004. *We Real Cool: Black Men and Masculinity*. New York, NY: Routledge.

Horowitz, Donald L. 1985. *Ethnic Groups in Conflict*. Berkeley, CA: University of California Press.

Horrace, William C., and Shawn M. Rohlin. 2016. "How Dark is Dark? Bright Lights, Big City, Racial Profiling". *The Review of Economics and Statistics* 98 (2): 226–32.

Horvat-Muc, Jožek. 2010. *20 let Romani Union Murska Sobota: 1990–2010*. RD Romani Union.

Horvat-Muc, Jožek. 2011a. Interview by Author. Voice Recording. Murska Sobota.

Horvat-Muc, Jožek. 2011b. *Romska Skupnost v Sloveniji: Zgodovina in Kultura Romov*. Murska Sobota, Slovenija: Zveza Romov Slovenije, Romani Union.

Hyde, Ann. 2006. "Systemic Exclusion of Roma from Employment". *Roma Rights: Quarterly Journal of the European Roma Rights Centre* 6 (1): 3–8.

Israel-Trummel, Mackenzie. 2015. "Politics at the Intersections: Race, Ethnicity, and Gender in Political Identity and Behavior". PhD thesis, Stanford University.

Imamura, Mari, Janet Tucker, Phil Hannaford, Miguel Oliveira Da Silva, Margaret Astin, Laura Wyness, Kitty W.M. Bloemenkamp, Albrecht Jahn, Helle Karro, Jøn Olsen and Marleen Temmerman. 2007. "Factors Associated with Teenage Pregnancy in the European Union Countries: A Systematic Review". European Journal of Public Health 17 (6): 630–36.

Ivanov, Andrey, Jaroslav Kling, and Justin Kagin. 2012. *Integrated House-Hold Surveys Among Roma Populations: One Possible Approach to Sampling Used in the UNDP-World Bank-EC Regional Roma Survey 2011*. Roma Inclusion Working Papers. Bratislava: United Nations Development Programme.

Jalušič, Vlasta. 2003. "Organizirana nedolžnost". In *Izbrisani: Organizirana nedolžnost in politike izključevanja*, edited by Jasminka Dedić, Vlasta Jalušič, and Jelka Zorn, 7–22. Ljubljana: Mirovni inštitut.

Jewkes, Rachel, et al. 2012. "What We Know and What We Don't: Single and Multiple Perpetrator Rape in South Africa". *South African Crime Quarterly* 41: 11–19.

Johnson, James, Sophie Trawalter, and John Dovidio. 2000. "Converging Interracial Consequences of Exposure to Violent Rap Music on Stereotypical Attributions of Blacks". *Journal of Experimental Social Psychology* 36 (3): 233–51.

Johnson, Noel, and Alexandra Mislin. 2011. "Trust Games: A Meta-Analysis". *Journal of Economic Psychology* 32 (5): 865–89.

Johnson, Roger, and David Johnson. 1981. "Building Friendships Between Handicapped and Nonhandicapped Students: Effects of Cooperative and Individualistic Instruction". *American Educational Research Journal* 18 (4): 415–23.

Jones, Camara Phyllis. 2000. "Levels of Racism: A Theoretic Framework and a Gardener's Tale". *American Journal of Public Health* 90 (8): 1212–15.

Jones, Edward, et al. 1984. *Social Stigma: The Psychology of Marked Relationships*. New York, NY: Freeman.

Jr., Franklin D. Gilliam, and Shanto Iyengar. 2000. "Prime Suspects: The Influence of Local Television News on the Viewing Public". *American Journal of Political Science* 44 (3): 560–73.

Juhaščíková, Ivana, et al. 2015. *The 2011 Population and Housing Census: Facts About Changes in the Life of the Slovak Population*. Bratislava: Statistical Office of the Slovak Republic, Bratislava.

Junn, Jane. 2017. "The Trump Majority: White Womanhood and the Making of Female Voters in the U.S." *Politics, Groups, and Identities* 5 (2): 343–52.

Kabananukye, Kabann, and Liz Wily. 1996. *Report On a Study of the Abayanda Pygmies of South West Uganda For Mgahinga and Bwindi Impenetrable Forest Conservation Trust, Mgahinga and Bwindi Impenetrable Forest Conservation Trust, Kampala*.

Kanižaj, Igor. 2004. "Predstavljenost Nacionalnih Manjina u Hrvatskim Dnevnim Novinama– Komparativni Pregled 2001–2003". *Politčka Misao* 41 (2): 30–46.

Karaja, Elira. 2013. "The Rule of Karlowitz: Fiscal Change and Institutional Persistence". Technical Report. University of Berkeley, BEHL Working Paper No. 2014–04.

Karaja, Elira, and Jared Rubin. 2017. "The Cultural Transmission of Trust Norms: Evidence from a Lab in the Field on a Natural Experiment", https://ssrn.com/abstract=2954336%20or%20http://dx.doi.org/10.2139/ssrn.2954336.

Karba, Pavla. 2010. *Program Osnovna Šola: Državljanska in Domovinska Vzgoja ter Etika*. Ljubljana: Ministrstvo za šolstvo in šport, Zavod RS za šolstvo.

Kastelic, Lovro. 2011. "Moril, ker so ga Romi ropali?" *Slovenske Novice* (). http://m. slovenskenovice.si/crni-scenarij/doma/moril-ker-so-ga-romi-ropali.

Kellermann, Scott, and Carol Kellermann. 2004. "Uganda Batwa Pygmies", https://web. archive.org/web/20070217003839/ http://pygmies.net:80/pages/history.html.

Khan, Sammyh, and James Liu. 2008. "Intergroup Attributions and Ethnocentrism in the Indian Subcontinent: The Ultimate Attribution Error Revisited". *Journal of Cross-Cultural Psychology* 39 (1): 16–36.

Kidd, Christopher. 2008. "Development Discourse and the Batwa of South West Uganda: Representing the 'Other': Presenting the 'Self'." PhD thesis, University of Glasgow.

Kindy, Kimberly, et al. 2015. "A Year of Reckoning: Police Fatally Shoot Nearly 1,000". December 26, 2015, *The Washington Post*.

Klopčič, Vera. 2012. Interview by Author. Voice Recording. Ljubljana. Ljubljana.

Klopčič, Vera. 2007. *Položaj Romov v Sloveniji: Romi in Gadže*. Ljubljana, Slovenia: Inštitut za narodnostna vprašanja.

Kluve, Jochen. 2010. "The Effectiveness of European Active Labor Market Programs". *Labour Economics* 17 (6): 904–18.

Knussen, Christina, and Catherine Niven. 1999. "HIV/AIDS and Health Care Workers: Contact With Patients and Attitudes Towards Them". *Psychology & Health* 14 (3): 367–78.

Kogovšek, Neža. 2010. "Uvod: Izbrisani včeraj, danes, jutri – Spodkopani stereotipi in nepovrnljiva pot k popravi krivic". In *Brazgotine izbrisa: Prispevek h kritičnemu razumevanju izbrisa iz registra stalnega prebivalstva Republike Slovenije*, edited by Neža Kogovšek and Brankica Petković. Ljubljana: Mirovni inštitut

Kramberger, Uroš Škerl. 2017. "Skoraj dva milijona evrov zanove romske centre". May 8, 2017, *Dnevnik*.

Krieger, Nancy. 1999. "Embodying Inequality: A Review of Concepts, Measures, and Methods for Studying Health Consequences of Discrimination". *International Journal of Health Services* 29 (2): 295–352.

Kruttschnitt, Candace, William Kalsbeek, and Carol House, editors 2014. *Estimating the Incidence of Rape and Sexual Assault*. Washington, DC: National Academies Press.

Lacatus, George. 2012. "Romanian Mayor Moves Hundreds of Roma to a Decommissioned Chemical Factor", http://www.romatransitions.org/romanian-mayormoves-hundreds-of-roma-to-a-decommissioned-chemical-factory/.

Lah, Lenart, Katja Rutar, and Irena Svetin. 2011. "Trg dela: Labour market". In *Statistične Informacije: Rapid Reports*, edited by Statistčni Urad Republike Slovenije, 1–23. 11. Ljubljana, Slovenia: Statisticni Urad Republike Slovenije

Laitin, David D. 1995. "Marginality: A Microperspective". *Rationality and Society* 7: 31–57.

Lajosi, Krisztina. 2014. "National Stereotypes and Music". *Nations and Nationalism* 20 (4): 628–45.

Law, Ian, and Martin Kovats. 2018. *Rethinking Roma: Identities, Politicisation and New Agendas*. London, UK: Palgrave Macmillan.

LeBas, Damian. 2013. "On the scrap heap". https://romediafoundation.wordpress.com/ 2013/09/20/on-the-scrap-heap/.

Le Bas, Damian. 2018. "The Romani Language: A Signpost to Home". In *Thinking Home: Interdisciplinary Dialogues*, edited by Sanja Bahun and Bojana Petrć. London, UK: Bloomsbury Academic

Lea, Stephen E.G., Paul Webley, and R. Mark Levine. 1993. "The Economic Psychology of Consumer Debt". *Journal of Economic Psychology* 14: 85–119.

Leach, Colin, Nastia Snider, and Aarti Iyer. 2002. "Poisoning the Consciences of the Fortunate." The Experience of Relative Advantage and Support for Social Equality." In

Relative Deprivation: Specification, Development, and Integration, edited by Iain Walker and Heather Smith, 136–63. Cambridge, UK: Cambridge University Press.

Lechner, Michael, and Conny Wunsch. 2009. "Are Training Programs More Effective When Unemployment is High?" *Journal of Labor Economics* 27 (4): 653–92.

Leskošek, Vesna. 2012. "Vpliv socialne države na (ne)odvisnost delavcev od tržnih pogojev zaposlovanja". *Časopis za kritiko znanosti, domišljijo in novo antropologijo*, no. 247: 103–12.

Levanič, Monika. 2018. "Uničujejo in razbijajo, za malo kovine povzročijo opustošenje". https://novice.svet24.si/clank/novice/slovenija/5b488e4d42 unicujejo-inrazbijajo-za-malo-kovine-povzrocijo-opustosenje.

Levin, Josh. 2013. "The Welfare Queen". December 19, 2013, *Slate*.

Lewy, Guenter. 2000. *The Nazi Persecution of the Gypsies*. New York, NY: Oxford University Press.

Ločar, Andreja, and Marko Rabuza. 2017. "Slovenija, socialna država ali država na sociali?" https://siol.net/novice/slovenija/slovenija-socialna-drzava-ali-drzavana-sociali-436176.

Lundberg, Johanna, et al. 2007. "Adverse Health Effects of Low Levels of Perceived Control in Swedish and Russian Community Samples". *BMC Public Health* 7: 314–25.

Madanipour, Ali, Goran Cars, and Judith Allen. 1998. "Introduction". In *Social Exclusion in European Cities: Processes, Experiences, and Responses*, edited by Ali Madanipour, Goran Cars, and Judith Allen, 7–23. London, UK: Jessica Kingsley Publishers Ltd.

Mansel, Tim. 2013. "Romain Sweden: A Nation Questions Itself", https://www.bbc.com/ news/magazine-25200449.

Maquet, Jacques. 1970. "Rwanda Castes". In Social Stratification in Africa, edited by Arthur Tuden and Leonard Plotnicov. New York, NY: The Free Press.

Mares, Isabela, Aurelian Muntean and Lauren Young. 2007. "Bought or Coerced? The Electoral Mobilization of Roma Voters in Eastern Europe." Manuscript.

Mares, Isabela, and Lauren E. Young. 2019. *Conditionality & Coercion: Electoral Clientelism in Eastern Europe*. New York, NY: Oxford University Press.

Mark, David. 2017. "Roma in European Politics, Looking to the Future". In *Realizing Roma Rights*, edited by Jacqueline Bhabha, Andrzej Mirga, and Margareta Matache, 223–34. Philadelphia, PA: University of Pennsylvania Press.

Marshall, Anna-Maria. 2014. "Idle Rights: Employees' Rights Consciousness and the Construction of Sexual Harassment Policies". *Law and Society Review*.

Martí, Teresa Sordé, and Fernando Macías. 2017. "Making Roma Rights a Reality at the Local Level: A Spanish Case Study". In *Realizing Roma Rights*, edited by Jacqueline Bhabha, Andrzej Mirga, and Margareta Matache. Philadelphia, PA: University of Pennsylvania Press.

Marushiakova, Elena, and Vesselin Popov. 2013. ' "Gypsy' Groups in Eastern Europe: Ethnonyms vs. professionyms". *Romani Studies* 23 (1): 61–82.

Marushiakova, Elena, and Vesselin Popov. 2016a. "Roma Culture: Problems and Challenges". In *Roma Culture: Myths and Realities*, edited by Elena Marushiakova and Vesselin Popov, 7–34. München, Germany: Lincom Academic Publishers.

Marushiakova, Elena, and Vesselin Popov. 2016b. "Who are Roma". In *Roma Culture: Myths and Realities*, edited by Elena Marushiakova and Vesselin Popov, 7–34. Munchen, Germany: Lincom Academic Publishers.

Marwell, Gerald, and Ruth E. Ames. 1979. "Experiments on the Provision of Public Goods. I. Resources, Interest, Group Size, and the Free-Rider Problem". *American Journal of Sociology* 84 (6): 1335–60.

Masclet, David, etal. 2003. "Monetary and Nonmonetary Punishment in the Voluntary Contributions Mechanism". *American Economic Review* 93 (1): 366–80.

Matache, Margareta. 2014. "The Deficit of EU Democracies: A New Cycle of Violence Against Roma Population". *Human Rights Quarterly* 36 (2): 325–48.

Matache, Margareta, and David Mark. 2014. "Confined by Narrow Choices: The Stories of Roma Adolescents". In *Human Rights and Adolescence*, edited by Jacqueline Bhabha. Philadelphia, PA: University of Pennsylvania Press.

Matras, Yaron. 2002. *Romani: A Linguistic Introduction*. Cambridge University Press. Cambridge, UK.

Mazziotta, Agostino, et al. 2015. "(How) Does Positive and Negative Extended Cross-Group Contact Predict Direct Cross-Group Contact and Intergroup Attitudes?" *European Journal of Social Psychology* 45 (5): 653–67.

McDowell, Allen, and Nicholas J. Cox. 2004. "How Do You Fit a Model When the Dependent Variable is a Proportion", http://www.stata.com/support/faqs/stat/logit.html.

McGarry, Aidan. 2017. *Romaphobia: The Last Acceptable Form of Racism*. London, UK: Zed Books Ltd.

Mendelberg, Tali. 2001. *The Race Card: Campaign Strategy, Implicit Messages, and the Norm of Equality*. Princeton, NJ: Princeton University Press.

Mendizabal, Isabel, et al. 2012. "Reconstructing the Population History of European Romani from Genome-wide Data". *Current Biology* 22 (24): 2342–49.

Messing, Vera, and Emília Molnár. 2011."Válaszok a pénztelenségre: szegény cigány és nem cigány családok megélhetési stratégiái". *Esély* 1: 53–80.

Michael, Billing, and Henri Tajfel. 1973. "Social Categorization and Similarity in Intergroup Behavior". *European Journal of Social Psychology* 3 (1): 27–52.

Mihailov, Dotcho. 2012. *The Health Situation of Roma Communities: Analysis of the Data from the UNDP/World Bank/EC Regional Roma Survey 2011*. Roma Inclusion Working Papers. Bratislava: United Nations Development Programme.

Miklč, Bojan. 2013. "Iz sveta Romov: Življenje v nezakonito postavljeni romski vasi Žabjak". https://www.rtvslo.si/lokalne-novice/iz-sveta-romov/foto-zivljenje-vnezakonito-postavljeni-romski-vasi-zabjak/319974.

Mirwaldt, Katja. 2010. "Contact, Conflict and Geography: What Factors Shape Cross-Border Citizen Relations?" *Political Geography* 29: 434–43.

Mo,Cecilia Hyunjung. 2017. "Perceived Relative Deprivation and Risk: An Aspiration Based Model of Human Trafficking Vulnerability". *Political Behavior* 40 (1): 247–77.

Montoya, Matthew, and Todd Pittinsky. 2011. "When Increased Group Identification Leads to Outgroup Liking and Cooperation: The Role of Trust". *The Journal of Social Psychology* 151 (6): 784–806.

Morton, Rebecca, and Kenneth C. Williams. 2010. *Experimental Political Science and the Study of Causality: From Nature to the Lab*. New York, NY: Cambridge University Press.

Moss-Racusin, Corinne A., et al. 2012. "Science Faculty's Subtle Gender Biases Favor Male Students". *PNAS* 109 (41): 16474–79.

Murdie, Amanda, and David R. Davis. 2012. "Shaming and Blaming: Using Events Data to Assess the Impact of Human Rights INGOs". *International Studies Quarterly* 56: 1–16.

Mutz, Diana C. 2016. "Harry Potter and the Deathly Donald". *PS: Political Science and Politics* 49 (4): 722–29.

Nasture, Florin. 2015. "Changing the Paradigm of Roma inclusion: From Gypsy Industry to Active Citizenship". *Roma Rights: Quarterly Journal of the European Roma Rights Centre* 18 (2): 27–32.

Nevels, Cynthia Skove. 2007. *Lynching to Belong: Claiming Whiteness Through Racial Violence*. College Station, TX: Texas A&M University Press.

Nielsen, Richard. 2014. "Case Selection via Matching". *Sociological Methods & Research*: 1–29.

Nosko, Andrej. 2013. "A Victory for Extremismin Slovakia, and What It Means", https://www.opensocietyfoundations.org/voices/victory-extremism-slovakia-and-what-it-means.

O'Higgins, Niall. 2012. *Roma and Non-Roma in the Labour Market in Central and South Eastern Europe*. Roma Inclusion Working Papers. Bratislava: United Nations Development Programme.

Olson, James, and Jeff Stone. 2005. "The Influence of Behavior on Attitudes". In *The Handbook of Attitudes*, edited by Dolores Albarracin, Blair Johnson, and Mark Zanna, 223–71. Mahwah, NJ: Lawrence Erlbaum Associates.

Olson, Kristina R., and Elizabeth S. Spelke. 2008. "Foundations of Cooperation in Young Children". *Cognition* 108 (1): 222–31.

Oprea, Alexandra. 2004. "Re-envisioning Social Justice from the Ground Up: Including the Experiences of Romani Women". *Essex Human Rights Review* 1 (1): 29–39.

Oprea, Alexandra. 2012. "Romani Feminism in Reactionary Times". *Signs* 38 (1): 11–21.

Osborn, Andrew. 2002. "Pygmy Show at Zoo Sparks Disgust". August 10, 2002, *The Guardian*.

Ostrom, Elinor. 1990. *Governing the Commons: The Evolution of Institutions for Collective Action*. Cambridge, UK: Cambridge University Press.

Page-Gould, Elizabeth, Rodolfo Mendoza-Denton, and Linda Tropp. 2008. "With a Little Help From My Cross-Group Friend: Reducing Anxiety in Intergroup Contexts Through Cross-Group Friendship". *Journal of Personality and Social Psychology* 95 (5): 1080–94.

Pager, Deva, Bart Bonikowski, and Bruce Western. 2009. "Discrimination in a Low-Wage Labor Market: A Field Experiment". *American Sociological Review* 74 (5): 777–99.

Pager, Devah. 2007. *Marked: Race, Crime, and Finding Work in an Era of Mass Incarceration*. Chicago, IL: University of Chicago Press.

Pager, Devah, and David S. Pedulla. 2015. "Race, Self-Selection, and the Job Search Process". *American Journal of Sociology* 120 (4): 1005–54.

Pager, Devah, and Hana Shepherd. 2008. "The Sociology of Discrimination: Racial Discrimination in Employment, Housing, Credit, and Consumer Markets". *Annual Review of Sociology* 34: 181–209.

Paluck, Elizabeth L., and Donald P. Green. 2009. "Deference, Dissent, and Dispute Resolution:An Experimental Intervention Using Mass Media to Change Norms and Behavior in Rwanda". *American Political Science Review*.

Paluck, Elizabeth Levy, Seth A. Green, and Donald P. Green. 2018. "The Contact Hypothesis Re-Evaluated". *Behavioural Public Policy*: 1–30.

Paolini, Stefania, Jake Harwood, and Mark Rubin. 2010. "Negative Intergroup Contact Makes Group Memberships Salient: Explaining Why Intergroup Conflict Endures". *Personality and Social Psychology Bulletin* 36 (12): 1723–38.

Papke, Leslie E., and Jeffrey Wooldridge. 1996. "Econometric Methods for Fractional Response Variables With an Application to 401(k) Plan Participation Rates." *Journal of Applied Econometrics* 11: 619–32.

Paradies, Yin. 2006. "A Systematic Review of Empirical Research on Self-Reported Racism and Health". *International Journal of Epidemiology* 35 (4): 888–901.

Pauley, Bruce F. 1992. *From Prejudice to Persecution: A History of Austrian Anti-Semitism*. Chapel Hill, NC: University of North Carolina Press.

Peffley, Mark, and Jon Hurwitz. 2007. "Persuasion and Resistance: Race and the Death Penalty in America". *American Journal of Political Science*.

Pepper, Gillian V., and Daniel Nettle. 2017. "The Behavioural Constellation of Deprivation: Causes and Consequences". *Behavioral and Brain Sciences* 40: 1–46.

Perić, Tatjana 2012. *The Housing Situation of Roma Communities: Regional Roma Survey 2011*. Roma Inclusion Working Papers. Bratislava: United Nations Development Programme.

Pettigrew, Thomas F. 1979. "The Ultimate Attribution Error: Extending Allport's Cognitive Analysis of Prejudice". *Personality and Social Psychology Bulletin* 5 (4): 461–76.

Pettigrew, Thomas F., and Linda R. Tropp. 2011. *When Groups Meet: The Dynamics of Intergroup Contact*. New York, NY: Psychology Press.

Pettigrew, Thomas F, and Linda R. Tropp. 2006. "A Meta-Analytic Test of Intergroup Contact Theory". *Journal of Personality and Social Psychology* 90 (5): 751–83.

Phelps, Edmund S. 1972. "The Statistical Theory of Racism and Sexism". *The American Economic Review* 62 (4): 659–61.

Phillips, Kristine. 2016. "The Nonprofit Director Who Called Michelle Obamaan 'Apein Heels' Has Lost Her Job—for Good". December 27, 2016, *The Washington Post*.

Pureber, Tjaša. 2012. "Segregacija danes: refleksija sistemskega nasilja nad Romi na Dolenjskem". *Časopis za kritiko znanosti, domišljijo in novo antropologijo*, no. 247: 54–66.

Radio Krka. 2011. "S tragedijo povezano izsiljevanje in dolg?" http://www.radiokrka.com/poglej_clanek.asp?ID_clanka=127062.

Rajšek, Bojan. 2011. "Med Romi v Žabjaku: Gospud, vodo in elektriko bi rabili!" March 28, 2011, *Delo*.

Rajšek, Bojan. 2014. "Romi ne znajo niti postevanke". March 31, 2014, *Delo*.

Ramos, Dandara, et al. 2013. "Future Discounting by Slum-Dwelling Youth Versus University Students in Rio de Janeiro". *Journal of Research on Adolescence* 23 (1): 95–102.

Rapoport, Anatol, and Melvin Guyer. 1978. "A Taxonomy of 2x2 games". *General Systems* 23: 125–36.

Reed, Richard. 1997. *Forest Dwellers, Forest Protectors: Indigenous Models for International Development*. Boston, MA: Allyn/Bacon.

Rege, Mari, and Kjetil Telle. 2004. "The Impact of Social Approval and Framing on Cooperation in Public Good Situations". *Journal of Public Economics* 88 (7): 1625–44.

Remec, Matija. 2005. "Življenjska raven: Level of living". In *Statistične Informacije: Rapid Reports*, edited by Statistični Urad Republike Slovenije, 1–10. 21. Ljubljana, Slovenia: Statisticni Urad Republike Slovenije.

Reskin, Barbara. 2012. "The Race Discrimination System". *The Annual Review of Sociology* 38: 17–35.

Riach, Peter A., and Judith Rich. 2002. "Field Experiments of Discrimination in the Market Place". *The Economic Journal* 112 (483): 480–518.

Riek, Blake, Eric Mania, and Samuel Gaertner. 2006. "Intergroup Threat and Outgroup Attitudes: A Meta-Analytic Review". *Personality and Social Psychology Review* 10 (4): 336–53.

Rios, Victor M. 2011. *Punished: Policing the Lives of Black and Latino Boys*. New York, NY: NYU Press.

Ripka, Stepan. 2010. Interview by Author. Notes. Prague.

Rivera, Lauren, and András Tilcsik. 2016. "Class advantage, Commitment Penalty: The Gendered Effect of Social Class Signals in an Elite Labor Market". *American Sociological Review* 81 (6): 1097–31.

Robb, Kathryn A., Alice E. Simon, and Jane Wardle. 2009. "Socioeconomic Disparities in Optimism and Pessimism". *International Journal of Behavioral Medicine* 16 (4): 331–38.

Rockenbach, Bettina, and Manfred Milinski. 2006. "The Efficient Interaction of Indirect Reciprocity and Costly Punishment". *Nature* 444 (718–723).

Rooney-Rebeck, Patricia, and Leonard Jason. 1986. "Prevention of Prejudice in Elementary School Students". The Journal of Primary Prevention 7 (2): 63–73.

Rostaş, Iulius, Márton Rövid, and Marek Szilvási. 2015."On Roma Civil Society, Roma Inclusion, and Roma Participation". *Roma Rights: Quarterly Journal of the European Roma Rights Centre* 18 (2): 7–10.

Rozenblit, Marsha L. 1983. *The Jews of Vienna, 1867–1914: Assimilation and Identity*. Albany, NY: State University of New York Press.

Sandreli, Monika. 2012. Interview by Author. Voice Recording. Murska Sobota.

Sardelić, Julija. 2015. "Romani Minorities and Uneven Citizenship Access in the Post-Yugoslav Space". *Ethnopolitics* 14 (2): 159–79.

Scacco, Alexandra, and Shana S. Warren. 2018. "Can Social Contact Reduce Prejudice and Discrimination? Evidence From a Field Experiment in Nigeria." American Political Science Review 112 (3) (2018): 654–77.

Schimmelfennig, Frank, Stefan Engert, and Heiko Knobel. 2005. "The Impact of EU Political Conditionality". In *The Europeanization of Central and Eastern Europe*, edited by Frank Schimmelfennig and Ulrich Sedelmeier, 29–50. Ithaca, NY: Cornell University Press.

Schmid, Katharina, et al. 2012. "Secondary Transfer Effects of Intergroup Contact: A Cross-National Comparison in Europe". *Social Psychology Quarterly* 75 (1): 28–51.

Scicluna, Henry. 2007. "Anti-Romani Speech in Europe's Public Space: The Mechanism of Hate Speech". *Roma Rights: Quarterly Journal of the European Roma Rights Centre* 10 (3): 47–55.

Scott, James C. 1985. *Weapons of the Weak: Everyday Forms of Peasant Resistance*. New Haven, CT: Yale University Press.

Sefton, Martin, Sobert Shupp, and James Walker. 2007. "The Effect of Rewards and Sanctions in Provision of Public Goods". *Economic Inquiry* 45 (4): 671–90.

Shapiro, Joel, and Stephen Wu. 2011. "Fatalism and Savings". *The Journal of Socio-Economics* 40 (5): 645–51.

Sheets, Rosa Hernández. 1996. "Urban Class Room Conflict: Student-Teacher Perception: Ethnic Integrity, Solidarity, and Resistance." *The Urban Review* 28: 165–83.

Sherif, Muzafer, and Carolyn Sherif. 1953. *Groups in Harmony and Tension: An Integration of Studies on Intergroup Relations*. New York, NY: Harper.

Sherif, Muzafer, et al. 1961. *Intergroup Conflict and Cooperation: The Robbers Cave Experiment*. Norman, OK: University of Oklahoma Book Exchange.

Shih, Margaret, Todd L. Pittinsky, and Nalini Ambady. 1999. "Stereotype Susceptibility: Identity Salience and Shifts in Quantitative Performance". *Psychological Science* 10(1): 80–83.

Sidanius, James, et al. 2008. *The Diversity Challenge: Social Identity and Intergroup Relations on the College Campus*. New York, NY: The Russel Sage Foundation.

Šiftar, Vanek. 1970. *Cigani: Minulost v Sedanjosti*. Murska Sobota: Pomurska Založba.

Šiftar, Vanek. 1994. "Knjigi na pot". In *Vzgoja in izobraževanje Romov na Slovenskem*, 9–14. Maribor: Obzorja.

Šiftar, Vanek. 1984. "Romi U Sloveniji 1941–1945". *Naše teme* 28 (7–8): 1324–34.

Šiftar, Vanek. 1978. "Romi v Sloveniji". *Dialogi*, numbers 7–8: 426–42.

Šiftar, Vanek. 1989. "Romi Vceraj . . . Pojutrišnjem?" *Znamenje*: 277–88.

Šiftar, Vanek. 1997. "Že dolgo so med nami - a smo še daleč narazen". *Pokrajinski muzej Murska Sobota, Katalog stalne razstave* 2: 12–37.

Sigmund, Karl. 2007. "Punish or Perish? Retaliation and Collaboration Among Humans". *Trends in Ecology and Evolution* 22 (11): 593–600.

Silk, Joan, and Bailey House. 2011. "Evolutionary Foundations of Human Prosocial Sentiments". *PNAS* 108 (Supplement 2): 10910–17.

Silverman, Lisa. 2012. *Becoming Austrians: Jews and Culture between the World Wars*. New York, NY: Oxford University Press.

Simonovits, Gábor, Gábor Kézdi, and Péter Kardos. 2018. "Seeing the World Through The Other's Eye: An Online Intervention Reducing Ethnic Prejudice". *American Political Science Review* 112 (1): 186–93.

Skiba, Russell J., et al. 2002. "The Color of Discipline: Sources of Racial and Gender Disproportionality in School Punishment". *The Urban Review* 34 (4): 317–42.

Solimene, Marco. 2015. " 'I Go for Iron': Xoraxané Romá Collecting Scrap Metal in Rome". In *Gypsy Economy*, edited by Micol Brazzabeni, Manuela Ivone Cunha, and Martin Fotta, 107–26. New York, NY: Berghahn Books.

Statistični urad Republike Slovenije. 2011a. "Povprečne mesečne plče po dejavnostih (SKD 2008), statistične regije". http://www.stat.si.

Statistični urad Republike Slovenije. 2011b. "Povprečne mesečne plače po: SKD dejavnost, statistična regija, mesec, plače, meritve". http://www.stat.si.

Statistični urad Republike Slovenije. 2011c. "Prag tveganja revščine po: meritve, top gospodinjstva, denarna enota, leto". http://www.stat.si.

Statistič urad Republike Slovenije. 2015a. "Posedovanje izbranih dobrin po:dohodek gospodinjstva - kvintil, leto, dobrina, meritve". http://www.stat.si.

Statistični urad Republike Slovenije. 2015b. "Stanovanjske razmere, glede na tip gospodinjstva, Slovenija, letno". http://www.stat.si.

Statistični urad Republike Slovenije (SURS). 2002. "Popis prebivalstva". http://www.stat.si.

Steele, Claude M. 1997. "A Threat in the Air: How Stereotypes Shape Intellectual Identity and Performance". *American Psychologist* 52 (6): 613–29.

Steele, Claude M., and Joshua Aronson. 1995. "Stereotype Threat and the Intellectual Test Performance of African Americans". *Journal of Personality and Social Psychology* 69 (5): 797–811.

Stejskalová, Michaela, and Marek Szilvási. 2016. "Coercive and Cruel: Sterilisation and its Consequences for Romani Women in the Czech Republic (1966–2016)". *European Roma Rights Centre:* 1–83.

Stewart, Tracie L., et al. 2010. "Consider the Situation: Reducing Automatic Stereotyping Through Situational Attribution Training". *Journal of Experimental Social Phsycology* 46: 221–25.

Štrukelj, Pavla. 1980. *Romi na Slovenskem*. Ljubljana, Slovenia: Cankarjeva Založba v Ljubljani.

Šuljić, Tomica. 2017. "Romi se bližajo Sončnim dvorom". June 17, 2017, *Novice*.

Sumner, William. 1906. *Folkways: A Study of The Soiological Importance of Usages Manners Customs Mores And Morals*. Boston, MA: Ginn / Company.

Svet24. 2010. "Ciganske zdrahe med Romi". https://novice.svet24.si/clanek/slovenija/581b35616e0d5/ciganske-zdrahe-med-romi.

Swaine, Jon, et al. 2015. "Young Black Men Killed by US Police at Highest Rate in Year of 1,134 deaths". December 31, 2015, *The Guardian*. https://www.theguardian.com/us-news/2015/dec/31/the-counted-police-killings-2015-young-black-men.

Tajfel, Henri, and John C. Turner. 1979. "An Integrative Theory of Intergroup Conflict". *The Social Psychology of Intergroup Relations* 33 (47): 74.

Tancer, Mladen. 1997. "Romi v Sloveniji". In *Strpnost do Manjšin: Zbornik Referatov Mednarodnega Znanstvenega Simpozija*, edited. by Zlatko Tišljar and Alojz Širec, 94–99. Pedagoška fakulteta Maribor, Inter-kulturo Maribor.

Tausch, Nicole, et al. 2010. "Secondary Transfer Effects of Intergroup Contact: Alternative Accounts and Underlying Processes". *Journal of Personality and Social Psychology* 99 (2): 282–302.

Taylor, Becky. 2014. *Another Darkness, Another Dawn: A History of Gypsies, Roma and Travellers*. London, UK: Reaktion Books.

Taylor, Christopher C. 2004. "Dual Systems in Rwanda: Have They Ever Really Existed?" *Anthropological Theory* 4 (3): 353–71.

ter Wal, Jessika. 2002. "Racism and Cultural Diversity in the Mass Media: An Overview of Research and Examples of Good Practice in the EU Member States, 1995–2000". *European Research Centre on Migration and Ethnic Relations*.

The Editorial Board. 2016. "The Racism at the Heart of Flint's Crisis". March 25, 2016, *The New York Times*.

The New York Times. 1916. "Ota Benga, Pygmy, Tired of America". July 16, 1916, *The New York Times*.

Thorat, Sukhdeo, and Joel Lee. 2005. "Caste Discrimination and Food Security Programmes". *Economic and Political Weekly* 40 (39): 4198–201.

Tichy, Brano. 2010. Interview by Author. Notes. Bratislava.

Tilcsik, András. 2011. "Pride and Prejudice: Employment Discrimination Against Openly Gay Men in the United States". *American Journal of Sociology* 117 (2): 586–626.

Tkach, Andrew. 2010. "Burned Girl a Symbol of Roma Hate and Hope", http: / / articles. cnn. com /2010-06- 25/ world / roma. prejudice_1_arson-attack-molotov-cocktail-attack-anti-roma?_s=PM:WORLD.

Tomasello, Michael. 2009. *Why We Cooperate*. Cambridge, MA: MIT Press.

Traynor, Ian. 2006. "Violence and Persecution Follow the Roma Across Europe". November 27, 2006, *The Guardian*.

Tredoux, Colin, and Gillian Finchilescu. 2010. "Mediators of the Contact-Prejudice Relation among South African Students on Four University Campuses". *Journal of Social Issues* 66 (2): 289–308.

Triandis, Harry C. 1994. *Culture and Social Behavior*. New York, NY: McGraw-Hill.

Tropp, Linda R., Thomas C. O'Brien, and Katya Migacheva. 2014. "How Peer Norms of Inclusion and Exclusion Predict Children's Interest in Cross-Ethnic Friendships". *Social Issues* 70 (1): 151–66.

Trump, Donald. 2015. "Presidential Announcement Speech". http://time.com/3923128/donald%20trump-announcement-speech/.

Tudija, Milena. 2012. Interview by Author. Voice Recording. Novo mesto.

Ture, Kwame, and Charles V. Hamilton. 1967. *Black Power: The Politics of Liberation*. New York, NY: Random House, Inc.

Turner, Rhiannon N., Miles Hewstone, and Alberto Voci. 2007. "Reducing Explicit and Implicit Outgroup Prejudice via Direct and Extended Contact: The Mediating Role of Self-Disclosure and Intergroup Anxiety". *Journal of Personality and Social Psychology* 93 (3): 369–88.

Twenge, Jean M., et al. 2007. "Social Exclusion Decreases Prosocial Behavior". *Journal of Personality and Social Psychology* 92 (1): 56–66.

Unoka, Zsolt, et al. 2009. "Trust Game Reveals Restricted Interpersonal Transactions in Patients With Borderline Personality Disorder". *Journal of Personality Disorders* 23 (4): 399–409.

Vaish, Amrisha, Malinda Carpenter, and Michael Tomasello. 2010. "Young Children Selectively Avoid Helping People With Harmful Intentions". *Child Development* 81 (6): 1661–69.

Van Oudenhoven, Jan Pieter, Jan Tjeerd Groenewoud, and Miles Hewstone. 1996. "Cooperation, Ethnic Salience and Generalization of Interethnic Attitudes". *European Journal of Social Psychology* 26 (4): 649–61.

Vermeersch, Peter. 2017. "Roma Mobilization and Participation: Obstacles and Opportunities". In *Realizing Roma Rights,* edited by Jacqueline Bhabha, Andrzej Mirga, and Margareta Matache, 209–222. Philadelphia, PA: University of Pennsylvania Press.

Vezzali, Loris, and Dino Giovannini. 2012. "Secondary Transfer Effect of Intergroup Contact: The Role of Intergroup Attitudes, Intergroup Anxiety and Perspective Taking". *Journal of Community & Applied Social Psychology* 22 (2): 125–44.

Vezzali, Loris, Sofia Stathi, and Dino Giovannini. 2012. "Indirect Contact Through Book Reading: Improving Adolescents' Attitudes and Behavioral Intentions Toward Immigrants". *Psychology in the Schools* 49 (2): 148–62.

Vezzali, Loris, et al. 2014. "Improving Intergroup Relations With Extended and Vicarious Forms of Indirect Contact". *European Review of Social Psychology* 25 (1): 314–89.

Vlada RS. 2014. "Tretje poročilo Vlade Republike Slovenije o položaju romske skupnosti v Sloveniji - priloga 4". *Poročilo o izvajanju Zakona o romski skupnosti v Republiki Sloveniji (Uradni list RS, št. 33/2007) in Nacionalnega programa ukrepov za Rome Vlade Republike Slovenije za obdobje 2010–2015.*

Vrh, Alenka. 2017. "Povprečne mesečne plače, Slovenija, december 2016". http://www.stat.si/StatWeb/News/Index/6502.

Vukovich, Gabriella. 2012. *Population Census 2011: 1. Preliminary Data.* Budapest: Hungarian Central Statistical Office.

Wagner, Ulrich, Oliver Christ, and Thomas F Pettigrew. 2008. "Prejudice and Group-Related Behavior in Germany". *Journal of Social Issues* 64 (2): 403–16.

Wald, Johanna, and Daniel J. Losen. 2003. "Editors' Notes". In *Deconstructing the School-to-Prison Pipeline: New Directions for Youth Development,* edited by Johanna Wald and Daniel J. Losen, 1–2. San Francisco, CA: Jossey-Bass.

Warneken, Felix, and Michael Tomasello. 2006. "Altruistic Helping in Human Infants and Young Chimpanzees". *Science* 311 (5765): 1301–03.

Werth, James, and Charles Lord. 1992. "Previous Conceptions of the Typical Group Member and the Contact Hypothesis". *Basic and Applied Social Psychology* 13 (3): 351–69.

Williams, David, and Selina Mohammed. 2009. "Discrimination and Racial Disparities in Health: Evidence and Needed Research". *Journal of Behavioral Medicine* 32 (1): 20–47.

Williams, Kipling D. 2007. "Ostracism". *Annual Review of Psychology* 58: 425–52.

Wimmer, Andreas. 2002. *Nationalist Exclusion and Ethnic Conflict: Shadows of Modernity.* Cambridge, UK: Cambridge University Press.

Woodburn, James. 1997. "Indigenous discrimination: The ideological basis for local discrimination against hunter-gatherer minorities in sub-Saharan Africa". *Ethnic and Racial Studies* 20 (2): 345–61.

Wright, Stephen C., et al. 1997. "The Extended Contact Effect: Knowledge of Cross-Group Friendships and Prejudice". *Journal of Personality and Social Psychology* 73 (1): 73–90.

Zajonc, Robert. 1968. "Attitudinal Effects of Mere Exposure". *Journal of Personality and Social Psychology* 9 (2, Pt. 2): 1–27.

Zorn, Jelka. 2003. "Politike izključevanja v nastajanju slovenske državnosti". In *Izbrisani: Organizirana nedolžnost in politike izključevanja*, edited by Jasminka Dedić, Vlasta Jalušič, and Jelka Zorn, 85–140. Ljubljana: Mirovni institut.

Zupan, Andrej, Katarina Vrabec, and Damjan Glavač. 2013. "The Paternal Perspective of the Slovenian Population and Its Relationship With Other Populations". *Annals of human biology* 40 (6): 515–26.

Index

Note: Figures, tables and maps are indicated by an italic "*f*", "*t*", and "*m*" respectively and notes are indicated by "n" or "nn" following the page numbers.